THE BEST OF

After Office Hours

EDITORS

Roy M. Pitkin
Editor Emeritus, *Obstetrics & Gynecology*

Rebecca D. Rinehart
Director of Publications
The American College of Obstetricians and Gynecologists

THE AMERICAN COLLEGE OF
OBSTETRICIANS AND GYNECOLOGISTS

Library of Congress Cataloging-in-Publication Data

The best of after office hours / edited by Roy M. Pitkin, Rebecca D. Rinehart.
    p. ; cm.
Includes bibliographical references and index.
  ISBN 1-932328-00-9 (alk. paper)
  1. Obstetrics--Miscellanea. 2. Gynecology--Miscellanea. 3. Medicine--Miscellanea. 4. Essays
  [DNLM: 1. Obstetrics--Collected Works. 2. Gynecology--Collected Works. 3. Medicine in Literature--Collected Works. 4. Religion and Medicine--Collected Works. WQ 5 B651 2003] I. Pitkin, Roy M. II. Rinehart, Rebecca D.

RG 103.B475 2003
618--dc21

            2003001436

Copies of *The Best of After Office Hours* can be ordered through the ACOG Distribution Center by calling toll free 800-762-2264. Orders can be placed from the ACOG web site at www.acog.org or sales.acog.org.

12345/76543

Contents

Editors acclaim...

The Best of After Office Hours

In an age when history is sometimes regarded as having little importance or interest, the editors of *The Best of After Office Hours* have put together a compendium of excellent articles that will stir an interest in our learned ancestors. A discipline that doesn't honor its predecessors is doomed to oblivion. This fascinating collection indicates that we are at little risk of this danger.

ALAN H. DeCHERNEY, MD
Editor, *Fertility and Sterility*

Who said doctors can't write? Fifty-seven essays, ranging from an analysis of the case for Shakespeare being an obstetrician, through how Fallopio's tubes were named, to an exploration of Shamanism, grace this wonderful collection from the first 50 years of the Green Journal.

GEORGE D. LUNDBERG, MD
Editor, *Medscape General Medicine*

This delightful collection of essays reminds us that there is more to medicine than strict science. Readers will find it interesting and entertaining.

JAMES R. SCOTT, MD
Editor, *Obstetrics & Gynecology*

rather than prematurity (see below). Philip, in *King John*, must be the reason why the World Health Organization placed the lower level of viability at 500 gm. Witness:

> And if he were, he came into the world
> Full fourteen weeks before the course of time.[36]

He must, at least, have been one of the very rare survivals of early premature labor in that age, if what Philip states was true. His brother, Robert, took a different approach and maintained that Philip was illegitimate.

Shakespeare also recognized that the delivered preterm infant reacted on many occasions as a normal term or was he referring to the end result of a somewhat-later-than-should-be marriage in this passage from *The Winter's Tale:*

> She is something before her time deliver'd.
> A boy?
> A daughter; and a goodly babe.
> Lusty and like to live.[37]

The problems of the teenage pregnancy caught his eye. In spite of that superb story of teenage love—*Romeo and Juliet*, the epitome of all love stories—he did not think that pregnancy in the teenager would always be salutary.

> Younger than she are happy mothers made.
> And too soon marr'd are those so early made[38]

He was partial to identical twins and his comedies that feature them are some of his best.

> ... Twinn'd brothers of one womb,
> Whose procreation, residence and birth,
> Scarce is dividant.[39]

> A joyful mother of two goodly sons;
> And, which was strange, the one so like the other
> As could not be distinguish'd but by names,
> That very hour, and in the self-same inn,
> A meaner woman was delivered
> Of such a burthen, male twins, both alike.[40]

He was, however, aware of the more common variety.

> By her he had two children at one birth[41]

The awareness of hypoxia to the unborn, albeit the various causes are not suspected, is evident from the following passage:

> By strangling thee in her accursed womb[42]

Even though this is an avowed wish for life to cease before birth, the fact that it could happen and that fetal death occurred before the onset of labor can readily be read into this short line.

Dystocia was of common occurrence in Elizabethan times, if we can believe Shakespeare, and I believe we should. Not only did he recognize the problems and all-too-common poor results of dystocia:

> A terrible child-bed hast thou had, my dear[43]

> ... The queen's in labour,
> They say, in great extremity; and fear'd
> She'll with the labour end.[44]

> For a more blusterous birth had never babe[45]

> A grievous burthen was they [sic] birth to me[46]

but also, he knew two methods to correct desultory labor.

One,[18] quoted above when referring to midwifery, consisted in a prayer of the goddess (Lucina) of midwives: the other is:

> Macduff was from his mother's womb
> Untimely ripp'd.[47]

This line substantiates the thought that he was the early modern obstetrician, using cesarean section. You may have the privilege of entertaining the idea of "prematurity" in this line in *Macbeth*, but to me it was as stated— "untimely ripp'd."

Did he presage the concept of postmaturity when he wrote

> The child was prisoner to the womb, and is
> By law and process of great nature thence
> Freed and enfranchis'd;[48]

The saddest of all deaths are recorded on at least two occasions by our noble obstetrician. In *A Midsummer Night's Dream* he briefly states

> But she, being mortal, of that boy did die[49]

In *Pericles* he portrays the pathos of a living child and maternal death:

> Here is a thing too young for such a place,
> Who, if it had conceit, would die, as I
> Am like to do: take in your arms this piece
> Of your dead queen.[50]

and

> Here's all that is left living of your queen,
> A little daughter;[51]

The anomalous infant impressed our obstetrical ancestor in many descriptive passages. Two of these were quoted above, when abortions were described.[33, 34] The most gripping passage is voiced by Richard III about himself:

> Cheated of feature by dissembling nature,
> Deform'd, unfinish'd, sent before my time

Into this breathing world, scarce half made up,
And that so lamely and unfashionable
That dogs bark at me, as I halt by them.[52]

Or do you prefer

Thy mother felt more than a mother's pain,
And yet brought forth less than a mother's hope;
To wit an undigested and deformed lump,
Not like the fruit of such a goodly tree.
Teeth hast thou in thy head when thou wast born,
To signify thou cam'st to bite the world.[53]

Short, but frightening in *Titus Andronicus* is

A joyless, dismal, black and sorrowful issue.
Here is the babe, as loathesome as a toad.[54]

And in The Tempest

Save for the son that she did litter here—
A freckl'd whelp, hag-born—not honor'd with
A human shape.[55]

His emphasis wanes in *Othello*

... Hell and night
Must bring this monstrous birth to the world's light[56]

The real desire of Shakespeare comes through beautifully in the following from *A Midsummer Night's Dream*. It is the prayer of all mothers, fathers and obstetricians:

And the issue there create
Ever shall be fortunate.
So shall all the couples three
Ever time in loving be;
And the blots of Nature's hand
Shall not in their issue stand;
Never mole, hare-lip nor scar.
Nor mark prodigious, such as are
Despised in nativity,
Shall upon their children be[57]

The genetic implications to the newborn are recognized in both the similarities and dissimilarities of one's ancestors.

... That bed, that womb,
That metal, that self-mold that fashioned thee
Made him a man[58]

and

... this teeming womb of royal kings,
Fear'd by their breed and famous by their birth[59]

and

Good wombs have borne bad sons.[60]

Maternal love and the psychological effect it plays on maternal behavior during pregnancy is beautifully demonstrated in *King Henry VI, Part III*. Could anyone have written so well about the psychology of being a mother without frequent association as a physician?

For love of Edward's offspring in my womb:
This is it that makes me bridle passion,
And bear with mildness my misfortune's cross;
Ay, Ay, for this I draw in many a tear,
And stop the rising of blood-sucking sighs,
Lest with my sighs or tears I blast or drown
King Edward's fruit, true heir to the English crown.[61]

It would be interesting to know where our obstetrician received his psychiatric training. Or would Sophocles be the training ground where he learned of the "Oedipus complex"? On two occasions he wrote:

Ay, rather than I'll shame my mother's womb[62]

and

... If she
Had partaken of my flesh, and cost me the dearest
Groans of a mother, I could not have owned her
A more rooted love.[63]

In spite of his many astute observations, on occasions he was blinded by the superstitions of the times—the witch's brew, the shrieking owl, the evil day.

... let wives with child
Pray that their burthens may not fall this day.[64]

The owl shriek'd at thy birth, an evil sign.[65]

Why, love forswore me in my mother's womb.[66]

The midwife wonder'd, and the women cried
'O! Jesus bless us, he is born with teeth'[67]

Indeed, he uses pregnancy and the uterus to express hate on several occasions in Richard III.[33, 34] And again in the same play:

From forth the kennel of thy womb hath crept
A hell-hound that doth hunt us all to death[68]

There was one sociologic problem with an obstetric implication that occupied his mind more than any other. Curiously, our own age is seeing a rapid upsurge in this social aberration. Illegitimacy was mentioned no less than on fifteen occasions in eight of his plays.[8, 10, 69-81] In *Measure For Measure* the main theme is illegitimacy, and it is mentioned on seven occasions.

> ... from whence he was whipped for getting the shrieve's fool with child,[69]
>
> ... But it chances
> The stealth of our mutual entertainment
> With character too gross is writ on Juliet
> With child perhaps?
>
> Unhappily, even so.[72]
>
> ... even so her plenteous womb expresseth his full tilth and husbandry.
> Someone with child by him? My cousin Juliet?[74]

On one occasion rape is specifically mentioned (not including the poem *The Rape of Lucrece*):

> If any woman wrong'd by this lewd fellow-
> As I have heard him swear himself there's one
> Whom he begot with child,[82]

After this evidence can anyone doubt that Shakespeare was an obstetrician?

BIBLIOGRAPHY

(Quoted from the Yale *Shakespeare*)

1. Measure For Measure. II:*iii*, 12.
2. King Henry VI, Part I. V:*iv*, 62–63.
3. A Midsummer Night's Dream. II:*i*, 131.
4. Pericles, Prince of Tyre. III: *Prol.*, 9–11.
5. Henry VIII. II:*iv*, 184–189.
6. Love's Labour Lost. V:*ii*, 676–677.
7. Love's Labour Lost. V:*ii*, 680–681.
8. The Winter's Tale. II:*i*, 59–61.
9. Henry VIII. IV:*i*, 76–77.
10. Love's Labour Lost. V:*ii*, 684–686.
11. All's Well That Ends Well. V:*iii*, 306–307.
12. Measure For Measure. II:*i*, 88–90.
13. Measure For Measure. II:*i*, 97–99.
14. Pericles, Prince of Tyre. III: *Prol.*, 51–52.
15. Henry VIII. V:*i*, 68–72.
16. Measure For Measure. II:*ii*, 14–15.
17. All's Well That Ends Well. I:*iii*, 155.
18. Pericles, Prince of Tyre. III:*i*, 10–14.
19. Richard II. II:*ii*, 61–65.
20. Titus Andronicus. IV:*ii*, 62–63.

21. Titus Andronicus. IV:*ii*, 125–126.
22. Titus Andronicus. IV:*ii*, 142–143.
23. Titus Andronicus. IV:*ii*, 155.
24. Richard III. II:*i*, 71–72.
25. Pericles, Prince of Tyre. III:*i*, 32–34.
26. Cymbeline. V:*iv*, 43–47.
27. The Tempest. I:*ii*, 269.
28. Henry VIII. V:*i*, 164–165.
29. King Lear. I:*iv*, 284–287.
30. Timon of Athens. IV:*iii*, 189–190.
31. Henry IV, Part II. V:*iv*, 10.
32. Henry IV, Part II. V:*iv*, 15.
33. Richard III. I:*ii*, 21–24.
34. Richard III. I:*iii*, 228 and 231.
35. Love's Labour Lost. I:*i*, 104.
36. King John. I:*i*, 112–113.
37. The Winter's Tale. II:*ii*, 25–27.
38. Romeo and Juliet. I:*ii*, 12–13.
39. Timon of Athens. IV:*iii*, 3–5.
40. The Comedy of Errors. I:*i*, 50–55.
41. King Henry VI, Part II. IV:*ii*, 151.
42. Richard III. IV:*iv*, 138.
43. Pericles, Prince of Tyre. III:*i*, 57.
44. Henry VIII. V:*i*, 18–20.
45. Pericles, Prince of Tyre. III:*i*, 28.
46. Richard III. IV:*iv*, 168.
47. Macbeth. V:*vii*, 44–45.
48. The Winter's Tale. II:*ii*, 59–61.
49. A Midsummer Night's Dream. II:*i*, 135.
50. Pericles, Prince of Tyre. III:*i*, 15–18.
51. Pericles, Prince of Tyre. III:*i*, 20–21.
52. Richard III. I:*i*, 19–23.
53. King Henry VI, Part III. V:*vi*, 49–54.
54. Titus Andronicus. IV:*ii*, 67–68.
55. The Tempest. I:*ii*, 282–284.
56. Othello. I:*iii*, 402–403.
57. A Midsummer Night's Dream. V:*i*, 414–423.
58. Richard II. I:*ii*, 22–24.
59. Richard II. II:*i*, 51–52.
60. The Tempest. I:*ii*, 120.
61. King Henry VI, Part III. IV:*iv*, 18–24.
62. King Henry VI, Part I. IV:*v*, 35.
63. All's Well That Ends Well. IV:*v*, 10–13.

THE BEST OF AFTER OFFICE HOURS

64. King John. III:*i*, 89–90.
65. King Henry VI, Part III. V:*vi*, 44.
66. King Henry VI, Part III. III:*ii*, 153.
67. King Henry VI, Part III. V:*ii*, 74–75.
68. Richard III. IV:*iv*, 47–48.
69. All's Well That Ends Well. IV:*iii*, 212–213.
70. Measure For Measure. I:*ii*, 73–74.
71. Measure For Measure. I:*ii*, 92–93.
72. Measure For Measure. I:*ii*, 156–159.
73. Measure For Measure. I:*iv*, 29.
74. Measure For Measure. I:*iv*, 43–45.
75. Measure For Measure. III:*i*, 476–477.
76. Measure For Measure. IV:*iii*, 173–174.
77. The Merchant of Venice. III:*v*, 40–43.
78. King Lear. I:*i*, 13–14.
79. Timon of Athens. I:*i*, 210–211.
80. As You Like It. III:*ii*, 207.
81. All's Well That Ends Well. III:*ii*, 60–61.
82. Measure For Measure. V:*i*, 511–513.

Obstet Gynecol 1964;24:491–6.

COMMENTARY

D. Frank Kaltreider (1912–1988), a long-time faculty member at the University of Maryland and later also at Johns Hopkins University, was chief of obstetric–gynecologic services at Baltimore City Hospital. He also must have been quite a Shakespearean scholar, for in this article he identifies, among the extensive writings of Shakespeare, those portions having obstetric allusions. The list is both long and impressive, leading Kaltreider to argue that Shakespeare must have been an obstetrician.

In an earlier After Office Hours article (Obstet Gynecol 1953;2:187–200), R. D. Bryant constructed a long and detailed obstetric case in which every single aspect was described with a Shakespearean quote.

Hamlet's Soliloquy on Allergy

E. L. Dimmick, MD

JULY 1962

To sneeze, or not to sneeze; that is the question.
Whether it is nobler in the mind to suffer
The stings and lachrymation of outrageous hay fever
Or to take shots against a sea of troubles
And by much needling end them? To cry, to sneeze
No more, and by a sneeze to end
The headache and the thousand devilish symptoms
The flesh is heir to; 'tis a consummation devoutly to be wished
To cry, to sneeze,
To sneeze, perchance to stream; ay, there's the rub
For in that sneeze allergic when it comes what streams
May run from noses and from eyes
Must give us pause. There's the aftereffects
That make the antihistamines of so long action
For who would bear the pills and sprays all the time,
The skin tests wrong, the proud man whealy,
The pangs of needles shoved, the doc's delays,
The impotence of medication and the side effects
The patient suffers from the things he takes
When he himself might his own relief obtain
With a sterilized Luer? Who would patch tests bear
To itch and scratch under an unknown allergy
But that the dread of something worse to come,
That undiscovered remedy by whose boon
No victim's yet been cured, puzzles the will
And rather makes one bear the wheals one has
Than risk some others that he knows not of?
Thus allergy doth make cowards of us all
And thus the native tan of healthy hide
Is sicklied o'er with pale lumps of "hives"
And proprietaries of great promise and advertisement
Their doses go awry and fail to get desired action.

Obstet Gynecol 1962;20:148.

The Adventure of the Three Abnormal Paps

Krishnansu S. Tewari, MD

November 2000

wing to ill weather on 2 October 1888, my friend Sherlock Holmes and I retired early to our familiar lodgings at 221B Baker Street. Parliament had risen and I entered into a brown study, pursuing a treatise on gynecologic infections.[1] Holmes was restless and in a rather black mood, recalling our time together on the dark and eerie Grimpen Moor.[2]

Holmes had grown bored deciphering the secret writings of the Freemasons and with the apocrypha of the agony column in the *Times*. The latest on the Whitechapel mystery held his interest momentarily; he remarked that the singular nature of the Jack the Ripper murders and the Masonic connections seemed to place it beyond even the realm of his evil doppleganger [sic], Professor James Moriarty, the Napoleon of Crime.[2] The world's only consulting detective took up his violin and subjected me to several unfamiliar and discordant airs before conducting a malodorous laboratory experiment that was not befitting the atmosphere of our domicile.

"Really, Holmes," said I, "You are rather trying at times."

Before he could make answer to my remonstrance, Mrs. Hudson appeared with the calling card of a visitor. I was thinking that the card appeared too small to carry the weight of the man's academic distinctions when our client burst suddenly into the room and collapsed.

THE TROUBLED DOCTOR

"Watson! What is it?" Holmes exclaimed as I felt for the elderly man's pulse.

Placing my brandy flask to his lips, I said, "Exhaustion, perhaps starvation. Nothing more."

Our visitor regained himself and begged forgiveness. "Gentlemen, my driver Netley has braved the elements to bring me through the gaslit city in a magnificent royal coach so that I may place my case before you." He was a large man with long, thick sideburns, so pompous in his black cloak and top hat and yet so dignified.

"I am Sir William Withey Gull, royal physician to Queen Victoria. My career has been one of distinction; you may recall my monograph on anorexia nervosa.[3] But now, during the autumn years of my life, I have been presented with three cases which are destined to be my undoing. Three ladies—three persistently abnormal Pap smears despite negative biopsy results! 0! Ye gods! What am I to do?"

"There may be several features of interest to your cases, but I am clearly out of the range of my expertise." Holmes lit his drop-stem pipe, the companion of his deepest meditations. Presently, he continued, "These initial shortcomings may be easily remedied. Unfamiliar as I may be with the mechanics of medicine, my biographer here will attest that there are common thought processes and drives necessary for both medical and detective work, including observation, analysis, and deduction, a devotion to details, labor, learning, energy, determination, and an overpowering desire to solve mysteries."[4] Holmes reached for his personal directory in which he recorded all things sensational. Scanning Volume E, he mumbled "... Prince Eddy ... Edinburgh ... Ah! Elephant Man! Let me see ... Merrick ... circus ... Treves ... Very well, then! Sir William, I must ask you to collect all of your slides and bring them to London Hospital tomorrow morning. I believe that a review of the pathology is warranted, during which time Dr. Treves may be able to educate me on these clinical tests. I trust you have heard of Sir Frederick Treves and his famous Elephant Man."[5]

After Sir William had left, Holmes asked, "So, Watson, what do you make of our dear Dr. Gull's obsessive and emotional state regarding these Pap tests?"

"The modern French psychologists have described a form of monomania called the *ideé fixe*.[2] Under its influence, a man may be capable of any fantastic outrage. Perhaps thoughts of failure when confronted with a difficult clinical puzzle constitute an Achilles' heel to the academician. I am grateful to have placed myself in private practice!"

THE GYNECOLOGY LESSON

The next morning, I opened my eyes to find Holmes fully attired, having already broken his fast. "There is coffee on the table," he said as I completed my toilet. A familiar fog enshrouded the city, vainly attempting to hide its secrets from my friend. We hailed a cab and soon were being driven through the cobbled arteries of London by two chestnut mares. Our destination, London Hospital, was set amidst the poorest populace in the city; however, there was no shortage of clinical material, and I had been told that the teaching was superb.

There was an intensity to Dr. Treves as he scrutinized the cytologic smears and histologic sections under the microscope. Through a heavy black moustache, he announced that everything was in agreement with what had been originally reported. He had nothing new to add.

"I am undone!" Gull ejaculated.

Holmes asked, "Kindly illuminate me on the singular nature of these lesions."

In a seasoned professorial manner, Dr. Treves explained that the cervical cancer epidemic has been controlled in developed countries by the screening tool known as the Pap smear. Cells are sampled from the transformation zone, where most cervical cancers arise. "Now, when a routine Pap test is abnormal, colposcopic viewing is the next step. Abnormal cervical regions saturated in a vinegar solution are detectable under magnification."

"Acetic acid," Holmes breathed, "Capital! The piling up of neoplastic cells containing an increased nuclear-to-cytoplasmic ratio would certainly make the abnormal areas stand out."

"My dear Holmes!" I exclaimed, astounded at his knowledge of modern cellular biology.

"My blushes, Watson! As ever, there are some points which escape even your Machiavellian intellect. While you lay sleeping, I read long into the night." Turning back to Treves, Holmes said, "Pray continue with your most interesting narrative."

"Abnormal acetowhite areas on the cervix should be sampled for biopsy and a scraping from within the canal obtained. A careful histologic evaluation determines the degree of correlation to the cytologic Pap test, and a treatment plan can be formulated."

"What causes these changes, Dr. Treves, these precancerous cells?" Holmes asked.

"High-risk strains of the human papillomavirus obtained through sexual intercourse have been implicated. The changes do not appear immediately; rather, years are required."

Silently, I concurred. In my recent readings I had come across this so-called human papillomavirus,[1] although while in the presence of so learned a man as Dr. Treves, I did not volunteer any specific details of what I had learned.

Suddenly Holmes stood up and addressed the crestfallen royal physician. "Sir, bring your patients separately to Baker Street." A ray of hope shone upon Sir William's face.

"Holmes, you have a theory?" I ventured.

"Yes, perhaps, my dear Watson. It is certainly a three-pipe problem."

If Sherlock Holmes had any defects, one must surely be that he was exceedingly loathe to communicate his reasoning to others until the instant of revelation or fulfillment.[2] This stemmed from his masterful nature to surprise those around him and the professional caution he maintained. The result, however, was very trying for those who were acting as his assistants.

And so we parted ways. Dr. Treves had graciously secured for me an audience with Mr. Joseph Merrick, the Elephant Man. Sir William left for the British Museum to view a newly arrived Egyptian mummy from the Fifteenth Dynasty. Holmes himself was bound for the concert hall to hear Richard Wagner's *Die Walküre* and to smoke an ounce of shag tobacco.

THE CASE OF MRS. O

For the next two days, Holmes pored over anatomical texts, medical journals, and diagrams concerning the lower female genital tract, often preparing fresh drawings. He had a horror of destroying documents,[2] and as explicit diagrams and atlases depicting female anatomy began to litter our floor and find their way into his Persian slippers or jack-knifed to the mantle, I grew concerned. What would guests say?

Sir William arrived on the third day with Mrs. O. Recently widowed, a diamond of the first water rested on her finger. Her first abnormal Pap test had been followed by negative results on biopsy and on loop electrical excision procedure (ie, LEEP). And yet her Pap tests were still abnormal.

Holmes told Mrs. O that he would like to repeat the colposcopy and asked our landlady, Mrs. Hudson, to serve as the chaperone. I will not bore the general reader with details of how Mrs. O assumed a position conducive to pelvic examination. Nor will I describe in depth the precision and skill accorded Sir William's masterful placement of the speculum into the vagina.

Holmes proceeded to apply acetic acid to not only the cervix but to the entire vagina, vulva, and perineum! With a lens he carefully evaluated all areas of Mrs. O's genitalia. Mrs. Hudson's expert commentary contained the terms "shocking behavior" and "blasphemous conduct."

"Ah!" Holmes exclaimed, pointing to a small abnormal area along the right vaginal side wall.

"This is astounding, Holmes!" I ejaculated.

"Elementary, my dear Watson!" As Sir William obtained a biopsy, Holmes explained, "All epithelial layers of the lower reproductive tract are likely to be susceptible to viral infection."

The following day, Dr. Treves confirmed the diagnosis of a grade II vaginal intraepithelial neoplasia. Sir William was a transformed man, and Mrs. O was scheduled for a wide local excision.

THE CASE OF MISS J

Before the week was up, Sir William appeared at our doorstep with Miss J. Holmes embarked upon the interview, while Sir William and I sat in abject silence. Miss J was 22 years of age and had her first abnormal Pap test last year. Negative results on cervical biopsy and endocervical scrapings were followed by another abnormal Pap test; this in turn was succeeded by negative LEEP, a negative cervical cone, another negative LEEP, and finally another abnormal Pap test. This sequence was particularly painful for Sir William to relive, as Miss J was unmarried and nulliparous.

"Have you had multiple sexual partners?"

"Really, Mr. Holmes! This is intolerable!" Mrs. Hudson had turned crimson.

Holmes was momentarily distracted by something on our patient's clothing. "A touch!" he exclaimed, "A distinct touch. It fits with the known risk factors. I see you are a connoisseur of Imperial cigarettes..." He was no doubt paying homage for perhaps the one hundredth time to his own monograph entitled *On the distinction between the ashes of various tobaccos.*[2]

"Now, at what age did you first engage in the act of coitus?"

"Mr. Holmes!"

Holmes terminated the interview in frustration under Mrs. Hudson's seething glare. He saturated the vagina and perineum with vinegar and moved through the colposcopic procedure as fluidly as though he had invented the steps. "Sir William has indeed succeeded in excising most of the transformation zone. After two LEEPs and a cone, only a nub of cervix remains!"

Our royal physician grew pale and started to fret. "Unlike our previous case," Holmes continued, "Miss J's vagina appears in satisfactory condition; in addition, the endocervical remnant, vulva, and perineum do not exhibit any remarkable abnormalities."

Holmes continued his methodical inspection, and I feared for Sir William; the perspiration was heavy upon his brow. And then finally, "I have it here!" Holmes exclaimed. Lying not within the endocervical canal but along the perimeter of the ectocervix at 2 o'clock, nearly completely hidden from view, was a distinct, punctated, acetowhite, lesion 2 to 3 mm in diameter! The three of us were caught up by the excitement of discovery and were all peering into Miss J's vagina, jostling each other for the use of the lens. Mrs. Hudson had become quite hysterical, and I had to calm her nerves before Sir William could perform the crucial biopsy.

Dr. Treves reported a diagnosis of grade I cervical intraepithelial neoplasia, and regular colposcopic surveillance was initiated. Miss J was advised to marry quickly and attempt pregnancy. I believe Sir William even broached the subject of prophylactic cervical cerclage.

THE CASE OF MRS. N

Now Holmes has rarely expressed sentimentality towards the gentler sex, but even he was touched beyond professional empathy by the predicament of the 26-year-old Mrs. N. Recently married to a sailor, the realms of passion had been previously uncharted for her. Annual Pap tests had always been normal until two weeks into her marriage, when she was found to have an abnormal Pap result. True to form, the ever-diligent Sir William had performed an unremarkable colposcopy, retrieved blind negative results on biopsy and scrapings, repeated the Pap test (which was abnormal), and proceeded in desperation to a negative LEEP. During the interview, Mrs. N abruptly burst into tears stating that her Eddy had left her earlier that day.

This case seemed to trouble Holmes more than either of the others. Sir William and I were on the edges of our seats as we watched him weigh the matter in his mind. Sir William wished to proceed with colposcopy, this time certain that he could detect the occult lesion.

Suddenly Holmes asked Mrs. N at which o'clock her sailor had left and where he was bound. She gave him the information, and Sir William urged us to get on with the colposcopy. "That will not provide the solution you seek, dear Gull!" Turning to me, Holmes said, "We must be swift of foot, Watson. Already precious time has been lost. I fear that this young lady has suffered from ill-use and mischief! The North Western line makes for Birmingham at 1:30.[2] Contact Scotland Yard and ask our friend Lestrade to meet us at the railway station!"

And with that, he donned his deerstalker cap and was off. I sent the required message and followed in pursuit. My sedentary life compelled me to fall far behind; Holmes, however, was always in training and had inexhaustable [sic] stores of nervous energy upon which to draw.[2]

At the railway station I searched frantically, but there was no sign of Holmes. Within minutes, Officer Lestrade arrived, as did Sir William and Dr. Treves. I began relating Holmes' incomprehensible actions when suddenly we heard his voice: "Help! Help! Murder!"

On Platform 4, a bulky man was strangling Holmes. Lestrade and I threw him to the ground. "He tried to molest me!" the man shouted pointing to Holmes. Sir William and Dr. Treves appeared frozen in time. "He tried to look at my John Thomas with a magnifying glass!"

This is it, I thought, all of his relentless work and 7% solutions,[2] finally they had caused my friend to lose all reason. But Holmes said, "Sir William, if prudence permits, I must recall to your memory that Mrs. N was a stranger to love until she married her sailor, who stands before us now. Her first abnormal Pap test occurred two weeks after the wedding. Dr. Treves would certainly concur that such a short period would be insufficient for the development of detectable neoplastic changes. As seafaring men readily answer the siren's call, our sailor was probably not uninitiated in the acts of passion and would have had multiple previous encounters with Aphrodite or her less virtuous cousins. Neoplastic cells shed from his organ of generation when the marriage was consummated or shortly thereafter would be inadvertently retrieved during the Pap test! Your presence, Lestrade, was requested because I suspected he would not readily agree to having his entire member submerged in a bucket of acetic acid to prove my theory."

"Absolutely brilliant!" Dr. Treves cried out.

"Remarkable!" said I.

"Surely my deductions are simplicity itself."

Officer Lestrade did not appear to be any clearer on the subject and looked at us suspiciously.

Sir William fainted right there on the spot. The strain of the past weeks' adventures had shattered his nerves. Before morning, he lay delirious in a high fever under the care of Dr. Treves. They were destined to travel the world together before Sir William would regain his senses.

We learned later that Dr. Treves had evaluated Mr. N and confirmed that Holmes had indeed faced a grade III penile intraepithelial neoplasia. Puffing on his pipe, Holmes remarked, "If Dr. Gull were here, I would advise him in the future to always look before he LEEPs."

EPILOGUE

On 10 November 1888, I was reviewing my notes during the early afternoon when I mentioned to Sherlock Holmes, "We have had several interesting medical cases. I may prepare a pamphlet containing ones such as our recent affair with Dr. Gull as well as the adventure of the conjoined triplets and the mystery of the persistent molar pregnancy." But Holmes wasn't listening. He was staring out of our windows, his eyes apparently fixed on some object or person. At his side lay his own monograph, *On the tracing of footsteps*,[2] and the latest edition of the *Times*, in which was reported the fifth Ripper victim.

"I wonder if they'll ever find this murderer," I ventured.

"What was that?" Holmes asked, somewhat annoyed as if I had interrupted a delicate train of thought. A seagull that had been perched on the rooftop across the street flew away.

REFERENCES

1. Shen LH, Rushing L, McLachlin CM, Sheets EE, Crum CP. Prevalence and histologic significance of cervical human papillomavirus DNA detected in women at low and high risk for cervical neoplasia. Obstet Gynecol 1995; 86:499–503.
2. Conan Doyle A. The complete Sherlock Holmes. New York: Bantam Doubleday Dell, 1999.
3. Gull WW. Anorexia nervosa (apepsia hysterica, anorexia hysterica). Trans Clin Soc London 1874;7:22–8.
4. Peschel RE, Peschel E. What physicians have in common with Sherlock Holmes: Discussion paper. J R Soc Med 1989;82:33–6.
5. Treves F. The Elephant Man. In: The Elephant Man and other reminiscences. London: Cassell, 1923:1–37.

Obstet Gynecol 2000;96:795–8.

Obstetrics and Ernest Hemingway

Charles R. King, MD

JULY 1989

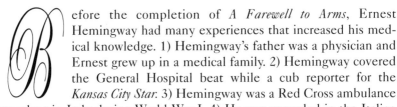efore the completion of *A Farewell to Arms*, Ernest Hemingway had many experiences that increased his medical knowledge. 1) Hemingway's father was a physician and Ernest grew up in a medical family. 2) Hemingway covered the General Hospital beat while a cub reporter for the *Kansas City Star.* 3) Hemingway was a Red Cross ambulance attendant in Italy during World War I. 4) He was wounded in the Italian campaign at Caporetto, and experienced medical treatment firsthand while he convalesced in Italy and at the family home in Oak Park, Illinois. 5) As a reporter for the *Toronto Star*, Hemingway reported medical stories among his dispatches. 6) Two of Hemingway's wives, Hadley and Pauline, delivered sons before he completed *A Farewell to Arms.* 7) Hemingway and Don Carlos Guffey, the Kansas City obstetrician who delivered both Patrick and Gregory Hemingway, were friends and frequently corresponded with each other. The medical knowledge realized from these events probably aided Hemingway in depicting medical scenes realistically in his fiction.[1, 2]

SON OF A PHYSICIAN

Today, Ernest Hemingway's father, Dr. Clarence Hemingway, would be considered a family practitioner, but Dr. Hemingway had unusual obstetric knowledge for a physician of the early 20th century. In 1896 he graduated from Chicago's Rush Medical College, which also graduated Joseph Bolivar DeLee, soon to become the foremost obstetrician in Chicago. Dr. Hemingway interned at the University of Edinburgh. When Ernest was nine, his father added to his credentials a 4-month training course in obstetrics at the New York Lying-In Hospital. During this training period in the summer of 1908, Dr. Hemingway wrote excitedly in a letter to his wife that he had "personally delivered 73 babies in the past 21 days."[3] Shortly after his return to Chicago, Dr. Hemingway became the head of obstetrics at Oak Park Hospital. Beginning in 1914, Dr. Hemingway listed his practice in the American Medical Directory as obstetrics.[4]

By the time of his death in 1928, the doctor had delivered more than 3000 babies, including all six of his own children. Ernest and his siblings were born at home because their mother was afraid of a "baby mix-up" with hospital birth.[5, 6] Dr. Hemingway delivered his first daughter, Marcelline, in January 1898, when the attending doctor suffered a heart attack during Grace's labor. Dr. Hemingway arrived home in a snowstorm and administered to the attending doctor, gave anesthesia to his wife, and performed the delivery with high forceps.

The Hemingway family assumed on more than one occasion that Ernest would become a physician. When he was nine, he signed the guest book at a family dinner party as "Ernest Hemingway, MD." Ernest's sister recalled that both she and Ernest were interested in medicine and that their "Daddy laughed about it, but he was pleased that the boy planned to be a doctor."[3] Similar episodes were to surface over the following years. For example, while Dr. Hemingway was attending a medical meeting at the Mayo Clinic, he wrote the adolescent Ernest: "It will only be a few years, before you and Papa will be visiting clinics together."[7] Although Ernest did not become a physician, he did actively integrate medical knowledge into his writing.

KANSAS CITY REPORTER

In the fall of 1917, the 18-year-old Ernest left Oak Park to become a cub reporter for the *Kansas City Star*. Within 1 month of joining the *Star*, Hemingway was assigned to the "shortstop run," including Kansas City General Hospital and the 15th Street police station. This beat was so named because the assigned reporter covered "much ground and needed quickness to do it," just like a baseball shortstop.[8]

Hemingway's first news stories of importance were based on the General Hospital beat, where he saw "hospital inefficiencies and ambulance laxity, and wrote with vigor about them."[9] Contemporaries confirm Hemingway's fascination with the ambulance run. Fellow reporter John Selby recalled that Hemingway was forever disappearing into "the receiving ward" or onto "the tail of an ambulance."[10]

None of Hemingway's newspaper stories report obstetric experiences, but it is likely that riding the ambulance and waiting in the receiving ward would have enabled him to develop additional firsthand experience of obstetric care. In 1918, obstetric complications and even maternal death were common. The growing science of obstetrics was working to remove birth from the home and to transplant the event to the more controlled hospital environment. Thus, a reporter on the shortstop run would be likely to encounter patients with obstetric complications during their transfer to the hospital.

RED CROSS AMBULANCE ATTENDANT

By the late spring of 1918, Ernest and fellow Star reporter Ted Brumbach were leaving Kansas City to join the Red Cross Ambulance Corps in Italy. Hemingway had reportedly been rejected for military service on numerous occasions before his entry into Red Cross service.[11] Within 1 month of his departure from Kansas City, and just weeks before his 19th birthday, Hemingway was wounded in the Italian retreat from Caporetto. His long convalescence in Italy, especially Milan, has been detailed in his biography[1] and forms the basis for the injuries suffered by Frederick Henry in *A Farewell to Arms*.

During his treatment and recovery, Hemingway experienced many medical events as both a patient and a firsthand observer of the medical care of other injured soldiers. He had daily contact with other injured patients, doctors, nurses, and civilians who entered the medical world of war-torn Milan. All of these events contributed to the further growth of his medical knowledge. He was attended by nurse Agnes von Kurowsky, who became part of the model for Catherine Barkley in *A Farewell to Arms*. Unfortunately, there is no record from Hemingway's Italian convalescence of specific events that may have contributed to his obstetric knowledge.

CONVALESCENCE IN OAK PARK

By the fall of 1918, Ernest had returned to Oak Park to complete his convalescence. He received an insurance payment of $1,400,[2] a significant sum at the time, which enabled him to recover without financial worries. He played the part of a war hero; he often appeared in public in a military uniform and frequently gave speeches to local clubs.

Hemingway's sister recalls that during his convalescence, Hemingway read all the time, even "the AMA journals from Dad's office."[12] The *Journal of the American Medical Association* for 1918 and 1919 reported many articles on fractures, war injuries, amputation, hemorrhage, shock, traumatic neuroses, and venereal disease. Of particular interest are the 15 full-length papers on childbirth reported in 1918 and the 20 papers in 1919. Reported are cases of hemorrhage as a cause of maternal death,[13] stillbirth,[14] birth trauma,[15] dystocia,[14] and nitrous oxide anesthesia for childbirth.[14, 16] McQuarrie,[14] for example, reported birth trauma from dystocia as the most common cause of stillbirth. However, more important is Joseph B. DeLee's discussion of the operative techniques, indications, complications, and high mortality of cesarean section.[16] Hemingway could hardly have overlooked the numerous obstetric articles, especially the lengthy article by DeLee, by this time the foremost obstetrician in Chicago. These medical reports provided information for Hemingway's later fictional use. They became secondary sources of obstetric knowledge, similar to the sources Hemingway is known to have used elsewhere in his fiction to depict, accurately and realistically, a war he did not fight.[17]

TORONTO REPORTER

By the early 1920s, Ernest Hemingway had formally begun his career as an author. His future wife, the tall, auburn-haired Hadley Richardson of St. Louis, furthered this process by giving him a typewriter, with which he honed his craft as a reporter for the *Toronto Star*. He continued to write medical articles; for example, "Tooth pulling no cure-all" appeared on April 10, 1920.[18] As he was to do later in his fiction, Hemingway recorded historical and medical details to depict a medical procedure realistically.

In mid-1923, the couple returned from Paris to Toronto for the birth of their first child, John (Bumby). Hemingway favored a Canadian birth, because he thought it would be easier to gain United States citizenship for the child, and he could also continue work with the *Toronto Star*. Hadley was happy to leave Paris, as she "believed that the doctors, nurses, and hospitals would be better in Toronto than in Paris."[7]

After a 3-hour labor on October 10, 1923, Bumby was born at 2 AM in Wellesley hospital in Toronto. Ernest missed the birth because he was sent to New York by the *Star* to cover the visit of Lloyd George to the United States.[19] He returned to Toronto later in the day; Hadley recalls that Ernest broke down when he saw the new baby, but "then pulled together, and was as sweet as you and I know he can be."[7] The ease and simplicity of this birth are in marked contrast to the difficult birth of Patrick Hemingway less than 5 years later.

By 1928, Ernest Hemingway had published short stories, completed the early novel *The Torrents of Spring*, and published the mature novel *The Sun Also Rises*. By the spring of 1928, he had abandoned another major work, and began the novel that would become *A Farewell to Arms*. The writing of the manuscript progressed rapidly even though the Hemingways traveled from Europe to Key West, to Kansas City, and to Wyoming during its composition.

DELIVERY BY CESAREAN SECTION

In early June 1928, Ernest consulted his father about his new wife Pauline's impending childbirth and suggested a possible birth in Michigan, but Dr. Hemingway recommended Kansas City or St. Louis "as the Petroskey Hospitals are really only best for local emergencies.... If you want to have me attend your wife at the Oak Park Hospital, I am glad to offer you my services."[5] The Hemingways declined his father's offer, and instead advised Dr. Don Carlos Guffey in Kansas City of their impending move to the city. Why the Hemingways selected Dr. Guffey is not known, but by

1928 Dr. Guffey had practiced obstetrics in Kansas City for 23 years, and was the first Chairman of Gynecology and Obstetrics at the University of Kansas School of Medicine. Most likely Ernest selected Dr. Guffey as Pauline's physician based on a recommendation from Kansas City relatives. Patrick Hemingway was born on June 28, 1928 at Research Hospital in Kansas City, Missouri. The delivery, of nine and one-half pound Patrick, followed an 18-hour labor. The child was described by the proud father in a letter to Maxwell Perkins, his editor at Scribner's, as "very big and dark and strong seeming."[20] As payment for the delivery, Dr. Guffey received a presentation copy (the third of ten) of *A Farewell to Arms*, which was dedicated to "Dr. Don Carlos Guffey with much admiration and grateful remembrance of a cesarean that was beautifully done and turned out splendidly. Written with the left hand due to fracture of right humerus, with open reduction, etc."[21]

Pauline experienced a difficult labor and delivery. Again in his letter to Perkins, Hemingway noted, "Pauline had a very bad time—cesaerian (can't spell it) and a rocky time afterwards."[20] Four days later in a letter to his old friend Guy Hickok, Hemingway noted, "They had to open up Pauline like a picador's horse to lift out Patrick. It is a different feeling seeing tripas (insides) of a friend rather than those of a horse to whom you have never been introduced."[22] A contemporary operative report by Dr. Guffey provides a description comparable to Hemingway's report of Pauline's delivery. The incision was made from "above the umbilicus to the pubic symphysis" and was followed by the escape of the intestines "from the upper edge of the incision" onto the "surface of the abdomen."

By August, Hemingway was averaging eight manuscript pages per day. The final climactic and concluding 34 pages of the manuscript were completed between August 20 and 22[2] in Sheridan, Wyoming. All of Hemingway's feelings about Patrick's birth eventually entered the description of Catherine's surgery in *A Farewell to Arms*:

> He held something in his two hands that looked like a freshly skinned rabbit and hurried across the corridor with it and in through another door. I went down to the door he had gone into and found them in the room doing things to a new-born child. The doctor held him up for me to see. He held him by the heels and slapped him....
>
> "He's magnificent. He'll weigh five kilos."
>
> ... They were washing him and wrapping him in something. I saw the little dark face and dark hand, but I did not see him move or hear him cry. The doctor was doing something to him again....
>
> I thought Catherine was dead. She looked dead. Her face was gray, the part of it that I could see. Down below, under the light, the doctor was sewing up the great long, forcep-spread, thick-edged wound. Another doctor in a mask gave the anaesthetic. Two nurses in masks handed things. It looked

like a drawing of the Inquisition. I knew as I watched I could have watched it all, but I was glad I hadn't. I do not think I could have watched them cut, but I watched the wound closed into a high welted ridge with quick skillful-looking stitches like a cobbler's, and was glad. When the wound was closed I went out into the hall and walked up and down again....[23]

Dr. Guffey's colleagues recognized his operative skill. Hemingway's depiction of Catherine's wound closure with "quick skillful-looking stitches like a cobbler's" is not unlike contemporary reports that Dr. Guffey routinely delivered babies by cesarean section within 30 seconds. Likewise, infant resuscitation with "suspension by the feet," immersion in "hot and cold water together," "flagellation of the feet," "artificial respiration," and "spirits of ammonia" were commonly practiced by Dr. Guffey (case records, University of Kansas School of Medicine). Such procedures are similar to Hemingway's description of the unsuccessful infant resuscitation in *A Farewell to Arms*.

The similarity of art and life suggests that Hemingway had built on his previous knowledge of obstetrics learned in Oak Park, Kansas City, Toronto, and Europe, and that he may have witnessed the birth of Patrick. Hemingway's letter to Maxwell Perkins and the fictional record speak strongly in favor of his presence at Patrick's birth. The long friendship of Hemingway and Dr. Guffey, including frequent poker games and common correspondence, also provided an opportunity for Hemingway to develop a considerable secondhand knowledge of obstetrics from the doctor, just as he had developed his knowledge of war from old soldiers.

The pivotal scene in *A Farewell to Arms* is in the final chapter, which centers on the delivery from Catherine of a stillborn child, and Catherine's subsequent death in hemorrhagic shock. Although an earlier work, Theodore Dreiser's *The Genius*, has been suggested as the literary source for the final chapter of *A Farewell to Arms*,[24] the real-life birth of Patrick Hemingway by cesarean section is a more important non-literary source. The death of Dr. Hemingway by a self-inflicted gunshot wound in early December 1928 may have influenced Hemingway's revision of the novel's conclusion,[25] but a cause for Catherine's death based on her "narrowness in the hips," which "biologically" traps the woman, must have been the final consideration.[26] This was an especially realistic conclusion in light of the frequency of maternal death and the obstetric knowledge of the day.

REFERENCES

1. Baker C. Ernest Hemingway: A life story. New York: Scribner's, 1969.
2. Reynolds MS. Hemingway's first war. The making of A Farewell to Arms. Princeton: Princeton University, 1976:25–118.
3. Sanford MH. At the Hemingways: A family portrait. Boston: Little, Brown, 1961:112–34.

4.   American medical directory. Chicago: American Medical Association, 1914:449.

5.   Hemingway L. My brother Ernest Hemingway. New York: World, 1961:21–37.

6.   Meyer J. Hemingway, a biography. New York: Harper, 1985:6.

7.   Kert B. The Hemingway women. New York: Norton, 1983:39–141.

8.   Griffin P. Along with youth: Hemingway, the early years. New York: Oxford, 1985:40.

9.   Wilson D. Hemingway in Kansas City. In: Bruccoli MJ, ed. Fitzgerald/ Hemingway annual. 1976:208–26.

10. Umland R. Ernest Hemingway: The cub reporter. The City Window 1974; 2:14–26.

11. *Kansas City Star* January 27, 1986:1C.

12. Brumbach T. With Hemingway before A Farewell to Arms. *Kansas City Star* December 6, 1936:20.

13. Gardiner JP. Acute dilatation of the post partum uterus as a cause of post partum hemorrhage. JAMA 1919;73:1915–6.

14. McQuarrie TG. Fetal death. JAMA 1919;73:15–8.

15. Heppner M. Postmortem cesarean section following an influenzal bronchopneumonia. JAMA 1919;72:727.

16. DeLee JB. The newer methods of cesarean section. JAMA 1919;73:91–5.

17. Hemingway E. Monologue to the maestro: A high seas letter. Esquire 1935; 4:21–6.

18. Hemingway E. Tooth pulling no cure-all. *Toronto Star* April 10, 1920:10.

19. Scholoff AH. Hadley, the first Mrs. Hemingway. New York: Dodd Mead, 1973.

20. Hemingway E. Letter to Maxwell Perkins July 23, 1928. In: Baker C, ed. Ernest Hemingway selected letters 1917–61. New York: Scribner's, 1981:278.

21. Hemingway E. A Farewell to Arms (special presentation copy). New York: Scribner's, 1929. (Manuscript owned by the University of Missouri, Kansas City).

22. Hemingway E. Letter to Guy Hickok July 27, 1928. In: Baker C. Ernest Hemingway selected letters 1917–61.[20] 280.

23. Hemingway E. A Farewell to Arms. New York: Scribner's, 1929:335–6.

24. McIlvanine RM. A literary source for the cesarean section in A Farewell to Arms. Am Lit 1971;43:444–7.

25. Oldsey B. Hemingway's hidden craft: The writing of A Farewell to Arms. University Park, Pennsylvania: Pennsylvania State University, 1979:37.

26. Friedman N. "Small hips, not war." In: Gellens J. Twentieth century interpretations of A Farewell to Arms. Englewood Cliffs, New Jersey: Prentice Hall, 1970:102–9.

Obstet Gynecol 1989;74:117–20.

Medicated Nursery Rhymes

Howard J. Bennett, MD

October 2000

 hildren have enjoyed Mother Goose nursery rhymes for hundreds of years. Now that I have two little Bennetts in my house, I spend as much time with children's literature as I do with the medical kind. So the other night, as I sat down to read Ms. Goose for the umpteenth time, I thought it would be fun to play around with the verses and give them a medical slant. Here's what I came up with.

LITTLE MISS MUFFET (IN THE DELIVERY ROOM)

> Little Miss Muffet
> Decided to rough it
> By shooing the drugs away.
> Then came a contraction,
> That caused a retraction,
> And "Bradley" was quickly passé.

MARY HAD A LITTLE LUMP

> Mary had a little lump,
> That soon began to grow;
> And everyone that Mary saw
> Said, "Boy, this lump should go."
> She went to see her doc one day,
> To get the lump removed;
> But since it was cosmetic,
> It couldn't be approved.

JACK AND JILL

> Jack and Jill went up the hill,
> The day she broke her water;
> Jack said "Push," and she said "Shush,"
> And soon they had a daughter.

Sing a Song of Clomid

Sing a song of Clomid,
A pelvis full of dye;
Four-and-twenty studies
Your HMO won't buy.
When the tests are finished,
The docs and nurses sing:
"By the time we get you pregnant,
You won't own a thing."

Bah, Bah, Beep, Beep

Bah, bah, beep, beep, have you any calls?
Yes, sir, yes, sir, three in all;
One from a primip, one from a sprain,
And one from the IVF who lives down the lane.
Bah, bah, beep, beep, have you any calls?
Yes, sir, yes, sir, here's three more.

Mistress Mary

Mistress Mary, quite contrary,
How does your baby lie?
It's ROA and minus one,
Get it out before I cry!

Little Boy Blue
(a medical student)

Little Boy Blue,
Come do this form,
The patient's in stirrups,
The kid's almost born.
But where is my student
Who handles the scut?
He's down in the ER,
Messing things up.
Will you scold him?
No, not I,
For if I do,
He's sure to cry.

Obstet Gynecol 2000;96:643.

COMMENTARY

This clever parody relates popular nursery rhymes to obstetric–gynecologic topics. The author, a pediatrician, has compiled and edited a popular book, The Best of Medical Humor, *now in its second edition (which, incidentally, includes at least nine selections from After Office Hours).*

Tips of the Slongue: The Enduring Legacy of W.A. Spooner

Ronald S. Gibbs, MD

JUNE 1997

*T*he title of this article is not an example of a typographical error, but rather a common and often amusing phonic error, referred to as a "Spoonerism." These slips of the tongue are named after William Augustus Spooner, Professor of Theology, Dean and Warden at New College, Oxford University.[1, 2] Spooner was born in 1844 and, by the time of his death in 1930, was alleged to have made some of the most celebrated of these errors.

Once, while officiating at a wedding ceremony, he noted that the groom was so nervous that he had overlooked an important part of the ritual and told him, "Son, it is kisstomary to cuss the bride."[3] At another time while addressing a group of farmers, it is alleged that he said, "Never before have I had the privilege of addressing so many tons of soil."[3] The good reverend, on another occasion, chided a group of students for having "hissed my mystery lecture"[3] and for later having "tasted the whole worm." Then, at the height of Victorian England, he raised his glass before his colleagues and proposed a toast to "the queer old dean."[3]

So well characterized are these unfortunate slips, that over the years they have come to be known as spoonerisms. But William Augustus was not the first or the only and surely is not the last speaker to launch these amusing transpositions publicly. One of the most well known from the days of radio includes the announcer who regaled Wonderbread as "the breast in bed." Even so esteemed an announcer as Lowell Thomas was not immune. In a wartime broadcast from London, he referred to British minister Sir Stafford Cripps as "Sir Stifford Crapps."[3] And the noted radio and TV announcer Harry von Zell, in the depths of the Depression, uttered, "Now from the White House, President Hoobert Heever."[3] These, indeed, can certainly give one a spear of public freaking.

One recent night while on call, I set my mind to work, transposing Spooner to our faculty in 1997, and wondered what a case presentation might sound like.

A young primigravida was referred with an unusual combination of toast perm pregnancy and multitwetal fins. Twin A had premature rupture of membranes, and I was immediately concerned because there was meconium as thick as sea poop. Because her personal hygiene was poor, we had her shake a tower. Immediately thereafter, she developed dyspnea and pest chain. Diagnostically, I left no tern unstoned.

My clinical diagnosis was Dave's grisease, and I placed a central line passed through a hypodeemic nerdle so that we could measure her central penous vressure. I proposed to determine the cardiac output by—I'll pass here—the Fick principle.

She went into spontaneous labor and asked for a cane pillar, but fetal tart hones became nonreassuring, and I knew we would need to carry out delivery city prune. We had vaginal deliveries of healthy twins, about which I certainly had no fad ceilings. To the referring physician, I quickly lent a setter. At the end of the hospitalization, when mother and babies were doing well, she gave me the most gratifying compliment. She turned to me and said, "Dr. Spooner, you must be one pretty fart smeller."

Enjoy Spoonerisms in your everyday communications, professional or social. The next time you leave a dinner party, thank the host for a lovely evening and the malicious deal.

REFERENCES

1. Crystal D. The Cambridge encyclopedia of the English language. Cambridge: Cambridge University Press, 1995.
2. Farb P. Word play, what happens when people talk. New York: Vintage Books Division of Random House, 1993.
3. Morris W, Morris M. Morris dictionary of word and phrase origins. 2nd Ed. New York: Harper-Collins Publishers, 1988.

Obstet Gynecol 1997;89:1047–8.

COMMENTARY

Ronald Gibbs, chair of obstetrics and gynecology at the University of Colorado in Denver, once gave an after-dinner talk on spoonerisms, the always-funny slips of the tongue involving transposing the initial letters of two words. With only a little encouragement, he agreed to submit it for publication. A decade before this piece was published, Gibbs served on the Green Journal Editorial Board (1985–1988).

The Death of Charlotte Brontë

Gerson Weiss, MD

October 1991

O ne of the controversies surrounding Charlotte Brontë's life and career concerns her death, which has been ascribed to hyperemesis gravidarum, a condition thought to be induced by neurosis. By implication, her work has been belittled as the product of a neurotic mind.[1] Thus, a better understanding of the cause of her death may affect our view of her life and, more important, our perceptions of her creativity, if such understanding quells the view that her writings were merely the ravings of a severe neurotic.

Brontë's life has attracted a great deal of biographical scrutiny. Since the publication of *Jane Eyre* in 1847, the literary world has been fascinated by this obscure woman of modest background. *Jane Eyre* and the later novel, *Villette*, were clearly works of great genius. They were particularly troubling novels for her Victorian contemporaries because the protagonists were strong-willed and independent-minded women[2] of talent and integrity whose natures altered the behavior of those around them. These women must have been quite shocking to the staid British gentry of the mid-19th century. The heretical nature of Brontë's views can be seen in this passage from Jane Eyre:

> Women are supposed to be very calm generally: but women feel just as men feel; they need exercise for their faculties, and a field for their efforts as much as their brothers do; they suffer from too rigid a restraint, too absolute a stagnation, precisely as men would suffer; and it is narrow-minded in their more privileged fellow-creatures to say that they ought to confine themselves to making puddings and knitting stockings, to playing on the piano and embroidering bags. It is thoughtless to condemn them, or laugh at them, if they seek to do more than custom has pronounced necessary for their sex.[3]

This statement of intellectual equality of the sexes is unusual for Victorian England.

BIOGRAPHY

Charlotte Brontë was born in 1816 in Haworth, Yorkshire, the third of six children (four sisters and one brother). Her mother died in 1821 and from that time on, the children were raised by their father, a strict disciplinarian who trained them to accept harsh conditions and instilled a strict sense of duty. In 1825, Maria and Elizabeth, Charlotte's older sisters, aged 12 and 10 years, died of a respiratory infection, probably tuberculosis, contracted at Cowan's Bridge School. The students' life was harsh; the school was crowded, the atmosphere damp, the food scarce and of poor quality. Despite these conditions, Charlotte and her sister Emily were sent to Cowan's Bridge School after their sisters' deaths.[4]

Between September 1848 and May 1849, Charlotte's remaining siblings all died of tuberculosis. Her brother, Patrick Branwell, a gifted artist, wasted his talents by living a dissolute life punctuated by alcohol and opium abuse and was the first to die. Both Emily and Anne had promising literary careers, but their lives were also cut short. None of the six Brontë children reached the age of 40.

Charlotte Brontë's writings are strongly autobiographical. The description of Lowood in Jane Eyre appears to represent the Cowan's Bridge School, and the character of Helen Burns appears to be based on her sister Maria.[5] Much of what is known about Brontë's life is recorded in *The Life of Charlotte Brontë* by Elizabeth C. Gaskell,[5] a famous 19th-century British novelist who befriended Brontë in 1850. Gaskell completed the biography in 1857 using documents provided by the Brontë family and friends as well as her own recollections. From this work we know that Brontë died on March 31, 1855, at the age of 39. Approximately 9 months before her death, she had married Arthur Bell Nicholls, a minister who replaced her father in Haworth Parsonage, Yorkshire. By most accounts, the brief marriage was a happy one.[4, 5]

HER FINAL MONTHS

A review of Brontë's health in the 4 months preceding her death will be helpful in hypothesizing the most likely cause of her death. Obviously, the definite cause of death cannot be determined by deductive reasoning alone, but several likelihoods can be postulated. I am grateful to John Maynard, Professor of English at New York University, for first bringing these issues to my attention. Professor Maynard has already clearly outlined and summarized the known facts regarding Brontë's health in her last months.[6] The information comes from physicians' statements, local letters, and Gaskell's biography.[5]

Brontë was married on June 29, 1854. In late November, she took a long walk along the moors with her husband. She enjoyed the walk "inexpressibly."[5] The weather had been cold and rainy; the ground was covered with melting snow. After returning home, she developed a lingering sore throat and cold that "hung about her, and made her thin and weak."[5] Her last Christmas was a happy one. She did, however, delay visits to two friends. It is possible but not certain that she suspected she was pregnant. On January 19, 1855, Brontë recounted to a friend that she was attacked by sensations of perpetual nausea and recurring fainting spells. Her physician assigned the symptoms to a "natural cause"; this is presumed to mean that she was pregnant. Indeed, her family and friends believed she was pregnant.[4, 5] The sickness increased until the very sight of food caused nausea, and according to Gaskell, "a wren would have starved on what she ate during those last six weeks."[5] Brontë's illness continued into February, when she became "completely prostrated with weakness and sickness and frequent fever."[6] She became emaciated and bedridden, and vomited persistently. She had difficulty speaking and writing and, after mid-February, no longer wrote letters. Gaskell writes, "about the third week in March there was a change; a low wandering delirium came on; and in it she begged constantly for food and even for stimulants. She swallowed eagerly now; but it was too late." On Saturday morning, March 31, 1855, Brontë died. The official cause of her death was given as phthisis,[4] an obsolete term for the wasting form of tuberculosis.

ANALYSES OF BRONTË'S DEATH

In 1920, Lucile Dooley, writing in the *American Journal of Psychology*, produced a psychoanalytic evaluation of Brontë's personality,[1] depicting her as an immature neurotic whose writings were simply the vivid description of her own life. Dooley states,

> ... she died in the eighth month of pregnancy, having suffered from much nausea, vomiting and prostration. The data recorded in the biographies are, of course, insufficient for diagnosis. Pernicious vomiting of the neurotic variety may be summarized to have been the illness of which she suffered during the early months of pregnancy, but nothing can now be stated with certainty. This complaint always has psychogenic features.

Dooley judged Brontë to be fearful, conflicted, and reluctant to accept her future marriage and childbearing. This evaluation is, however, at odds with Brontë's own correspondence and with Gaskell's biography. Dooley states, "Without under-rating the true organic factors in her illness we may assume with certainty that her condition was aggravated by psychogenic reactions, derived, probably, from the fear and reluctance she felt at this new facing of life."

In 1932, Edgerley[7] abstracted the causes of death of the Brontës based on death certificates. In his opinion, Charlotte Brontë died of a combination of vomiting, pregnancy, and tuberculosis. In 1934, MacNalty[8] commented on the infectious nature and epidemiologic factors of tuberculosis in the death of all the Brontë children. He wrote, "Charlotte was the most resistant of the family. Her disease was probably of the chronic fibrotic type, with slight exacerbations of activity from time to time." He adds, "The strain of impending maternity broke down her resistance to tuberculosis."

In 1972, Rhodes in "A medical appraisal of the Brontës"[9] wrote, "too often her death has been ascribed to tuberculosis. But it was not. The evidence is quite clear that she died of hyperemesis gravidarum, the pernicious vomiting of pregnancy. The picture painted by Mrs. Gaskell is classic as a description of the disease." Rhodes states that hyperemesis gravidarum "only seems to be excessive in those who display neuroticism and they require firm, kind, treatment to get them better. But this was not known in 1855." He goes on to state, "Some doctors have suggested that hyperemesis gravidarum is an unconscious rejection of the baby on the part of the woman, and this might have been so in Charlotte's case." In his opinion, "her more frequent outgoings from the family home probably built up a resistance to tuberculosis and so she survived it."

Maynard's 1983 report[6] suggests that Brontë died of a terminal wasting disease. Gallagher[10] concluded in 1985 that Brontë likely died of a combination of hyperemesis gravidarum and tuberculosis, stating, "Abdominal tuberculosis can cause cessation of menstruation and abdominal distention, but I know of no tuberculous lesion that causes wretching and vomiting of the type and severity described by Charlotte." Gallagher suggests that a hydatidiform mole may have occurred, which in turn produced the severe vomiting. He felt that there would be continuing debate as to whether the vomiting was physical or psychological.

WAS BRONTË PREGNANT?

I have reviewed the rather slim evidence with Dr. Maynard.[6] There was a presumption among Brontë's family and household servants that she was pregnant. Her physician ascribed her illness, which was characterized by weakness and vomiting, to pregnancy in late January 1855. If her symptoms were due to pregnancy, then they likely began at roughly the sixth week,[11] suggesting that conception occurred at approximately the second week of December 1854. Thus, she would have died no later than the fourth month of her pregnancy. Therefore, Dooley[1] was wrong in claiming that she was 8 months pregnant, a presumption apparently made from the date of her marriage. There was never any evidence that Brontë felt quickening, was heavy with child, or had any symptoms beyond wasting. How would a general practitioner in a rural Yorkshire parsonage in the mid-19th century diagnose pregnancy? It is unlikely that a pelvic examination was done at home. Even if it had been, it is not clear that a 6-week pregnancy could have been diagnosed. Clinical signs of pregnancy such as Chadwick sign (discoloration of the vagina) were not recognized at that time[12]; laboratory verification of pregnancy would await developments of the next century. A physician would probably have depended upon well-known symptoms associated with pregnancy, such as vomiting and amenorrhea. We have no evidence as to whether amenorrhea was present but, had it been, it could have been a result of many wasting illnesses, as described below. The symptom of vomiting could also be attributed to wasting.

The diagnosis of hyperemesis gravidarum can only be entertained if, in fact, a pregnancy had occurred. This is an open question. If hyperemesis was the terminal event, then the mode of death would have been from dehydration and electrolyte imbalance. The cure would have been normal fluid and food intake. In fact, 2 weeks before her death, Brontë regained her appetite and constantly begged for food. At that point, she was able to swallow and eat. If her major problem had been hyperemesis, she would have corrected it by improving her intake; this clearly did not happen.

Gallagher's[10] diagnosis of hydatidiform mole is unsupported. Had Brontë been pregnant, a diagnosis of hyperemesis could be entertained without any further diagnoses. There is no need to hypothesize a molar gestation. Most women with hydatidiform moles have uteri that are much larger than expected for the duration of pregnancy. There is no record of this. The major symptom of hydatidiform mole is not vomiting but persistent, heavy, and sometimes life-threatening bleeding.[13] There is no evidence of this symptom.

The family believed Charlotte to be pregnant, but it is not clear that she was. All of her symptoms can be explained without invoking this diagnosis.

DID BRONTË DIE OF TUBERCULOSIS?

What is the evidence that Brontë's terminal wasting illness was, in fact, tuberculosis? There was a strong family history of tuberculosis, and all five of her siblings, with whom she shared a home, died of tuberculosis.[8] Her own physician believed that she had tuberculosis. His assigned cause of death was "phthisis, duration—2 months."[8] This was certainly a disease with which he was most familiar, as it was endemic and a common cause of death in young women in Victorian England. Brontë's final illness started with a cold and respiratory infection several months before her death. She continued to cough intermittently and became weak and emaciated. She had intermittent fevers. Severe vomiting was a part of her illness and the major symptom for some time. After the nausea and vomiting abated, Brontë died in extreme weakness and exhaustion. This terminal wasting illness is most consistent with tuberculosis.

Although severe vomiting is not a part of most cases of pulmonary tuberculosis, weakness, wasting, and vomiting may easily be signs of Addison disease caused by adrenal tuberculosis. This may have been part of fulminant tuberculosis involving extra-pulmonary sites. Amenorrhea, if present, can clearly be explained by any severe illness, as well as by a tubercular pituitary lesion. Addison disease was described in 1855,[14] and its most common cause was tuberculosis.[15] As described by Addison,[14] the leading features of the disease are "anemia, general languor and debility, remarkable feebleness of the heart's action, irritability of the stomach and a peculiar change of colour of the skin." The records do not document skin discoloration, but this may not have been a major characteristic of Brontë's disease. Pituitary involvement by tuberculosis could have produced a similar picture without skin pigmentation. Addison[14] described a case report with symptoms similar to Brontë's (case VI). A diagnosis of tuberculosis secondary to Addison disease would explain all the symptoms without the need to postulate additional diagnoses. Although we will never have complete information regarding the cause of Brontë's death, there is much to favor the single, simple unitary diagnosis of fulminant tuberculosis involving the adrenal glands.

COMMENT

If Brontë's death was originally ascribed to tuberculosis and if that diagnosis could explain her symptoms, why did many authors feel it necessary to ascribe some of her disease to neurosis? One explanation is that they may not have appreciated that all of her symptoms could be explained by a unitary diagnosis. Some observers may have felt a need to further explain all the symptoms rather than admit ignorance. Thus, a diagnosis of neurosis may have tied any loose ends and linked her symptoms and her work.

Another explanation may be that it was unacceptable to many in the 19th and early 20th centuries that achievement of the magnitude of *Jane Eyre* could be attained by a woman. That humbling realization may have been intolerable. The argument that this was not a work of genius but simply the description of a neurotic may have been comforting to those of lesser talent.

Brontë experienced much anguish caused by the rampant sexism of her age. She asked only that her work be judged on its own merits. The message for the modern physician is clear: Ascribing unexplained symptoms to either neurosis or hysteria is as inappropriate today as it was in the mid-19th century.

REFERENCES

1. Dooley L. Psychoanalysis of Charlotte Brontë, as a type of the woman of genius. Am J Psychol 1920;31:221–72.
2. Gilbert SM, Gubar S. The madwoman in the attic. New Haven, Connecticut: Yale University Press, 1975.
3. Brontë C. Jane Eyre. New York: Bantam, 1988:101.
4. Fraser R. The Brontës: Charlotte Brontë and her family. New York: Fawcett Columbine, 1988.
5. Gaskell EC. The life of Charlotte Brontë. London: Penguin Books, 1985.
6. Maynard J. The diagnosis of Charlotte Brontë's final illness. Biography 1983; 6:68–75.
7. Edgerley CM. Causes of death of the Brontës. Br Med J 1932;1:619.
8. MacNalty AS. The Brontës: A study in the epidemiology of tuberculosis. Br J Tuberculosis 1934;28:4–7.
9. Rhodes P. A medical appraisal of the Brontës. Brontë Society Transactions 1972; 16:101–9.
10. Gallagher HW. Charlotte Brontë: A surgeon's assessment. Brontë Society Transactions 1985;18(part 95):363–70.
11. Eastman NJ, Hellman LM. Williams obstetrics. 12th ed. New York: Appleton-Century-Crofts, 1961:275–6.
12. Chadwick JR. Value of the bluish coloration of the vaginal entrance as a sign of pregnancy. Trans Am Gynecol Soc 1886;11:399–423.
13. Cunningham FG, MacDonald PC, Gant NF. Williams obstetrics. 18th ed. Norwalk, Connecticut: Appleton and Lange, 1989:5434.
14. Addison T. On the constitutional and local effects of disease of the supra-renal capsules. London: Samuel Highley, 1855.
15. Rowntree LG, Snell AM. A clinical study of Addison's disease. Mayo Clinic Monographs. Philadelphia: WB Saunders, 1931.

Obstet Gynecol 1991;78:705–8.

COMMENTARY

Those interested in the medical aspects of literature have long been fascinated with the Brontë family, especially Charlotte, who is regarded conventionally as having died of hyperemesis gravidarum. In this detailed and scholarly analysis of various sources of information, Gerson Weiss constructs a convincing argument that she was in fact not pregnant, but rather succumbed to Addison's disease secondary to tuberculosis. Weiss, who has had a distinguished career as department chair at the University of Medicine and Dentistry of New Jersey in Newark, wrote this article while serving on the Green Journal Editorial Board (1988–1991).

Religion

The three masters of Jewish medicine: Isaac, Constantine and Halvabbas. Print published in Lyons, 1515. (Library of the Old Faculty of Medicine, Paris, France. Photo © J.L. Charmet.)

Religion, like literature, has been greatly concerned—some might even say obsessed—with reproduction and the birth process. Articles selected for this chapter relate to all three of the great monotheistic religions.

Clinical Research in Ancient Babylon: Methodologic Insights from the Book of Daniel

David A. Grimes, MD

DECEMBER 1995

*A*round 600 BC, Daniel of Judah conducted what is widely regarded as the earliest recorded clinical trial. His trial compared the health effects of a vegetarian diet with those of a royal Babylonian diet over a 10-day period. The strengths of his study include the use of a contemporaneous control group, use of an independent assessor of outcome, and striking brevity in the published report. Weaknesses include probable selection bias, ascertainment bias, and confounding by divine intervention. Although Daniel probably never achieved tenure, he did get "learning and skill in all letters and wisdom ... and understanding in all visions and dreams" (well before Freud). Despite the trial's dramatic findings, over 4 centuries elapsed before publication of Daniel's results. Daniel apparently perished, then published.

* * * * *

Experts have suggested a 32-point structured format for reporting randomized trials,[1] to improve the quality of this type of research. To demonstrate the usefulness of this format, I used it to evaluate the earliest known report of a clinical trial.[2] In this trial,[3, 4] Daniel and three colleagues compared the immediate health effects of a vegetarian diet with those of a rich diet, including meat and wine, enjoyed by the Babylonian royalty.

1. *State the unit of assignment.* The trial allocated participants to two treatment groups with the individual being the unit. Four young men from Judah (Daniel, Hananiah, Mishael, and Asariah, also known as Belteshazzar, Shadrach, Meshach, and Abednego) comprised one treatment arm, and an unspecified number of Babylonian youths comprised the other.

2. *State the method used to generate the intervention assignment schedule.* The experimental group self-selected their exposure, a vegetarian diet. No random assignment occurred. Randomization is important to avoid selection bias and both known and unknown confounders[5]; subsequently, confounding played an important role in

this trial's results.[6] The trial did, however, feature a contemporaneous comparison group.

3. *Describe the method used to conceal the intervention assignment schedule from participants and clinicians until recruitment was complete and irrevocable.* Assignment to treatment groups was transparent, raising the strong possibility of selection bias, as has been documented in the modern literature.[7] Large treatment effects, as seen in this trial, are more common when the allocation schedule is transparent.

4. *Describe the methods used to separate the generator and executor of the assignment.* Not applicable. Daniel both generated and executed the treatment assignments with the willing complicity of a steward (Melzar) appointed by the chief eunuch, Ashpenaz. The trial was a secret, because discovery might have led to the death of Ashpenaz. King Nebuchadnezzar had made the chief eunuch responsible for the well-being of Daniel and his colleagues; Ashpenaz considered the vegetarian diet potentially dangerous to the trial participants and, hence, indirectly to himself.

5. *Describe an auditable process of executing the assignment method.* Adequate records of the allocation of participants in the active treatment arm have survived for over 2 millenia. However, reconstructing events in the Book of Daniel is challenging because the clinical trial in chapter 1 was recorded in Hebrew, whereas other chapters are in Aramaic or Greek.[8] Deciphering trials not published in English remains problematic today.

6. *Identify and compare the distributions of important prognostic characteristics and demographics at baseline.* Limited data are available concerning baseline characteristics of those in the experimental arm. None, however, suffered from acne; the king had ordered Ashpenaz to bring from Israel certain "youths without blemish, handsome and skillful in all wisdom, endowed with knowledge, understanding learning and competent to serve in the king's palace, and to teach them the letters and language of the Chaldeans."[3] The Chaldeans were the intelligentsia of Babylon; they taught astrology, mathematics, and magic, for which Babylon was famous.[6] No information is available concerning participants in the other treatment arm, except for their chronic exposure to the king's "rich food."[3]

7. *State the method of masking.* Not applicable. Even a double-dummy approach would not avoid distinguishing between the vegetarian and royal diets. Whereas the revised standard version of the Bible[3] describes Daniel's diet as one of "vegetables," the King James version[4] reports more specifically that the diet consisted of "pulse."

Unrelated to cardiac activity, "pulse" refers to the seeds of peas, beans, lentils, and similar plants bearing pods. A modern equivalent may be succotash, invented by the North American Indians.

8. *State how frequently care providers were aware of the intervention allocation, by intervention group.* The steward Melzar was aware of treatment allocation; whether the chief eunuch knew is not clear. Nebuchadnezzar presumably was blinded (even to the existence of the trial). Melzar apparently skirted any requirement Nebuchadnezzar might have had for the protection of human subjects.

9. *State how frequently participants were aware of the intervention allocation, by intervention group.* All members of the active treatment group knew their assignment, although it is not clear that participants in the comparison group were even aware that they were participating in a formal trial. Lack of blinding in the experimental group could have led to overcompensation on the part of participants regarding exercise, weight reduction, or personal grooming, which would not have occurred in the control group.

10. *State whether (and how) outcome assessors were aware of the intervention allocation, by intervention group.* The steward Melzar was the outcome assessor for both treatment groups, and he was aware of the intervention allocation for both. Blinding the evaluator to treatment allocation is highly desirable, but the steward might not have accepted this condition, given that his survival (and that of his boss) depended on the trial's outcome. Here, both the evaluator and the investigator had an urgent interest in the trial's outcome, raising the strong possibility of ascertainment bias.

11. *State whether the investigator was unaware of trends in the study at the time of participant assignment.* This information is not available. Because of the trial's short duration (10 days), this deficiency may be unimportant.

12. *State whether masking was successfully achieved for the trial.* Not applicable.

13. *State whether the data analyst was aware of intervention allocation.* The outcome assessor also served as the data analyst, and he knew the treatment assignments. The lethal consequences of an unfavorable assessment of the vegetarian diet probably heightened the potential bias toward favoring the "new treatment."[1] Again, ascertainment bias is likely in this situation.

14. *State whether individual participant data were entered into the trial data base without awareness of intervention allocation.* No blinding was done.

15. *State whether the data analyst was masked to intervention allocation.* See no. 13.

16. *Describe fully the numbers and flow of participants, by intervention group, throughout the trial.* Full accounting of the four participants in the experimental arm is available; the report provides no information on participants in the comparison group.

17. *State clearly the average duration of the trial, by intervention group, and the start and closure dates for the trial.* The trial lasted 10 days. Because of the favorable outcome, the steward continued the vegetarian diet for Daniel's group for the entire 3 years of their preparation for service to the king.[3]

    Biblical scholars disagree on the exact dates of the trial, which reportedly took place in the "third year of the reign of Jehoiakim king of Judah."[3] One commentator reports that the Jewish nation fell in 586 BC and the Babylonian empire ended in 539 BC, when Cyrus, King of Persia, conquered Babylon.[9] Another places the trial in either 606 or 597 BC.[10] Nevertheless, the author of the Book of Daniel did not publish these results until the time of Antiochus IV Epiphanes, which was most probably around 168–165 BC.[8, 10] Delay in publication of research findings is not a new problem: Daniel apparently perished, then published.

18. *Report the reason for dropout clearly, by intervention group.* No dropouts occurred in the experimental arm, and no details are available concerning the other group.

19. *Describe the actual timing of measurements by intervention group.* The steward apparently performed all evaluations simultaneously: "At the end of ten days it was seen that they [Daniel's group] were better in appearance and fatter in flesh than all the youths who ate the king's rich food."[3] This feature helps to avoid bias.[1] Paradoxically, "fatter" refers not to skinfold thickness but to attractiveness.[4]

20. *State the predefined primary outcome(s) and analyses clearly.* The a priori hypothesis was that a 10-day course of vegetarian food would result in an improvement in physical appearance: "Then let our appearance and the appearance of the youths who eat the king's rich food be observed by you...."[3] However, the definition of the primary outcome measure was not clear, specific, or measurable. No interim analyses occurred, despite the high stakes involved.

21. *Describe clearly whether the primary analysis has used the intention-to-treat principle.* The report describes no deviations from the assigned treatment in the experimental group, so compliance with the regimen was presumably complete. Daniel and his colleagues would have avoided food that violated Mosaic law or that had been offered to idols.[10] Hence, all those assigned to the experimental group were appropriately analyzed with the group to which they

had been originally assigned. No information is available concerning the comparison group.

22. *State the intended sample size and its justification.* The sample size was one of convenience. Regrettably, the small number of participants in the experimental group (four) severely limited the power of the trial to show a significant difference, a common deficiency even today.[11] For example, with "appearance" as a dichotomous outcome variable, to detect a relative risk of 2.0 with an outcome rate of 50% in the unexposed group and four participants in each arm, the power (α = .05) would be less than 1%.[12] With 20 Babylonians and the four men from Judah, the power would still be only 24%.

23. *State and explain why the trial is being reported now.* The trial ended as planned, and confirmatory evidence grew during its 3-year extension.[3] Written during the oppression of Antiochus IV Epiphanes, the Book of Daniel gives hope to those suffering from persecution.[8] Although he belonged to a conquered people, Daniel had great power and influence in Babylon. An innovator in other areas, Daniel interpreted dreams centuries before Freud.

24. *Describe and/or compare dropouts and completers.* No dropouts occurred in the experimental arm, and no data are available for the comparison group.

25. *State or reference the reliability, validity, and standardization of the primary outcome.* No definition is available for the "appearance" outcome variable. Given the subjective nature of such a determination and the potentially lethal consequences for the outcome assessor, ascertainment bias seems likely.

26. *Define what constituted adverse events and how they were monitored by intervention group.* This was not explicitly stated. However, at the trial's completion, those in the control group did not fare as well as did those in the experimental group. The latter received "learning and skill in all letters and wisdom; and Daniel had understanding in all visions and dreams." When Nebuchadnezzar tested Daniel and his colleagues, he found them "ten times better than all the magicians and enchanters that were in all his kingdom."[3] The prospect of better outcomes remains a powerful inducement for volunteers in clinical trials today.

27. *State the appropriate analytical techniques applied to the primary outcome measure(s).* Not done. The trial clearly antedated modern statistical theory, and, presumably, few software packages were available for an abacus or other computers of the day. However, at the trial's conclusion, Daniel and colleagues were better in appearance than "*all* [emphasis mine] the youths who ate the king's rich food."[3]

28. *Present appropriate measures of variability (eg, confidence intervals for primary outcome measures).* Data provided do not allow these calculations to be made.

29. *Present sufficient simple (unadjusted) summary data on primary outcome measures and important side effects so that the reader can reproduce the results.* A numerator and denominator were available for the experimental group only.

30. *State the actual probability value and the nature of the significance test.* Not done; see no. 27.

31. *Present appropriate interpretations (eg, not significant, no effect; P < .05, proof).* Despite the small sample size and short treatment course, the trial's author found the evidence of benefit compelling, as did the steward.

32. *Present the appropriate emphasis in displaying and interpreting the statistical analysis, in particular controlling for unplanned comparisons.* Not applicable.

DISCUSSION

Daniel's trial anticipated the essence of the scientific method: an experimental group exposed to the factor of interest compared with contemporaneous unexposed controls. However, after Daniel's study, clinical experimentation languished until the 16th century, when Pare [sic] compared a "bland digestive" to boiling oil (the standard treatment) for battle wounds.[2] In his famous 1747 study, Lind followed Daniel's precedent of a small dietary trial in preventing scurvy among British sailors. Despite six different treatment arms and a total of only 12 participants, citrus fruit supplementation was strikingly effective. The trial led to effective prophylaxis and the nickname "limeys" for British seamen.[2]

In the 1600s, several thousand years after the Babylonian trial, van Helmont first suggested a randomized controlled trial.[13, 14] He proposed, "Let us take out of the hospital, out of the camps, or from elsewhere, 200 or 500 poor People that have Fevers, Pleurisies, etc. Let us divide them into halfes, let us cast lots, that one half of them may fall to my share, and the other to yours: ... we shall see how many funerals both of us shall have."[13, 14] Because van Helmont's challenge was not accepted, he failed to win the 300 florins he was prepared to wager on the outcome.

Although randomization in agricultural trials began in the 1920s, Hill[15] was first to use the powerful technique of randomizing participants in clinical trials. In Daniel's trial, randomization would have avoided the selection bias and the confounding that apparently occurred. Several nutritional skeptics[6, 10] have noted that, "Ten days is too short a time for any natural effect of a difference in diet; the noticeably healthier appearance of the four youths must be attributed to divine approval of their loyalty."[6] Divine intervention was associated with the predictor variable (vegetarian diet) and caused the outcome (healthy appearance).

By contemporary standards,[1] Daniel's trial had numerous deficiencies. However, many of these weaknesses persist in clinical research today.[16, 17] Indeed, some modern investigators have drawn causal inferences without the use of appropriate controls.[18] Similarly, the published report of this trial[3, 4] would not meet contemporary standards of peer review.[1] In the author's defense, he had no "Instructions for Authors." On the other hand, he was concise: The entire account runs less than a page of printed text[3] (presumably longer when handwritten on clay tablets).

Examples from the Bible illuminate human behavior; the Book of Daniel is no exception. After thousands of years, excellent clinical research still brings great rewards[19]—and much fun. Although contemporary investigators who conduct excellent studies[1] may no longer gain "understanding in all visions and dreams," they may well be "ten times better than all the magicians and enchanters" who use inferior research methods.[20]

REFERENCES

1. The Standards of Reporting Trials Group. A proposal for structured reporting of randomized controlled trials. JAMA 1994;272:1926–31.

2. Feinstein AR. Clinical epidemiology: The architecture of clinical research. Philadelphia: WB Saunders, 1985:683–718.

3. The Book of Daniel. In: The Holy Bible. Revised standard version. New York: Thomas Nelson & Sons, 1953:686–98.

4. The Book of Daniel. In: The Holy Bible. King James version. Nashville: Regency Publishing House, 1976:1301–26.

5. Altman DC. Randomization: Essential for reducing bias. BMJ 1991;302:1481–2.

6. Knight GAF. The Book of Daniel. In: Laymon CM, ed. The interpreter's one-volume commentary on the Bible. Nashville: Abingdon Press, 1971:438–9.

7. Schulz KF, Chalmers I, Hayes RJ, Altman DG. Empirical evidence of bias. Dimensions of methodologic quality associated with estimates of treatment effects in controlled trials. JAMA 1995;273:408–12.

8. Kodell J. The Catholic Bible study handbook. Ann Arbor, Michigan: Servant Books, 1985:111–2.

9. Dummelow JR. ed. A commentary on the Holy Bible. New York: Macmillan Publishing Co, 1975:525–44.

10. Barr J. Daniel. In: Black M, Rowley HH, eds. Peake's commentary on the Bible. Nashville: Thomas Nelson Publishing, 1962:591–602.

11. Moher D, Dulberg CS, Wells GA. Statistical power, sample size, and their reporting in randomized controlled trials. JAMA 1994; 272:122–4.

12. Dean AG, Dean JA, Coulombier D, et al. Epi Info, version 6: A word processing, database, and statistics program for epidemiology on microcomputers. Atlanta: Centers for Disease Control and Prevention, 1994.

13. Doll R. Darwin lecture. Development of controlled trials in preventive and therapeutic medicine. J Biosoc Sci 1991;23:365–78.

14. Doll R. Sir Austin Bradford Hill and the progress of medical science. BMJ 1992;305:1521–6.

15. Hill AB. The clinical trial. N Engl J Med 1952;247:113–9.

16. Schulz KE, Chalmers I, Grimes DA, Altman DG. Assessing the quality of randomization from reports of controlled trials published in obstetrics and gynecology journals. JAMA 1994;272:125–8.
17. Grimes DA, Schulz KE. Randomized controlled trials of home uterine activity monitoring: A review and critique. Obstet Gynecol 1992;79:137–42.
18. Caillouette JC, Koehier AL. Phasic contraceptive pills and functional ovarian cysts. Am J Obstet Gynecol 1987;156:1538–42.
19. Lamas GA, Pfeffer MA, Hamm P, et al. Do the results of randomized clinical trials of cardiovascular drugs influence medical practice? N Engl J Med 1992; 327:241–7.
20. Altman DG. The scandal of poor medical research. BMJ 1994;308:283–4.

Obstet Gynecol 1995;86:1031–4.

COMMENTARY

This article represents the classic example of what an After Office Hours article should be. It is interesting, entertaining, and scholarly (one of the reviewers of the original submission was a biblical scholar), and it has deft touches of humor. But it is also instructive, being based on the Standards for Reporting Trials (SORT). The SORT criteria were modified and became CONSORT (Consolidated Standards of Reporting Trials) criteria, standards with which, incidentally, Obstetrics & Gynecology *has had a close connection. The Editor was a member of the group that promulgated CONSORT in 1996, and the Green Journal was among the first of many journals to adopt the standards as policy.*

The author, David A. Grimes, is an authority in epidemiology who served on the Green Journal Editorial Board (1989–1992) and more recently was appointed Consultant Editor (Epidemiology).

Doctor James Young Simpson, Rabbi Abraham De Sola, and Genesis Chapter 3, Verse 16

Jack Cohen, MD

NOVEMBER 1996

When new ideas or concepts are introduced in science or medicine, religious objections or controversies may be raised. Examples today include the use of sperm donors, surrogate mothers, and in vitro fertilization. Smallpox vaccination, introduced by Edward Jenner in 1797, created a religious backlash against its use. Almost 100 years later in Montreal, it took a smallpox epidemic that claimed 3000 lives, most of them Catholic, to make the Church in Quebec change its stand against vaccination.[1] For promoting the heliocentric theory, Galileo was brought before the Inquisition, and escaped long-term imprisonment only by the intervention of powerful friends.[2] When anesthesia was first used for women during childbirth, a similar hue and cry was raised against its use.

The "official" debut of anesthesia occurred on October 16, 1846, when an operation was performed with ether anesthesia at the Massachusetts General Hospital. Two months later, Robert Liston became the first surgeon in Europe to use general anesthesia on a patient undergoing an amputation.[3] That surgical procedures could now be done without pain was accepted by most physicians and the general population as a great boon to mankind. Its use in obstetric cases, however, created a religious ethical dilemma for many.

James Young Simpson (1811–1870) was one of the earliest users of anesthesia in Great Britain, and became an immediate enthusiastic supporter of it. He was born into modest means, the seventh son of a baker. With the financial aid of an older brother, he attended the medical faculty of Edinburgh University, graduating at the age of 21. Within 8 years, he had been appointed professor of midwifery at the University of Edinburgh. A brilliant teacher and dynamic doctor, he soon became the busiest obstetrician in all of Scotland.[4]

Simpson began to use anesthesia in his obstetric cases as well as for his surgical patients. Although he first used ether, he soon switched to chloroform because of ether's lingering odor and what he felt was the bronchial irritation it caused. As he began to lecture and publish his experiences of anesthesia in childbirth, he found himself at the center of an increasing debate. For various medical reasons, many physicians were against anesthesia's use during labor. Much more acrimonious was the religious controversy over the use of these agents. Genesis chapter 3, verse 16, stated, "I will greatly multiply thy sorrow and thy conception; in sorrow thou shalt bring forth children." This was Eve's punishment for eating the fruit of the tree of knowledge, and it implied that childbirth had to be painful. To alleviate this pain by the use of anesthetic agents was to directly contravene the word of God!

Dr. Charles Meigs, professor of obstetrics in Philadelphia, voiced the medical concerns of many in articles he wrote for American and British medical journals and in an exchange of correspondence with Simpson. If forceps were required during labor, pain was the best guide to their exact placement; this would be lost with anesthesia. Other objections were that the pain of natural childbirth was a physiologic one, and a "most desirable, salutary, and conservative manifestation of life force." If women were sustained by "cheering counsel and promises," most could endure, without great complaint, their labor pains. "To be in natural labor, is the culminating point of the female somatic forces." Meigs also was worried that the anesthetic agent would slow down the uterine contractions and prolong the delivery. And if one patient in 1000 died because of the use of anesthesia, he would never forgive himself—the relief of physiologic pain of the other 999 women would not mitigate his sorrow. There was, after all, no danger to the health or life of the mother from having to endure labor pains.[5]

Simpson replied that pain should never be a guide to the use of forceps—only one's knowledge of anatomy. Anesthesia made it easier to examine the patient and place the forceps properly. When properly administered, anesthesia relieved the pain but did not stop the uterine contractions. Simpson felt that labor pains were not physiologic and were not essential to the delivery of the baby—only the uterine contractions were. Hundreds of babies had been delivered safely and painlessly in the previous year with the use of anesthetics. It also was not true that there was no danger to the life of the mother who was enduring labor pain. In one study done in Dublin, the number of maternal deaths was in proportion to the length of labor. Thus, the mortality rate for women in labor more than 36 hours was one in six, versus a rate of one in 320 for those who had labor lasting less than 2 hours. Thus, by shortening labor, anesthesia could save lives. Simpson felt that the benefits of anesthesia in childbirth far outweighed the rare risks of complications or death.[6]

Much more acrimonious dissent was encountered by Simpson from those against the use of anesthesia in childbirth on religious grounds, not only by the clergy and general public, but from many doctors as well. One well-known teacher of midwifery in Dublin wrote to Simpson stating that the feeling in Dublin was against the use of anesthesia in labor, and with this he entirely concurred. After all, it was the Almighty who had seen fit to allot pain to natural labor "and most wisely we cannot doubt." An editorial in the *Edinburgh Medical and Surgical Journal*, which was summarized by Simpson in his pamphlet described later, criticized the use of anesthesia because pain during operation was desirable in most cases, and the prevention of it was hazardous to the patient. This was even more true in the lying-in room. "Pain is the mother's safety and its absence her destruction ... it has been *ordered* that 'in sorrow shall she bring forth.'" In one medical school, the use of anesthesia was publicly denounced as an attempt to contravene the decrees of Providence, and was to be avoided by all properly principled students and practitioners.[7]

Simpson answered these criticisms in a pamphlet in which he gave a detailed analysis of Genesis 3:16. The first half of this verse in the King James version is: "Unto the woman He said, I will multiply thy sorrow and thy conception; in sorrow thou shalt bring forth children." As reference, he used mainly the works of Henrich Friedrich Wilhelm Gesenius (1786–1842), professor of theology at Halle. This scholar was the first Christian in the field of biblical Hebrew and the study of the Bible to free these subjects from theologic considerations, basing his studies only on objective scientific methods. According to Simpson, Gesenius and other recent Christian Hebraists and Bible authorities believed that the sentence "I will greatly multiply thy sorrow and thy conception" was a case of hendiadys, and could be rendered more correctly as "I will greatly multiply the sorrow *of* thy conception." (Hendiadys is a figure of speech in which a single complex idea is expressed by two words connected by a conjunction, which in this case would render the translation as he stated rather than as "thy sorrow and thy conception.") Also, in the original Hebrew version, the words for sorrow used were *etzebh* and *itztzabhon*. Gesenius traced the origin of the root of these words to *atzabh*, meaning "to labor." One could thus translate *etzebh* as labor or toil. Because of the upright position of the human body and the anatomic arrangements of the pelvis, vagina, and uterus, much more muscular effort (ie toil or labor) was required to push the fetus out. Simpson went on to say that the word *etzebh* occurred six times in the Old Testament, in which it did not imply physical pain. There were other words used in the Old Testament that specifically denoted actual pain and agony as might occur in childbirth—*hhil* and *hhebhel*. Thus, he felt that Genesis 3:16 really implied that in toil or labor shall women bring forth children.[7]

The religious controversy went on in Canada as well. In 1849, to help clarify the religious issue, the editors of the *British American Journal of Medical Science* asked Abraham De Sola, Canada's first rabbi, to write an article on the meaning of Genesis 3:16 for the benefit of their readers. De

Sola arrived in Canada in 1847 to become the first official rabbi of Canada's oldest Hebrew congregation, the Spanish and Portuguese of Montreal (Shearith Israel). He came from a long line of rabbis, and he had obtained a good classical education in London, where his father was senior minister of the Bevis Marks Synagogue. Although only 21 years old, he quickly threw himself into the duties of rabbi of the congregation and into the affairs of the small Jewish community of Montreal (slightly over 500 people; the entire Jewish population of Canada was about 600 at the time). He also began to take part in the various cultural and scientific organizations of the city. Because of his knowledge of the subject, he was soon appointed lecturer of Hebrew language and literature at McGill University.[8]

The title of De Sola's three-part article was "Critical Examination of Genesis III.16. Having Reference to The Employment Of Anaesthetics in Cases Of Labour." Probably, he was chosen more because he was the lecturer in Hebrew at McGill than because he was a rabbi. He had to tread warily because he was not a Christian and because some of his interpretations differed from the accepted views of Christian biblical scholars. Moreover, some of his analyses also differed from those of Simpson.

To begin with, De Sola disagreed with Simpson on his opinion that "thy sorrow and thy conception" represented a case of hendiadys, and could be rendered as "the sorrow of thy conception." Moreover, although Gesenius stated that the words *etzebh* and *itztzabhon* could be translated as labor, toil, pain, or sorrow, he had translated Genesis 3:16 with the word "sorrow" rather than the other meanings. In the original Hebrew version of this phrase, one finds the words *etzebonech veheronech*. (I have changed the spelling of de Sola's transliterations to correspond with Simpson's.) Philologically, the Hebrew letter *vov* in front of a word as represented by the *v* in *veheronech* indicated any of the conjunctives "or," "and," or "if." Therefore, the phrase must be translated as "thy pain *and* thy conception." Also, for hendiadys to apply in Hebrew, not only must the two nouns be in juxtaposition, but the first word must be in the genetive case and have the symbol for "of" added to it. Otherwise, each noun is separate. Although the word *etzebonech* was in the genetive case, the added last Hebrew letter *kof*, as represented by the *ch* endings in *etzebonech* and *veheronech*, rendered the translations as "the trouble or labor of thee" or "thy trouble," and "the conception of thee" or "thy conception."

De Sola then gave his explanation of the roots of *etzebh* and *itztzabhon*, using as his main source the eminent Hebrew philologist and scholar Rabbi David Kimchi (1165–1235), a talmudic scholar who lived in Provence. Among his works were a philologic treatise that had a grammar section and a lexicon of biblical Hebrew. His works were often used by Christian Hebraists of the Renaissance. There were eight passages in the Bible using variations of these words in which Kimchi felt the words meant "labor" and "toil" rather than "sorrow." The words used by him for his explanations were *hemal (amal) vehaigiyeh*. From the scriptural examples quoted using the derivations of *amal*, one could conclude that *etzebh*, with the same meaning as *amal*, meant "toil." Gesenius, Simpson's source, quoted nine other biblical passages in which he believed *etzebh* did mean "sorrow" or "anger," including Genesis 3:16. Earlier, Kimchi had come to the same conclusion with eight of these, but felt that in Genesis 3:16 the word meant "toil" and not "sorrow." If "sorrow" were meant to be conveyed in that passage, De Sola explained, there were Hebrew words used in the Bible that expressed "sorrow" or "pain," and had no other meaning. These were *ke'eb* (dolor, pain, grief), *tsarah* (trouble, distress), *yagohn* (sorrow, sadness, affliction), and *anachah* (groaning, sighing).

Based on his research, it was De Sola's opinion that Genesis 3:16 should be translated as "Unto the woman he said, I will greatly multiply thy travail and thy conception: with travail shalt thou bring forth children." De Sola agreed with Simpson that *etzebh* referred to the uterine and other muscle contractions in labor. Thus, he concluded that to remove the pain but not the uterine contractions was not going against the scriptures, and, therefore, one should not withhold anesthesia during childbirth on religious principles. If the use of anesthesia during childbirth was sinful, then so were the efforts of obstetricians and midwives, for was not their purpose to speed delivery of the infant and help the mother with problems in labor, thereby relieving pain? De Sola told his readers that although it was not propitious for him to speak of anesthesia in childbirth from the medical viewpoint, he exhorted them to "weigh calmly and unprejudicially the arguments adduced on both sides of the question before they decide on the employment of anaesthetics in cases of labour to be unscriptural and irreligious."[9]

EPILOGUE

The religious debate on the use of anesthesia continued for several more years. In 1853, Dr. John Snow, a London physician and one of the earliest specialists in anesthesia, used chloroform anesthesia during the delivery of the eighth child of Queen Victoria. This helped to end the controversy in the British Empire, at least. After all, what was good enough for the Queen was good enough for everybody else. (Moreover, the Queen was the head of the Church of England.) The controversy of the exact meaning of Genesis 3:16 is still with us today, as evidenced by the translations of various Bibles of our era. For comparison, the King James and De Sola's versions are the first and second of these, respectively: 1) Unto the woman He said: "I will greatly multiply thy sorrow and thy conception; in sorrow thou shalt bring forth children." 2) Unto the woman he said, I will greatly multiply thy travail and thy conception: with travail shalt thou bring forth children.

All the following versions begin with "Unto the woman He (or he) said." Jewish sources: 3) I will greatly multiply thy pain and thy travail; in pain thou shalt bring forth children.[10] 4) I will make severe your pangs in childbearing. In pain shall you bear children.[11] 5) I will multiply, multiply your pain (from) your pregnancy, with pains shall you bear children.[12] 6) I will make most severe your pangs in childbearing; in pain shall you bear children.[13] In three other sources, the word in the second half was translated as "pain," ie, in pain shall you bear children.

Christian sources: 7) I will increase your labour and your groaning, and in labour shall you bear children.[14] 8) I shall give you intense pain in childbearing, you will give birth to your children in pain.[15] 9) I shall give you great labour in childbearing; with labour you will bear children.[16] 10) I will intensify the pangs of your childbearing; in pain shall you bring forth children.[17]

As can be seen, there is still no agreement on the meaning of *etzebh*. Also, in some versions, hendiadys is used (ie, "your pangs in childbearing" in version 4 and "great labour in childbearing" in number 9), but it is not used in others (ie, "thy pain and thy travail" in version 3 and "your labour and your groaning" in version 7).

REFERENCES

1. Bliss M. Plague. A story of smallpox in Montreal. Toronto: Harper Collins Publishers Ltd. 1993.
2. Encyclopedia Americana. Vol. 12. 1972:240.
3. Gordon R. The alarming history of medicine. New York: St. Martin's Press, 1993:78.
4. Major RH. A history of medicine. Springfield, Illinois: Charles C. Thomas, 1954:818–20.
5. Meigs C. Obstetrics: The science and the art. Philadelphia: Blanchard and Lea, 1863:356–60.
6. Simpson JY. Anaesthesia or the employment of chloroform and ether in surgery, midwifery, etc. Philadelphia: Lindsay and Blakiston, 1849:230–48.
7. Simpson JY. Answer to the religious objections advanced against the employment of anaesthetic agents in midwifery and surgery. Edinburgh, Scotland: Sutherland and Know, 1843:3–14.
8. Encyclopedia Judaica. Vol. 12. Jerusalem: Keter Publishing House Ltd., 1973: 1562–3.
9. De Sola A. Critical examination of Genesis III.16. Having reference to the employment of anaesthesia in cases of labour. Br Am J Med Sci 1849–50:227–9, 259–62, 290–3.
10. The Holy Scriptures according to the Masoretic text. Philadelphia: The Jewish Publication Society of America, 1975.
11. Birnbaum P. The Torah and Haftoroth. New York: Hebrew Publishing Company, 1983.
12. Fox E. In the beginning. New York: Schocken Books, 1983.

13. The Torah. Philadelphia: The Jewish Publication Society of America, 1967.
14. The New English Bible. The Old Testament. New York: Oxford University Press, 1970.
15. The New Jerusalem Bible. Garden City, New York: Doubleday and Company, Inc., 1985.
16. The revised English Bible with the Apocrypha. New York: Oxford University Press, 1989.
17. The Catholic study Bible. New York: Oxford University Press, 1990.

Obstet Gynecol 1996;88:895–8.

COMMENTARY

Written by a plastic surgeon from Montreal, this is an excellent piece of historical and religious scholarship tracing the controversy that raged over the use of obstetric anesthesia in the mid-19th century. The principal protagonist was James Y. Simpson, the eminent Professor of Midwifery at the University of Edinburgh, Scotland, and against him was arrayed a formidable collection of medical and theological authorities. Ultimately, the issue was put to rest by none other than Queen Victoria, the icon of propriety, who announced her decision to have anesthesia for an impending delivery: "We are having the baby; we will have chloroform."

Man's Primal Sin

Allan C. Barnes, MD

December 1964

At least insofar as his health is concerned, man's primal sin would seem to be not the eating of an apple in the Garden of Eden, but rather his insistence on walking in an upright position. It is remarkable the number of our ills that stem from this conceited gesture of rearing up on our hind legs. Even a partial list serves to illustrate that the medical profession lives very handsomely from the sequelae of the upright position; possibly, indeed, as a profession we would starve in a quadruped society.

Starting from the bottom, there are fallen arches and flat feet, varicose veins and hemorrhoids, indirect inguinal hernia, slipped disc, low back pain and sciatica, and cervical whip-lash. The obstetrician-gynecologist broods about such things because so much of his work involves dealing with by-products of uprightness. That portion of the anatomy which was meant to be the east end of the animal as it traveled west has now inherited the job of holding in the pelvic contents and of withstanding the weight of the abdominal organs and the pull of gravity. Because our patients insist on walking on their back legs, we must deal with relaxed pelvic floor, stress urinary incontinence, cystocele, rectocele, and uterine procidentia. On all fours there is no such entity as retroversion of the uterus—even though it is largely asymptomatic—and much of the sting is taken out of pelvic thrombophlebitis (those valveless veins!).

More important is the fact that the eclamptogenic toxemias of pregnancy are a biped disease, and—most of all—we have labor itself. My dog can whelp four pups in the easy chair without an attendant, whereas my patient needs hospitalization and careful medical attention simply because of the upright position adopted by the species *Homo erectus*.

My dog, you will recall, does not have the pubic bone opposite the sacrum, and when the pups are passing over the sacrum they have the soft belly muscles below them; as they go over the pubic bone the soft rump tissues are above them. But some benighted ancestor of ours—feeling unduly superior to his neighbors, one presumes—reared up on his hind legs. This was the Fall of Man. The weight of his trunk gradually forced the sacrum down, and the thrust of his acetabulum gradually forced the pubic bone up until man has become *the only animal to pass through a bony ring in being born.*

Here, then, lies our primal sin, and the curse which was laid upon us was accurate in the extreme: "In sorrow shalt thou bring forth children."[1] The ancient storyteller knew wherein the trouble lay, and disguised the truth but thinly in his allegory ... the tempter was made the flattest of vertebrates and the act of picking an apple required the victim to stand straight and reach up. Hate not the apple, gentle reader, hate the position (and add subdeltoid bursitis to the list of inherited ills). From the evolutionary point of view, one is forced to conclude that the upright position came first and the ability to think came second; if cerebration had come first, man would have presumably had the sense to estimate the medical hazards and would have remained a quadruped.

Faced with this list of aches, pains, and physical disabilities which attend uprightness, one might well ask, with great seriousness: What benefits are there? Is it truly worth it?

The minister immediately answers: "Man stood up to see the horizon." This of course is arrant nonsense—my dog can also see the horizon. His is closer to him than mine is to me, but everyone has his own horizon nevertheless.

The anthropologist says: "Man stood up to gain the use of his forelegs." As I watch the skill with which a chipmunk picks up, examines, and consumes a piece of popcorn, I wonder if some compromise similar to the chipmunk's wasn't possible to gain a quick and useful foreleg and still retain quadruped status. Certainly as I watch my cat worry a mouse, I wonder—and skillful as that forepaw is, it has never yet built a revolver, bazooka, or atom bomb.

Rejecting these presumed advantages as specious, one comes down to but a single gain which repays us for the ills, aches, and pains of uprightness; one attribute which recompenses all this difficulty: Man faces his sexual partner.

This, over the millennia, has presumably made it worth the medical complications!

REFERENCE

1. Genesis, 3:16.

COMMENTARY

This clever and delightful essay is the first of seven in this anthology written by Allan C. Barnes (1911–1982). A towering figure of American obstetrics and gynecology of the 20th century, Barnes chaired three university departments of obstetrics and gynecology, Ohio State University, Columbus (1947–1953), Case Western Reserve University, Cleveland, Ohio (1953–1960), and Johns Hopkins University, Baltimore, Maryland (1960–1970). The last is particularly noteworthy because it entailed combining the previously separate and highly reputed programs in obstetrics and gynecology. After retiring from Johns Hopkins, he took a position with The Rockefeller Foundation in New York, shifting his focus to international health, for a decade.

His professional accomplishments were probably unmatched, before or since, but their remarkable extent is only part of the story of Allan Barnes. He was, in every sense of the term, a Renaissance person, for which there is no better evidence than the 13 articles he wrote for After Office Hours between 1953 and 1971. The subjects were wide-ranging; most were characterized by strong historical scholarship, and all by a deft touch of cleverness and a certain piquant humor. All 13 were appropriate for this collection, and choosing seven to include presented no small challenge to the editors. It bears mention that among Barnes's many important professional obligations during the time he contributed so prolifically to After Office Hours was the editorship of the American Journal of Obstetrics and Gynecology.

Before Kubler-Ross: Lessons About Grief from the Book of Job

Deborah S. Lyon, MD

July 2000

Much current medical theory owes its existence to careful research techniques of this century, but ancient manuscripts give us a great deal to remember on the art of healing. We recently have been reminded that the controlled trial is not new to this century.[1] By the same token, Elisabeth Kubler-Ross[2] beautifully defined stages of grief, and her theoretic framework has been expanded since to include many losses besides one's own death: loss of a loved one, loss of a pet,[3] personal disability,[4] exile from one's home,[5] and even job loss.[6] Although Kubler-Ross' work is clear, brief, and broadly applicable, there are many older evidences of human progress through suffering. One of the best-known ancient texts on this subject is the biblical book of Job.

Job lived in a patriarchal era, sometime around 2000 1000 BC.[7] The book was written somewhat later, anytime from the time of Solomon (around 900 BC) to that of the Babylonian Exile (6th century BC). The story told is that of a wealthy, upright man living a comfortable life who suddenly is confronted with the loss of his family, his possessions, and his health. Job's precise disease is unknown but may have been some form of leprosy or parasitic infestation. Symptoms included pruritis, ulceration, wasting, bone pain, loss of teeth, and recurring nightmares. In the book of Job, the brief prologue setting forth the story and the brief epilogue completing it sandwich a lengthy series of dialogues and monologues regarding the nature of and reasons for suffering. Job's visiting friends come to provide comfort and serve as both discussants and foils for his soliloquies.

Each of the five stages of grief identified by Kubler-Ross may be clearly seen within the text of Job. His early denial of the gravity of his condition may be seen in 1:21 ("...The Lord gave and the Lord has taken away; may the name of the Lord be praised.'" [New International Version]) and in 2:10 ("'... Shall we accept good from God, and not trouble?'") Job's anger becomes apparent in 7:11–15: "'Therefore I will not keep silent; I will speak out in the anguish of my spirit, I will complain in the bitterness of my soul. Am I the sea, or the monster of the deep, that you put me under guard? When I think my bed will comfort me and my couch will ease my complaint, even then you frighten me with dreams and terrify me with visions, so that I prefer strangling and death, rather than this body of mine.' " He begins to think about bargaining with God in 9:33–34: " 'If only there were someone to arbitrate between us, to lay his hand upon us both, someone to remove God's rod from me, so that his terror would frighten me no more.' " Depression, evident throughout the book, is represented in 10:18: " 'Why then did you bring me out of the womb? I wish I had died before any eye saw me.' " Acceptance comes less bluntly, but in an oft-quoted passage (13:15) Job states: "Though he slay me, yet will I hope in him." After a long conversation with God designed to remind Job that his suffering is not the focal point of the universe, Job responds: "... Surely I spoke of things I did not understand, things too wonderful for me to know" (42:3).

Job also shows us another of the characteristics of grief identified by Kubler-Ross. He moves back and forth between these five stages of dealing with his suffering throughout the 42 chapters of the book. Job wishes he'd never been born (the closest a traditional Jew could acceptably come to verbalizing suicidal ideations), wishes he could have an arbitration session with God, and flares up at the seeming injustice of God and his inadequate comforters. These themes are recurrent and sometimes confluent.

Thus, it would appear that, although less pristinely laid forth than Kubler-Ross' work, information about grief and suffering has been available for several millennia to those willing to seek it. Overlooking the ancient sources of medical and general human knowledge forces us (and our patients with us) to relearn the art of medicine in each generation. Job tells us very clearly what sufferers need from those who render aid and comfort to them. In 19:4 he responds to charges that his suffering is his own fault (for presumed sins): "If it is true that I have gone astray, my error remains my concern alone." Thus Job reminds us that when dealing with sufferers, it is not helpful to remind them of how their own poor choices might have contributed to their current condition. In 13:4–5, exasperated with well-meant but injurious counsel, Job explodes: "You are worthless physicians, all of you! If only you would be altogether silent! For you, that would be wisdom." This reminds us of the value of sympathetic silence in dealing with someone else's deep grief. It is indeed a deep truth that silence often represents wisdom, and sometimes there are no words capable of providing the same comfort as a hand on the shoulder or shared tears. Lastly, in 21:2 Job pleads, "Listen carefully to my words; let this be the consolation you give me. Bear with me while I speak." The patient's history is, at its medically purest, the most often neglected portion of the assessment. In its broader sense, the history of a patient's life might not be of vital medical significance, but it is the essence of the being that is seeking medical care and of profound significance to the patient. If we would be of real help to our suffering patients, we might begin by doing less explaining and more listening. These lessons in suffering are no different now than they were 3000 years ago.

REFERENCES

1. Grimes DA. Clinical research in ancient Babylon: Methodologic insights from the book of Daniel. Obstet Gynecol 1995;86:1031–4.

2. Kubler-Ross E. On death and dying. New York: Macmillan, 1973.

3. Archer J, Winchester C. Bereavement following death of a pet. Br J Psychol 1994;85:259–71.

4. Langer KG. Depression and denial in psychotherapy of persons with disabilities. Am J Psychother 1994;48:181–94.

5. Munoz L. Exile as bereavement: Socio-psychological manifestations of Chilean exiles in Great Britain. Br J Med Psychol 1980;53:227–32.

6. Archer J, Rhodes V. The grief process and job loss: A cross-sectional study. Br J Psychol 1993;84:395–410.

7. Hartley JE. The book of Job. Grand Rapids, Michigan: Eerdmans, 1988.

Obstet Gynecol 2000;96:151–2.

Biblical Twins

Isaac Blickstein, MD, and
Edith D. Gurewitsch, MD

APRIL 1998

𝒯he Bible includes accounts of the pregnancies, labors, and deliveries of two sets of twins: Esau and Jacob, the sons of Rebekah and Isaac (Genesis 25:21–6), and Pharez and Zarah, the illegitimate sons of Tamar and her father-in-law, Judah (Genesis 38:27–30) (Figure 1). The details of these twin deliveries are far more explicit than other obstetric accounts in the Bible, providing vivid narration of ancient obstetrics. Indeed, from these passages (all quotations in this article are from the King James version), it is apparent that the biblical author was well-versed in the importance of the perception of fetal movement, the normal length of gestation,

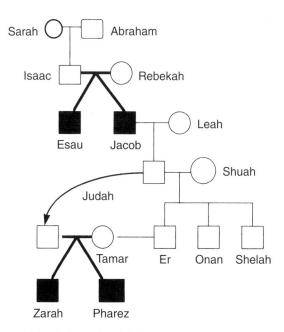

Fig. 1. Pedigree of the biblical twins. *Solid squares* = twins; *open squares* = male relatives; *open circles* = female relatives.

the general art of midwifery, and both the antenatal and intrapartum diagnosis of twins. Although much has been written about ancient and biblical midwifery,[1-6] the depiction of the intrapartum events of the deliveries of these sets of twins continues to challenge interpretation, because they clearly are not straightforward when viewed from the context of modern obstetric knowledge.

THE TWINS OF REBEKAH

Isaac and Rebekah suffered from primary infertility: "And Isaac intreated the Lord for his wife, because she was barren" (Genesis 25:21). His prayers resulted in Rebekah's conceiving twins. It is written that during her pregnancy, "the children struggled together within her." Although it is not surprising that fetal activity was known in biblical times, the text implies that the movements Rebekah perceived were somewhat intense and perhaps frightening to her: "And she said, 'If it be so, what am I thus?'" (Genesis 25:22). According to biblical narration, knowledge of the twin gestation was given to Rebekah before delivery in the form of a prophecy: "And the Lord said unto her: 'Two nations are in thy womb, and two manner of people shall be separated from thy bowels; and the one people shall be stronger than the other people; and the elder shall serve the younger.'" Interestingly, according to Josephus, a Jewish historian from the first century AD who recounted biblical events in his work *Jewish Antiquities*, it was Isaac, not Rebekah, who inquired of the Lord because he was concerned that her womb became so hard. This interesting revision suggests that Isaac may have perceived preterm contractions (more common in twins) or perhaps knew about an association between uterine hypertonus and poor outcome, as in placental abruption.

We know directly from the biblical text that the delivery of Esau and Jacob occurred at term but was otherwise quite unusual: "And when her days to be delivered were fulfilled, behold, there were twins in her womb. And the first came out red, all over like a hairy garment.... And after that came his brother out and his hand took hold on Esau's heel" (Genesis 25:24–6).

How are we to interpret the ability of the second twin to grasp the heel of the first twin during delivery? The prophet Hosea, referring to Jacob, states, "He took his brother by the heel in the womb...." (Hosea 13:3). That this act took place in utero, implies that this must have been a case of monoamniotic twins. Yet, the biblical author is painstaking in his depiction of the twins' differing phenotypes, which would suggest dizygotic twinning. One possible reconciliation of this apparent phenotypic difference within a monozygotic gestation is that the ruddy complexion in one twin and not the other may have been the result of twin-to-twin transfusion syndrome. However, this syndrome is extremely rare in the monoamniotic condition of monozygotic twins, and thereby confounds the monoamniotic assumption. Furthermore, the phenotypic differences persist in later descriptions of the twins: "Behold, Esau my brother is a hairy man, and I am a smooth man" (Genesis 27:11). It appears more plausible that the text is describing a set of dizygotic twins.

Another possible explanation is that the twins were pseudo-monoamniotic; that is, the dividing membrane ruptured before birth. However, the 12th-century biblical scholar Ibn Ezra comments that this is a most unusual occurrence.[7] It is also possible that the interval between Esau's and Jacob's deliveries was very short. Esau was delivered from the vertex presentation, so Jacob's hand may have prolapsed from a compound presentation and with a grasp reflex taken hold of his brother's heel before it cleared the birth canal or the field of the delivery. The last option is to abandon the literal interpretation for a metaphoric one, describing the future relationship between the twin brothers, in which Jacob pursued Esau.

THE TWINS OF TAMAR

According to the biblical narrative, Tamar, the daughter-in-law of Judah, who was Jacob and Leah's fourth son, was widowed before bearing any children. By the ancient Semitic custom of *yi'bum*, she was entitled to have children by her younger, unmarried brother-in-law, Shelah. Tamar disguised herself as a harlot and set out to seduce her recently widowered father-in-law, "for she saw that Shelah was grown, and she was not given unto him to wife" (Genesis 38:14). The outcome of her meeting with Judah was the twin pregnancy, Pharez and Zarah.

A detailed description of a rather bizarre twin delivery follows: "And it came to pass in the time of her travail, that, behold, twins were in her womb. And it came to pass, when she travailed, that the one put out his hand; and the midwife took and bound upon his hand a scarlet thread saying, 'This came out first.' And it came to pass, as he drew back his hand, that behold, his brother came out: and she said, 'How has thou broken forth? this breach be upon thee:'... And afterwards came out his brother, that had the scarlet thread upon his hand...." (Genesis 38:27–30).

There are some notable contrasts between this twin pregnancy and that of Rebekah. First, the gestational age at delivery is not mentioned, and because it was not described that "her days to be delivered were fulfilled," as in Rebekah's case, it might be assumed that Tamar had a preterm delivery and therefore Pharez and Zarah were low birth weight neonates. Second, the existence of twins is not mentioned until "the time of her travail." Indeed, when Tamar's relatives informed Judah of her pregnancy, the text reads, "behold she is with child by whoredom" (Genesis 38:24), whereas the narrator states clearly in Rebekah's case, "the children struggled together within her." The midwife in this case must have been quite experienced because she made the diagnosis of twins intrapartum. Otherwise, she could not have been ready to apply the scarlet thread to the firstborn, the identification of whom was of critical importance because, according to biblical law, the firstborn (whether singleton or twin) is entitled to a double portion of inheritance. Indeed, much Talmudic debate surrounds the question of whether a prolapsed hand can be considered a valid birth for such purposes.

The delivery of Pharez and Zarah, similar to the delivery of Jacob and Esau, is not understood easily. According to one theory,[7] the infants were in vertex-vertex presentation, with the arms of Zarah next to the head of Pharez. During descent, both the head of twin A, Pharez, and the arm of twin B, Zarah, were advancing, with twin B's arm prolapsing ahead of twin A. After the scarlet thread was applied to the prolapsed hand of twin B, the arm retracted, and twin A was delivered.

An alternative explanation takes into account the presumption that Tamar delivered prematurely by invoking a shoulder presentation of one twin, with its arm prolapsing alongside the vertex of the other twin. It is equally possible that the transverse twin could have been either the first or second; however, because the prolapsed arm did not prevent the head of a small co-twin from further descent, the vertex was delivered first, after the arm of the transverse lying twin retreated back to the birth canal. Obviously, such an explanation involves some degree of *conduplicato corpore* of the transverse lying twin, which results usually in fetal damage. An interesting consideration, suggesting that there was trauma during the delivery, is the phrase "this breach be upon thee." A careful deduction by Slevogt, cited by Preuss,[7] suggests that the breach refers to a perineal tear caused by the forceful delivery of twin A. Support for this assumption comes from the Hebrew meaning of the name given to the first twin, Pharez, or "spread apart" in the sense of "tearer of the perineum." The outcome for the malpresenting twin is not specified. Indeed, the genealogy given in a later chapter in Genesis lists Pharez' descendants, but conspicuously omits those of Zarah, suggesting perhaps that Zarah (the twin with the scarlet thread around his hand) did not survive to father children (Genesis 46:12).

Of the three possible combinations discussed above, namely vertex-vertex, vertex-transverse, and transverse-vertex, only the last does not involve rupture of the dividing membrane before the delivery of twin A. Because it is unknown if Pharez and Zarah had discordant phenotypes, as did Jacob and Esau, one cannot exclude monoamniotic twinning in this case. However, because monoamniotic twins and rupture of the dividing membrane are extremely rare situations, the most likely combination is transverse-vertex.

COMMENT

The motif of mother with child was common in the iconography of the Near East in ancient times. However, the motif of mother with twins is known only from the Bible and from the Canaanite Ugarit mythology that preceded it.[8] According to the Ugarit mythology, the Father of Gods (El) had two godly twin sons, Shahar ("Sunrise") and Shalem ("Sunset"), who were born to him by mortal mothers and were given to Asherah, the Mother of Gods, to be nursed by her. The red color associated with the rising and setting sun appears to be preserved in the stories of biblical twins—Esau who "came out red," and Zerah (Hebrew: sunrise), who was given the red thread by the midwife.

In the Greek mythology, divine twins were very popular, and many important figures had divine fathers, mortal mothers, and twin brothers. It is no wonder that the Philistines, who were of Greek Aegean origin, found interest in the Ugarit goddess Asherah nursing godly twins. Figure 2 shows a mold-made clay figurine from the Canaanite period (about 13th century BC), found in Israel. The two arms create a roundish frame symbolizing the womb in which twins, each nursing from a different breast, are seen. Each thigh is decorated with an ibex standing beside a palm tree, symbolizing growth and fertility. Of interest is the rather graphic depiction of the woman's hands opening her vagina to deliver from the breech-breech combination.

Fig. 2. Mold-made nude fertility figurine found near Kibbutz Revadim (Israel) in 1980. (Courtesy of the Israel Museum, Jerusalem; reprinted with permission from Blickstein I. Introduction to the 9th International Workshop on Multiple Pregnancy. Isr J Obstet Gynecol 1994;5:1[s].)

The application of modern obstetric knowledge to biblical narration adds new dimension to the storytelling, deepening our connection to these events of antiquity.

REFERENCES

1. Gordon B. The midwife in biblical history and legend. I. Old Testament mid wives. Midwife Health Visit 1968;4:3822–4.
2. Bash DM. The midwives Shifra and Punah: Biblical heroines. Bull Am Assoc Hist Nurs 1993;37:7.
3. Ceccarelli C. Obstetrics and neonatology in the Bible. Minerva Med 1993; 84:565–70.
4. Dumont M. La gynecologie et l'obsterique dans la Bible II. De l'accouchment a ses suites. J Gynecol Obstet Biol Reprod 1990;19:145–53.
5. Levin S. Obstetrics in the Bible. J Obstet Gynaecol Br Empire 1960;67:490–9.
6. Dubovsky H. The Jewish contribution to medicine. Part I, Biblical and talmudic times to the end of the 18th century. S Afr Med J 1989;76:26–8.
7. Preuss J. Biblical–Talmudic medicine. 2nd ed. New York: Hebrew Publishing Company, 1983:428–30.
8. Margalith O. A new type of Asherah figurine? Vetus Testamentum 1994; 44:109–13.

Obstet Gynecol 1998;91:632–4.

COMMENTARY

Isaac Blickstein, one of the authors of this obstetric analysis of the Bible's two cases of twins, is an Israeli obstetrician who has long been interested in multifetal gestation and is arguably one of the world's foremost authorities on twin–twin transfusion. It seems curious that only two cases of twins are described in the Bible, but of course the biblical era antedated the development of ovulation-inducing agents.

The Historic Significance of Circumcision

Stephen J. Waszak, MD

APRIL 1978

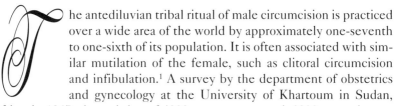he antediluvian tribal ritual of male circumcision is practiced over a wide area of the world by approximately one-seventh to one-sixth of its population. It is often associated with similar mutilation of the female, such as clitoral circumcision and infibulation.[1] A survey by the department of obstetrics and gynecology at the University of Khartoum in Sudan, Africa, in 1967, showed that of 4000 women surveyed, 3800 were circumcised or infibulated, and 200 were not.[1] However, the present discussion will be limited to male circumcision.

Circumcision is known to have been practiced on all continents and among virtually all sociologic groups.[2] Among the earliest peoples to practice circumcision were the Egyptians. Evidence of their practice of this operation is found in their bas-reliefs and in mummies dating as early as 2300 BC.[3] Wall paintings from ancient Egypt date circumcision several thousand years earlier than this.[4]

It is from the ancient Egyptians that the Jews derived the practice of circumcision. The ritual became such a crucial element of the Jewish religion that one can actually trace the biblical development of Judaism by the motif of circumcision alone. The practice was also a crucial issue in the development of the early Christian church.

The first reference to circumcision in the Bible is in the Book of Genesis. In fact, it was believed to be important enough to warrant an entire chapter (Ch. 17) because circumcision was to represent the covenant between Jehovah and the Jewish people.[5] The circumcision of Abraham and all the males in his family, related in that chapter, took place about 1713 BC, according to biblical scholars.[3]

The main historic significance of circumcision for the Jewish people is pointed out with great insight by Bertrand Russell.[6] He notes that the earliest point in Jewish history that can be verified by documents other than the Old Testament is when the two kingdoms of Israel and Judah already existed. In 722 BC, the Assyrians conquered the northern kingdom, and the kingdom of Judah alone preserved the Jewish religion and tradition. In the sixth century BC, however, Nebuchadnezzar captured Jerusalem, destroyed the Temple, and removed a large part of the population to Babylon. The Babylonian empire was subsequently conquered by Cyrus, king of the Medes and the Persians, who issued an edict in 537 BC allowing the Jews to return to Palestine. The Temple was rebuilt, and Jewish orthodoxy crystallized.

During the period of Babylonian captivity, Judaism underwent an important development: The prophets Jeremiah and Ezekiel proposed the idea that all religions except one are false and that the Lord punishes idolatry. A fiery nationalism was developed in the Jews that distinguished them from other nations of antiquity.

As the Temple had been destroyed, the Jewish ritual during captivity became nonsacrificial because sacrifice could be offered only in the Temple. Synagogues began at this time, with readings from such portions of the Scripture as already existed, and the importance of the Jewish Sabbath was first emphasized. Moreover, circumcision came to be the indelible, nationalistic mark of the Jew. It was a period of extreme exclusiveness among Jews, and at this time marriage to gentiles came to be forbidden.

The Jewish people then underwent a period of hellenization by the Greek conqueror Alexander the Great. However, after the reign of Alexander, Palestine became a disputed territory between the Seleucids centered in the North, with their capital in Antioch, and the Ptolemies in the south, with their capital in Alexandria.

In 168 BC, the Seleucid King Antiochus IV took over the province of Judah, determined to hellenize the Jews and to extirpate the Jewish religion. He forbade observance of Jewish laws relating to food; he forbade worship in the Temple; and most relevant to the present discussion, he strictly forbade circumcision, making it punishable by death.[7]

Thus, circumcision became a symbol of Jewish national identity, for which nationalists were willing to die. The rural Jews, or Hasidim, revolted under the leadership of Judas Maccabaeus, who recaptured Jerusalem in 164 BC. To this day, faithful Jews celebrate the victory of Judas Maccabaeus as Hanukkah, the Festival of Lights.

To think that a war could take place over the issue of circumcision or the question of eating pork seems almost unbelievable, but Russell points out the significance of this period in Jewish history:

"But for the heroic resistance of the Hasidim, the Jewish religion might easily have died out. If this had happened, neither Christianity nor Islam could have existed in anything like the form they actually took."[6]

From this point on, ritual procedures prescribed by Holy Law—observance of the Sabbath, abstinence from unclean meats, and especially circumcision—held the Jews together as a nation. The importance they attached to the Law steadily increased until the time of Christ, and their observance became intensely rigid and conservative.

Even today in Israel, 70 circumcisions are performed daily, on the average, by the Jewish Mohel, persons especially trained to perform ritual circumcision.[8]

THE MOTIF IN EARLY CHRISTIANITY

The motif of circumcision can be followed further, through the beginnings of Christianity and even into the Middle Ages. The intensity of adherence to the Law that was characteristic in the time of Paul makes his revolt against its domination very remarkable. One of the main obstacles Paul faced in converting gentiles to his new religion was convincing them that they need not be circumcised to enter the Heavenly Kingdom.

Paul argued that foreskin status was not a relevant variable in his discriminant function of salvation.[9, 10] Thus, in almost every one of the Epistles, Paul dealt with this problem, propagating the concept that it was "circumcision" of the heart and not of the flesh that was the true way to salvation.

Nevertheless, even by the 17th century, church fathers were unconvinced by the arguments of Paul, as can be seen in the painting (Figure 1) depicting circumcision as a religious ritual performed by a bishop. The rit-

Fig. 1. Circumcision performed by a bishop of the Church. Painted by Discorhecido, Portuguese School, 16th century (courtesy of the Museum Nacionel de Arte Antiga, Lisbon).

ual is still recognized by the Roman Catholic Church and other Christian churches as a feast day, based on the circumcision of Christ,[11] and celebrated on January 1.

It comes as rather a surprise that Michelangelo's sculpture of the biblical hero, David, on which he worked from 1501 to 1504, depicts David (Figure 2) as uncircumcised,[12] given the historic, religious, and cultural significance of the circumcision. Michelangelo certainly must have been familiar with the Bible.

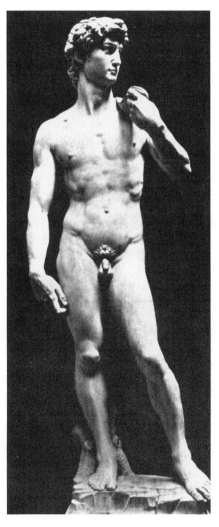

Fig. 2. Michelangelo's statue of David.

REFERENCES

1. Shandall A: Circumcision and infibulation of females. Sudan Med J 5:178, 1967
2. Bolande RP: Ritualistic surgery—circumcision and tonsillectomy. N Engl J Med 280:591, 1969
3. Speert H: Circumcision of the newborn. Obstet Gynecol 2:164, 1953
4. Gairdner D: The fate of the foreskin: A study of circumcision. Br Med J 2:1443, 1949
5. Genesis 17:1–24. Holy Bible. New York, Daughters of St Paul, 1961, p 34
6. Russell B: A History of Western Philosophy. New York, Simon and Schuster, 1945, p 316
7. First Book of Maccabees 1:63–64. Holy Bible. New York, Daughters of St Paul, 1961, p 1216
8. Shulman I, Ben-Hur N, Neuman Z: Surgical complications of circumcision. Am J Dis Child 107:85, 1964
9. Romans 4:9–12. Holy Bible. New York, Daughters of St Paul, 1961, pp 214–215
10. Phillipians 3:2–6. Holy Bible. New York, Daughters of St Paul, 1961, p 280
11. Luke 2:21–22. Holy Bible. New York, Daughters of St Paul, 1961, p 84
12. Delacroix H, Tansey R (eds): Gardner's Art Through the Ages. New York, Harcourt, Brace and World, Inc, 1970, p 468

Obstet Gynecol 1978;51:499–501.

COMMENTARY

This short essay traces the long history of male circumcision, emphasizing particularly its importance in Judaism. Religious implications aside, the practice of circumcising male newborns has become a focus of great controversy in recent years.

The Birth of Mohammed

Selcuk Erez, MD

JULY 1965

"Mevlid" is the name of a ritual ceremony performed in most of the Muslim countries. Originally, it was a festival celebrating the birthday of the Prophet of Islam.[3]

The earliest poem written to be read on this occasion is in Arabic; its author, Ibn-i Hisham, died in 834.[7] From the 13th Century onwards, the number of poems and essays of this kind increased. The most popular poem written to be recited on this ceremony is that of Suleyman Chelibi, who was one of the earliest Ottoman poets. On the overthrow of one of the Ottoman sultans, the Thunderbolt, by Tamerlane, Suleyman is known to have founded an asylum as the Chief Imam (priest) of the Great Mosque at Bursa, at that time the Turkish capital and not far from Istanbul.[3] His death took place here in the year 1421, and his tomb is still revered in that city.

The original copy of the poem is said to have been dated at Bursa in the year 1409. It was entitled *Vesilatun Nedjat* (The Means of Deliverance) and consists of a number of sections or cantos, usually separated by couplet and response, which served as chorus. The birth of Mohammed is described in the ninth section.

The English translation of some parts of this poem is given below. It must be remembered, in reading it, that some couplets are given in the first person and as spoken by Lady Amine, the mother of Mohammed, in the form of an introspection, the account of which is given afterwards:

> But in that night when he to earth descended,
> A host of herald signs bespoke his coming,
> It was the happy month, Rebi-ul-evel,
> And of this month, the twelfth, Isneyn, the Blessed.

* * * * *

> "I saw," said she, "a wondrous light up springing,
> and streaming from my house, with blaze increasing.
> Round it the sun revolved, moth-like and dazzled,
> While earth and sky gave back this matchless splendour

Heaven's radiant doors stood wide and Dark was vanquished.
There came three angels bearing shining banners.

* * * * *

"So clear before my eyes appeared these visions,
That all my heart o'erflowed with glowing wonder."

* * * * *

Here Amine made ending, for the hour
In which should come that best of men had sounded.
"I thirst," she cried, "I thirst, I burn with fever!"
A brimming glass to her at once was proffered.
White was this glass, than snow more white, and colder;
No sweetmeat ever made held half such sweetness.
I drank it, and my being filled with glory,
Nor could I longer self from light distinguish.

Fig. 1. The infant Mohammed surrounded by his mother, Amine, and three angels. The inscriptions on the wall are connected with the event of the nativity. This minia-ture, taken from the manuscript Siyer-un-Nebi (Progress of the Prophet) represents a compromise between the traditions of East and West concerning representation in human form of sacred figures: only the face of the child Mohammed and his mother are veiled, with the rest of the bodies shown. Also noteworthy is the flaming, golden light surrounding the child, a customary substitute for the halo above the heads of the holy figures seen in the religious art of the West.

It is clear from this account that Amine experienced visual aura as well as a sensation of hotness and thirst during her labor. The couplet that follows the last couplet cited above states that she was exhausted and fainted, and that when she recovered, there were no fairies, phantasmagoric birds, etc., to be seen.[1] We also know that some versions of this poem carry references to noises that she had heard that filled all the atmosphere.[1]

This tableau, described by the poet[,] can medically be interpreted in a number of ways: (1) It may be the account of eclampsia of pregnancy; (2) it may be the account of an epileptic seizure precipitated by labor; (3) It may be the account of a state of hyperpyrexia secondary to an intrapartum infection.

Clayton and Oram state that the symptoms of idiopathic epilepsy usually appear in the first or second decade, but sometimes not until later. They may, indeed, occur first during or just after a pregnancy and in that event, idiopathic epilepsy would have to be differentiated from eclampsia or from cerebral thrombophlebitis.[4]

Was it eclampsia? There are some points in favor of this possibility. According to Dieckmann, primiparas comprise 63–83% of the patients who have eclampsia and preeclampsia: Amine was a primipara when she gave birth to Mohammed. On the other hand, the incidence of toxemia among the unmarried women and widows is said to be higher; and we know that Abdulla, the father of Mohammed[,] had died before the latter was born.

But some points are against toxemia. It is widely known that the incidence of eclampsia shows marked variations throughout the world and that changes in climate, diet, and habits of people affect it. According to Dieckmann, Von Kondrad has stated that eclampsia is rare in Egypt and in people inhabiting the date-tree oases.[5] The same is true of the Arabian peninsula. Eclampsia is said to be very rare in the country then inhabited by the Arabian tribe called Quraish, of which Abdulla, the Prophet's father[,] was a member.

Eclampsia is, however, of frequent occurrence in Turkey. The common people know that such a disease exists and this medical term has its synonyms, such as *havale*, in the Turkish language used in everyday life. If, in Suleyman Chelibi's poem, Amine, the Prophet's mother[,] compares the liquid presented to her during her labor to snow, which is practically absent in the district where the birth took place, but ever present on the top of Mount Olympos, at whose feet Bursa, where this poet lived, is situated, why should he not interpret and describe the birth of his Prophet in terms of the phenomena with which he is quite familiar?[2]

In addition, amnesia usually occurs in the eclamptic patients and they not infrequently have a loss of memory. Hence, it would be difficult for her to remember that "So clear before [her] eyes appeared these visions" and give such a detailed account of them.

There are more points in favor of epilepsy. Visual disturbances attributed to eclampsia are usually described as "spots before eyes," "blurring of vision," or "a partial blackout due to retinal edema"; the use of these terms is insufficient to describe those visions seen by the Prophet's mother, while visual and psychic aura, a typical symptom of epilepsy[,] seems the right designation for them.

We know that some epileptic patients have within one framework of a very complex seizure that visual hallucination of a threatening figure. Still others see and hear very complicated dreamlike sequences.[6]

Certainly hyperpyrexia, secondary to an intrapartum infection, would be a likely event centuries before Semmelweis was born. It is also clear that one, without overworking one's imagination, can easily attribute the "hotness and the thirst" reported by the parturient to this cause. Certainly this would not be the first nor the last piece of art which describes hallucinations experienced in states of high fever: Goethe's famous *Erlkönig* may be cited as a well-known example.

Finally, to end this effort at differential diagnosis attempted hundreds of years after the event, I would like to quote a passage from the book *Comparative Religion* by Dr. A. C. Bouquet, about Mohammed's hearing voices during his meditations in the barren deserts around Mecca, for I believe that these words also hold true for Lady Amine in the process of delivery.

"[His] credit was not weakened by these strange events for they were the price which sensitive souls have to pay for the intensity of their vision."[2]

These gifted persons enlightened and morally elevated millions of people and yet they themselves did suffer from human illnesses.

REFERENCES

1. Ates, Ahmet. Vesiletu'n-Necat Mevlid. Turk Dil Kurumu. C. 11. 33. Ank 1954, pp. 109, 178.
2. Bouquet, A. C. *Comparative Religion*. Pelican Books. Baltimore, Md., 1941, p. 267.
3. Chelibi, Suleyman. "The Mevlidi Sherif." Translated by Lyman MacCallum; Ed. by L. Crammer-Byng. Wisdom of the East Series, Edinburgh, 1943, pp. 4, 11.
4. Clayton, S., and Oram, S. *Medical Disorders During Pregnancy*. Churchill, London, 1951, p. 239.
5. Dieckmann, W. J. *The Toxemias of Pregnancy*. Mosby, St. Louis, 1941, p. 38.
6. Straus, H. "Epileptic Disorders." In *American Handbook of Psychiatry*. Ed. by Silvano Aneti. Vol. 11, Basic, New York, 1959, pp. 1112, 1120.
7. Alangu, Tahir. Bizde Mevlut Torenleri. Vatan. 8 Nisan. 1959, p. 2.

History

Erasistratus. Engraving taken from *Spiegel der Arzt [sic]*, 1532. (Library of the Old Faculty of Medicine, Paris, France. Photo © Lib. OFMP.)

The relationship between history and medicine has two facets. One is how medicine and disease can influence the course of history, as exemplified in the first article of the series, and the other is the rich history of medicine itself, about which Fielding Garrison (1876–1935) wrote, "The history of medicine is, in fact, the history of humanity itself, with its ups and downs, its brave aspirations after truth and finality, its pathetic failures." Most of the articles in this group are primarily of this second type.

Diagnosis in Retrospect: Mary Tudor*

Allan C. Barnes, MD

MAY 1953

*T*he physician, so often accused of "talking shop" is often also guilty of "thinking shop." As he reads in other fields, he is often observing symptoms and making diagnoses. Meeting the somnolent, fat coach boy in *The Pickwick Papers* he thinks "Cushing's disease"; and with biography or history the temptation is even stronger. What illness plagued the Great Man? Of what did he die? Did Napoleon have cancer of the stomach, and over how long a period of time were the symptoms evident? Such questions become almost inevitable, and not infrequently the same physician who would hesitate to make a diagnosis over the telephone sets out to see if he can establish a diagnosis over the centuries, relaxed in the knowledge that the patient's fate has been decided and a diagnostic error will hurt only his professional vanity.

For the gynecologist, this pursuit of a diagnosis in retrospect has a special two-fold challenge: (1) the relative rarity of women as influential historical personages, and (2) the tendency to keep secret the type of symptomatology with which the gynecologist deals. What of Lola Montez? Or of Catherine de Medici? It is difficult not to speculate on their gynecologic status or to try to determine what diseases they may have had and the effect on their careers. The history of medicine has been covered again and again; but the medicine of history will eternally present new fascinations.

The present papers arose primarily from a long-standing interest in, and attempt to establish, a gynecologic diagnosis for Queen Elizabeth.

---

*To increase the ease, and (I would hope) the enjoyability of reading, no footnotes [sic] are included, and the text is not interrupted with annotation numbers. Obviously, however, many authorities have been consulted over the years leading to the writing of these papers, and many of them (as is necessary when returning to original sources) have been cheerfully plagiarized. Most of these authorities are referred to by name in the text; the absence of a formal bibliography does not imply any lack of recognition of my indebtedness. In fact, of this one could say with Montaigne: "I have gathered a bouquet of flowers from other men's gardens: naught but the string that binds them is my own."

Since to achieve this with any degree of adequacy we must go back at least to her father, we shall consider in this paper the last three of the Tudor monarchs—Henry VIII; Edward, his son; and Mary Tudor. We shall then turn to Elizabeth, the Virgin Queen, in a succeeding article.

HENRY VIII

The fact that this great monarch suffered from syphilis is so generally agreed on by medical authorities who have studied his reported symptoms that there is little need to re-examine the point here. Certainly, an obstetrician-gynecologist would probably be the last to dispute it. The record of Henry's efforts at parenthood is almost a textbook picture of the effect of untreated syphilis on the reproductive process; it is the story of stillbirths late in pregnancy, rather than of miscarriages early in pregnancy, of neonatal deaths, and of sickly children. Further, we can trace a decline in the virulence of the infection, reproductively speaking, as the years wore on and its manifestations in other body symptoms became more pronounced.

The obstetric history of Catherine of Aragon provides a case in point. On January 31, 1510, she gave birth to a 7-month stillborn daughter. On January 1, 1511, she produced a son who died at the age of 3 days (it is said from a cold caught at the prolonged christening, but much more likely it was spirochetal pneumonitis). In September of 1513 there was a second son who was either stillborn or who died immediately after delivery. In June, 1514, a third son was born who survived only long enough to be christened (the third day for a Prince). On February 18, 1516, was born the Princess who was to become the first woman since Matilda to rule England, and who is unfortunately remembered as "Bloody Mary." During 1517 it is probable that there was at least one ill-starred pregnancy, and on November 18, 1518, Catherine's last pregnancy produced a stillborn prince. She was now 40 and the menopause followed close upon this last delivery. Catherine provides us, however, with other confirmatory medical evidence. After her death a postmortem was performed, actually under Spanish influence and in hopes of proving that Henry had had her poisoned. This examination revealed that she was unpoisoned and was essentially intact except for a "black and hideous excrescence on the heart." This, of course, is the description of an (ruptured?) aneurysm of the aorta, tending to confirm the diagnosis as far as Catherine is concerned.

Anne Boleyn continues the record. Her first pregnancy produced the Princess Elizabeth. She was at her least infected at this point, but as the disease process took firmer hold on her, the stillborn pattern was resumed, with at least one and possibly two before she was slain. Jane Seymour likewise was able to carry her first and least infected pregnancy to term, producing Edward. Her death, from the record, was undoubtedly from puerperal sepsis, which must have claimed a startling number of women in the sixteenth century. Henry fathered no further pregnancies: much earlier, however, he was father to the illegitimate Duke of Richmond, who seems to have shared with Mary and Edward the penalty of a sickly constitution and poor general health.

With respect to Henry's health, one must also note the dreadful mental and moral degeneration that seized him during his fifth decade. Actually, Henry was an able and accomplished man during his early years, and the behavior so usually associated with his name set in quite rapidly during his forties. This is entirely compatible with the principal diagnosis we have ascribed to him. Although the recurrent ulcerating sinus on his leg may have been a syphilitic periostitis, as Dr. MacLaurin and others have felt, it equally well could have been a simple varicose ulcer. For the chief support of this diagnosis one need only look at a portrait of Henry. His costume included tight garters around the legs, and he was growing fatter and fatter. Years of a constricting garter just below the knee plus his corpulence would be enough to produce varicose veins in the lower leg, and, untreated, these could well lead to a superficial ulcer in the region of the ankle which would "close" or temporarily heal whenever the garters were omitted for a time and the leg elevated to promote venous drainage. The present writer would be inclined to attribute Henry's death in stupor and coma to uremia—either from a chronic nephritis which could not tolerate his increasing obesity, or (less likely, perhaps) from simple prostatic obstruction. While the blood pressure could not be taken at the time, Henry's size, his episodes of "cholera" of the face, and his death in uremia all suggest an elevated blood pressure and associated arteriosclerosis as additional reasonable diagnoses.

Let us close this diagnosis of Henry Tudor as the pathologist would close his protocol after completing a postmortem examination with a succinct listing of the diagnosis:

1. Acquired syphilis with central nervous system involvement.

2. Hypertension with arteriosclerosis and nephrosclerosis.

3. Leg ulceration probably on the basis of varicose veins.

4. Gross obesity.

5. Death from uremia, possibly with associated hypertrophy of the prostate.

The pathologist would not have added, as we may, that a man of intellectual capability, a man of fine literary learning and musical talent, a man who was a good athlete, with a decisive though imperious mind, such a man had been robbed of almost 20 years of valuable service to his country because of illness. History records the behavior of a diseased man, and one finds it difficult to remember the man on the one hand and the disease on the other.

EDWARD VI

This child, who ruled from his tenth to his sixteenth years, actually displays few direct evidences of hereditary syphilis other than a general susceptibility to other diseases. Since it was a matter of tremendous importance to his father that this sole male heir of the Tudors survive and be well, one is able to determine a great deal about his health.

Edward was thin and anemic looking from infancy, and from Thomas Cromwell's report to the Court it appears that he actually lost weight as he grew older. The evidences of luetic stigmata, including a dactylitis, while few and minor in nature seem unmistakable. Indeed his end may have been hastened by a Herxheimer reaction resulting from a mercury ointment applied by what Dickens mistakenly refers to as a "woman-doctor." Froude even comes to the conclusion that this healer was poisoning the young king.

His death, however, would seem to be clearly tubercular. He had a productive cough; he had fevers and sweats; he continued to lose weight. The blood-lettings of the Court Physicians could not cure these symptoms, and our pathologist would presumably have concluded his protocol:

1. Pulmonary tuberculosis, bilateral, far advanced.

2. Secondary anemia (both from the disease and the bleedings).

3. Evidence of congenital syphilis, with marked evidence of recent overtreatment.

4. Cachexia (and alopecia medicamentosa).

5. Dactylitis, possibly syphilitic, probably toxic.

QUEEN MARY

After 10 days of Lady Jane Grey's nominal rule with the Duke of Northumberland in power, Mary, the next-to-the-last of the Tudor Monarchs, ascended the throne to round out an unhappy life with 5 years of unhappy reign. She was 37 at the time of her coronation and died in her forty-fourth year.

As Henry's reproductive history is the prototype of acquired syphilis, Mary's constitution and appearance is the prototype of inherited syphilis. Small in stature and slight, she had a pinched and wizened face, which appeared prematurely old. A writer in the British Medical Journal in 1910 records her ill health and general susceptibility to illness as characteristic of congenital lues, and Sir Clifford Allbutt diagnoses her extremely bad eyesight as interstitial keratitis, which occurs predominantly in hereditary syphilis. Dr. MacLaurin says: "The 'storms of puberty' that had shattered the frail barque of Edward VI, and brought his latent spirochetes to the surface, beat hard upon Mary's body, and left her an embittered and sickly woman, with an intellect below her station, and a conscience above it." But actually, if this is the most apparent diagnosis with respect to Mary, it should be pointed out that its influence was at most indirect insofar as her death is concerned; nor is it the most influential medical diagnosis with reference to her life.

Mary died in 1558, the victim of an epidemic which was then sweeping England. It was referred to in the contemporary records as "the new burning ague" and had started in the fall of the year (Mary died in November), killing literally thousands of people. Epidemiologists have concluded that it was probably epidemic influenza. Our imaginary pathologist, concluding his postmortem examination of Mary[,] would have reported only:

1. Influenza, with pulmonary inflammation and consolidation.

2. Evidences of hereditary syphilis, including probable interstitial keratitis.

But the pathologist cannot see, and the microscope does not reveal, the diagnosis of the disease which principally afflicted Mary Tudor. It was an acquired disease which affected the mind and the psyche, rather than one which produced tumors and growths. But if the pathologist, looking at fixed and stained pieces of dead tissue cannot see this diagnosis, the gynecologist, who deals with living women, will recognize it.

Let us start with her childhood training. Mary, like her sister Elizabeth, experienced rapid increases and declines in official popularity. One year she would find herself declared a bastard by a law which her father forced through the Commons; the next year she would be taken into Court, legitimatized, and treated with favor. Shortly she would be "farmed out" and effectively banished from Court. Insecurity dogged her footsteps, and she had not the ability to attract personal friends that Elizabeth had; there were fewer devoted followers to stand firm during the precarious days.

When she was 17 she saw her mother discarded and banished from Court. Preceding that there had been many years of family bickering and Catherine's tragedy in the face of Henry's quest for Anne Boleyn. By contrast with Elizabeth, who could not even remember her mother, Mary was acutely conscious of her father's behavior and of her mother's fate. When she was approximately 20 her father forced her to sign a testimonial that his marriage with Catherine of Aragon had been "by God's law and man's incestuous and unlawful," thereby declaring herself illegitimate. Here is severe psychic trauma for a young girl to experience!

In her schooling she was subjected to the same rigorous training which was the lot of all of Henry's children. He himself knew a great deal, and he insisted that his children be taught a great deal. But Mary was slow in learning, and her eyesight was already not good. This was tolerated in the early years, when she was the sole heir and hope of the throne, but with the start of Elizabeth's schooling, and the glowing reports from the tutor Ascham as to *her* ability to learn, Mary's father grew short with her, although Edward's similar aptitude at learning brought no official rebukes; she was no longer important with a Prince available. Although she was a grown woman, comparisons were undoubtedly made by the tutors; and even had she not heard them, she would have made them herself.

She had always from childhood felt herself insecure; she felt that she and her mother had been wronged; she felt, in comparison with her half-brother and half-sister, dull and stupid. It is bad enough for a child to grow up with these feelings, but Mary had still another cross to bear: it was quite evident that she was unattractive. There were no spontaneous suitors, and indeed few close friends. When she became queen, a husband was arranged for by the Council; it was not possible to obtain the consent of the man of her first choice, Charles V, and Philip was the husband contracted for. He did little to supply the affection and attention she was starved for. He spent less than a year with her after the marriage, retiring for 19 months to the Continent away from her, to return only for a short time to the English court.

The girl had grown up anxious, tense, embittered; but predominantly she grew up starved for affection. The emotional and physical demands of her nature were frustrated; sexual tensions and personal anxiety were the predominant manifestations of her adult years. And many of the symptoms of this state, as the gynecologist would have predicted, centered around her pelvis and the reproductive organs.

All her life Mary suffered from dysmenorrhea. The pain associated with her menstrual periods tended apparently to grow more severe with the years, and was at its worst during her thirties. During her late teens and early twenties her menses were exceedingly scanty—a phenomenon attributed to excessive studying. In addition, her cycle was irregular, with a tendency toward prolonged intervals or missed periods. On two occasions this led Mary to the psychosomatic disease of pseudocyesis. It has often been said of this entity that it is particularly likely to occur in young brides who are afraid of pregnancy and in women in the early menopause who are reluctant to lose their reproductive ability. Mary Tudor had one episode of pseudopregnancy at each of these times, but she was a bride and a menopausal woman within a span of a few short years.

The first of these episodes (Neale's description) ran through the winter and spring of 1554 and 1555. It was predicated not only on her recent marriage (in July of 1554, when she was 38 years old) but also on the religious ecstasy of re-establishing her church in England. Cardinal Pole, the Pope's personal representative, had not felt it safe to re-enter England until well after the marriage. On November 30 he appeared before Parliament, and to the Queen's sobs, absolved the nation. And it was at that time, and to Pole rather than to her husband, that Mary announced her pregnancy! One might have doubted an announcement at such a time from a woman passionately anxious for off-spring and known to have menstrual irregularity. And some doubters there were, one of them attaching a paper to the palace door at Hampdon Court which read: "Shall we be such fools, good Englishmen, to believe that our Queen is with child."

But Cardinal Pole believed, and the appropriate sermons were preached. Philip believed, and stayed in England with his wife rather than returning to the Continent he preferred. Mary believed, and the signs of pregnancy advanced through the winter. As the pregnancy advanced, Mary became haunted with fears of death in childbirth, and the available physicians of note were summoned to recount to her stories of deliveries successfully accomplished by women in the twilight of their reproductive life.

On April 30 a false rumor swept London that she had been delivered. Throughout May the letters which were to announce the birth to foreign courts were made ready. In June, Mary took to bed.

Nothing happened. The weeks passed. Ambassadors arrived with speeches prepared and gifts ready. Tongues wagged throughout June and by July it was a court farce. But England continued to wait for the news and the religious processions continued. By the end of July the abdominal swelling had subsided; it was quite evident that there was not and had not been a physical pregnancy (and probably not even the ovarian tumor diagnosed by some subsequent physicians). To get rid of the crowds at Hampdon Court and to allow Mary to re-emerge, the Court was moved in August to Oatlands, and on August 26 Philip left for the Continent.

From childhood Mary had always been prone to tears, and during the ensuing months she gave way to them often. Her letters to Philip reveal a love-sick, affection-starved woman who was deeply frustrated, for whom nothing seemed to prosper. After 19 months' absence Phillip returned to her in March of 1557, to stay this time only 3 1/2 months. Nevertheless, early in 1558, although she had not been with her husband for 6 months, she again thought herself pregnant. Again it evaporated, and the influenza that carried her away in November of that year was a merciful friend—a brief organic disease which concluded a long functional disorder and brought peace to Mary Tudor and to England.

Obstet Gynecol 1953;1:585–90.

COMMENTARY

Allan C. Barnes (see biographical information, page 61) demonstrates his versatility with this scholarly and interesting essay (the very first After Office Hours article) on the medical aspects of the Tudor monarchs. Mary Tudor, with her chronic menstrual abnormalities and two episodes of pseudocyesis, is especially interesting to gynecologists. Facing death, Mary accepted, albeit reluctantly, her half sister Elizabeth as her successor. The rest, as they say, is history. Barnes dealt with Elizabeth's medical history in a second article that appeared the next month (Obstet Gynecol 1953;1:702–11).

The Great Eighteenth Century Obstetric Atlases and Their Illustrator

John W. Huffman, MD

JUNE 1970

he publication in 1969 of a magnificent facsimile of William Smellie's *Sett of Anatomical Tables* again emphasizes the effect which Smellie and William Hunter and their obstetric atlases had upon the teaching and practice of midwifery during the eighteenth century. It was an effect which extended to continental Europe and America; it is still found in some of the basic obstetric principles taught today. Both men made notable contributions to obstetrics; they probably would not occupy the eminence they do, however, if their books had not been illustrated by Jan van Riemsdyk, an extraordinary Dutch artist who worked in England between 1745 and 1780. Little is known about him as a person, but the 1969 facsimile edition of Smellie's atlas again confirms the widely held opinion that Riemsdyk's work is the acme of the medical illustrator's art. The part he played in the development of modern obstetrics and his contribution to medical education in America entitle him to wider recognition than he has received up to this time.[3]

Smellie's *Sett of Anatomical Tables* and Hunter's *Anatomy of the Gravid Uterus* were used by both men to teach the many physicians who attended their classes in midwifery. Modern obstetrics was born in their classrooms and at the bedsides of their patients. For decades Smellie's atlas, republished and plagiarized, was a basic part of the obstetric student's library (Fig 1 and 2). It is interesting to note that the first edition of the *Encyclopaedia Britannica*, in its article on midwifery, used the Riemsdyk plates from Smellie's book, but the drawings were reversed and their source was not acknowledged, although credit was given to Smellie's work in the introduction. Modifications of some of Riemsdyk's drawings, originally made for Smellie and Hunter, were still found in obstetric textbooks published in the twentieth century.

It is ironic that we know so little about Riemsdyk. He is mentioned for the first time in a review of Smellie's *Treatise of the Theory and Practice of Midwifery* (1751). The reviewer does not call him by name but merely states that Smellie intended to publish a set of anatomical figures,

Fig 1. One of the plates drawn by van Riemsdyk for Smellie's atlas. The position and appearance of the fetus, the lower uterine segment, and the partially dilated cervix have been faithfully portrayed.

"engraved after the Drawings of a very able artist.... In point of Design and Anatomical Exactness we ... pronounce them to be superior to any Figures of the kind hitherto made public." Smellie's atlas, published in 1754, contains 39 life-sized plates; 26 of them were drawn by Riemsdyk.

Riemsdyk's name and the character of his work indicate that he came to England from the Netherlands. The name van Riemsdyk is a common one in Holland but it cannot be traced back genealogically prior to 1780. No one with the given name of Jan and the surname of van Riemsdyk is listed in the genealogic tables which I examined in the Library of the Royal University in Leyden. Lint, who described several drawings in mezzotint made by Riemsdyk for Charles Jenty's *Uteri praegnantis et at partem maturi demonstrations* (1758), states that Jenty, a London anatomist and surgeon, "executed his plan [for the plates] with Johannes van Riemsdyk, a Dutchman who lived in London, who later made drawings for Hunter."

The fact that Riemsdyk used mezzotint at all strongly suggests that he had been under the influence of Jan Ladmiral, who made colored anatomic illustrations in mezzotint for Albinus in Leyden; Ladmiral's work was pub-

Fig 2. Illustration by van Riemsdyk of forceps to the aftercoming head; the technic was one of Smellie's major contributions. From Smellie's *Anatomical Tables.*

lished between 1736 and 1741, and it is quite possible that Riemsdyk learned the technic from Ladmiral in Leyden. Furthermore, Reimsdyk's [sic] skillful manipulation of lights and shadows and his use of perspective suggest that he either came from the same school as Wandelaer, who did the excellent plates in Albinus' anatomies, or was, perhaps, trained by Wandelaer. Unlike Wandelaer, however, Riemsdyk did not embellish his drawings with extraneous artistic decorations. Also, unlike Wandelaer, he depicted the fetus in utero in a lifelike way (Fig 3) instead of in the awkward and unnatural frog-like position that had been used by his predecessors. Johnstone, describing Riemsdyk's work, said: "Van Riemsdyk's drawings are chalk drawings ... in a bright rose red or vermilion colour on 'off-white' paper. His work is masterly and finished and exhibits a sureness of touch even in the smallest details."

There are no known examples of Riemsdyk's work in any Dutch book nor at the Printzcabinet in Leyden. For many years I have tried to find plates by Riemsdyk in medical books published in Europe between 1700 and 1750; none have been found. Nothing is known about when he went to England nor what work he was doing before Smellie brings him to our attention. Smellie was a well-known obstetric teacher when he decided to produce an atlas to accompany his successful book on the practice of mid-wifery. In the advertisement for the second edition of that book it is noted that he had "with great care and expense employed Mr. Riemsdyk." Riemsdyk must have already displayed evidence of his ability before Smellie commissioned him to do the illustrations; it is inconceivable that an unknown artist would have been employed for such an important task. If Riemsdyk had done any work of note before he became associated with Smellie, it presumably was done in the Netherlands, most likely at Leyden and before 1748, when Pieter Camper the anatomist visited Smellie in London. Although Smellie wrote to Camper about his book, there is no mention of Riemsdyk in the correspondence between the two men in the Camper Collection at the Library of the University of Amsterdam. We cannot be certain when Riemsdyk started to work for Smellie. In the preface to the *Tables* Smellie says that "Mr. Riemsdyk had finished 22 of the illustrations two years before." That would have been in 1752. According to Glaister, however, "The preparation of the plates for this work occupied some years and even at the date of publication of the *Treatise* several of them had been completed." The *Treatise* was published in 1751. Glaister, whose biography of Smellie is considered the most com-plete, does not mention the relationship between Riemsdyk and Smellie. Yet they must have spent many hours together comparing the artist's sketches with Smellie's dissections.

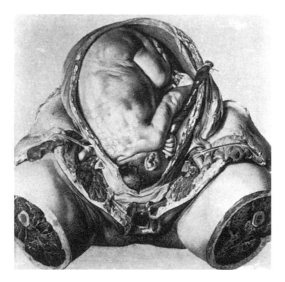

Fig 3. William Hunter did the dissection, van Riemsdyk the drawing, and Robert Strange the engraving for this illustration from Hunter's atlas (1774). It was published by the Baskerville Press and is the acme of the medical illustrator's art.

William Hunter's *Anatomy of the Gravid Uterus* is one of the great events not only in obstetric literature but in the art of medical illustration. It contains 34 life-sized plates; Riemsdyk drew 31 of them. The first dissection was drawn in 1751 and additional plates were added, as dissections became available, until 1765, when Hunter gave the manuscript and plates to John Baskerville of Birmingham for printing. The book, one of two medical works published by the famous Baskerville Press, was not published until 1774. The illustrator is not named in the preface to Hunter's atlas. The author mentions "the ingenious artists who made the drawings and engravings," and emphasizes that the illustrations are exact duplicates of the dissections. However, although he never publicly, insofar as we know, thanked Riemsdyk, the fact that Hunter purchased the Smellie plates and gave them to the University of Glasgow suggests he admired the artist's work. Fox, in his life of Hunter, best described the engravings:

> The plates are of much beauty and all of natural size and are drawn with marvelous fidelity to nature, not allowing, as Hunter tells us, the imagination to vary the actual appearances in order to render the object more useful as a demonstration ... in other words they are not mere diagrams but, as it were, photographic in their reality. The delicacy and softness of Riemsdyk's work bespeak a labor of love in which neither time nor cost were an object.

Very few people realize the contribution which Riemsdyk made to medical education in the American colonies. In 1762 William Shippen, Jr used drawings and casts in his classes in anatomy and midwifery at the Pennsylvania Hospital (Fig 4). The drawings and casts had been sent by John Fothergill, an English Quaker physician, as a gift to the Pennsylvania Hospital. They were used as teaching material in the first classes in anatomy and obstetrics in the first medical school in the United States. According to Scott, who described the plates in 1903, Caspar Wistar stated: "The paintings were done by Riemsdyk, one of the first artists of Great Britain. Jenty, an anatomist of London, is said to have made the dissections from which these pictures were taken." The plates, all of which are in excellent condition, are kept in the Library of the Pennsylvania Hospital. They are drawn in colored crayons, with the arteries shown in red and the veins in blue. One is signed by Riemsdyk, another by Burgess. The others, although not signed, give unmistakable evidence of Riemsdyk's ability to portray anatomic material graphically.

As far as we know, Riemsdyk's total accomplishments as a medical artist consisted of the 26 plates he made for Smellie, the 31 plates he made for Hunter, the 17 anatomic drawings for the Pennsylvania Hospital, the 5 mezzotint plates for Charles Jenty, and an illustration, reproduced by Radcliffe, showing the pelvis of the dwarf who underwent the first recorded cesarean section in England. He is known to have done several portraits, but I have

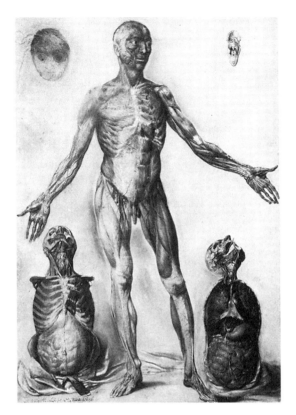

Fig 4. One of the anatomic paintings by van Riemsdyk which Fothergill gave to the Pennsylvania Hospital in 1762.

been unable to trace any but one—the portrait of Smellie drawn by Riemsdyk in 1753, which is in the Royal College of Physicians in London. In addition, he and his son, Andrew, published a volume in 1778 showing some of the curiosities in the British Museum. He is said to have died in Bath, England.

A great many beautifully illustrated medical books appeared during the eighteenth century. None of the others, however, equalled in scientific accuracy and careful reproduction Smellie's *Sett of Anatomical Tables* and Hunter's *Anatomy of the Gravid Uterus*. These were the offspring of a happy union of master obstetric anatomists and dissectors, an extraordinary medical illustrator, and skillful engravers. Riemsdyk's drawings are scientifically accurate. His ability in the use of perspective gives his figures an almost three-dimensional quality. His drawings of fetuses reproduced the subjects with startling accuracy, and for the first time the female genitalia, the intrapartum uterus, and the fetus were portrayed as they appear in the human subject. His drawings in colored crayon, in the Pennsylvania Hospital, are the equal in accuracy of those found in anatomic textbooks of today.

We may wonder about Reimsdyk's [sic] personal life, where he was born, who trained him, where he lived, how Smellie came to find him, and what his relationships were with Smellie and Hunter, but there is no question about his impact on obstetrics. The books he illustrated will always be towering milestones on the road of obstetric progress.

REFERENCES

1. Fox R: William Hunter. Lewis, London, 1901
2. Glaister J: Dr. William Smellie and his Contemporaries. J. Maclehose and Sons, Glasgow, 1894
3. Huffman 1: Jan van Riemsdyk, medical illustrator extraordinary. JAMA 208:121, 1969
4. Hunter W: The Anatomy of the Gravid Uterus Exhibited in Figures. J Baskerville, Birmingham, 1774
5. Jenty C: Uteri praegnantis et at partem maturi demonstrations. London, 1758
6. Johnstone R: William Smellie the Master of British Midwifery. E & S Livingstone, Edinburgh, 1952
7. Lint J de: The plates of Jenty. Janus 21:129, 1916
8. Monthly Review (London) 5:465 (Dec) 1751, quoted by Glaister
9. Radcliffe W: Milestones in Midwifery. John Wright & Sons Ltd, Bristol, 1967
10. Scott J: Concerning the Fothergill pictures at the Pennsylvania Hospital. Univ Penn Med Bull 16:338, 1903–1904
11. Smellie W: Set of anatomical tables with explanations and an abridgement of the practice of midwifery, with a view to illustrate a treatise on that subject and collection of cases. London, 1754
12. Smellie W: Facsimile edition of set of anatomical tables mentioned above. Philadelphia. W B Saunders & Co, 1969

Obstet Gynecol 1970;35:971–6.

COMMENTARY

John W. Huffman (1903–1989) attempts in this detailed and richly illustrated article to set the record straight and give credit where credit is due. Anatomic books by William Smellie and John Hunter, published in 1754 and 1774, respectively, are regarded as two of the most remarkable publications in all of history, but Huffman points out that the artist received little if any recognition. This surely does seem to be an oversight, for it is the incredible quality of the illustrations that makes the books the priceless gems they are. Huffman practiced in Chicago where he had an association with the Northwestern University medical school spanning a half century as medical student, resident, and faculty member. He was recognized around the world for his pioneering work in pediatric and adolescent gynecology, and he could justly be regarded as the founder of that subspecialty.

An Obstetric Record from *The Medical Record*: Report of Largest Human Birth

Allan C. Barnes, MD

FEBRUARY 1957

he Medical Record was a publication appearing during the 1870's and subtitled "A Weekly Journal of Medicine and Surgery." It was published by William Wood & Company of 27 Great Jones Street, New York. Its editor was George F. Shrady, A.M., M.D.

To that journal, Dr. A. P. Beach, a physician of Seville, Ohio, submitted a case report which was published in the issue of March 15, 1879. The case report is apparently completely reliable and is reproduced herewith through the courtesy of the Cleveland Health Museum.

At the request of many readers of The Medical Record, I am persuaded to report a case of labor which I attended a few weeks ago. The great size of the child at birth was the remarkable feature of the case, it being probably the largest human birth on record. It would be well to state here, that when we take into consideration the immense proportions of the parents (Fig. 1), the size of the child need not astonish us. The mother, Mrs. Captain M. V. Bates, whose maiden name was Annie Swan of Nova Scotia, stands 7 feet 9 inches in height. Captain M. V. Bates, formerly of Kentucky, is 7 feet 7 inches in height. These large people have, undoubtedly, been visited by many readers of this journal, as they have given public receptions in nearly all of the large cities and towns of Europe and America.

At 12M, January 15, 1879, I was called upon to attend this lady in confinement, it being her second labor. I found her surrounded with competent attendants, and everything in order and at hand that would in any way add to her comfort and convenience. Her pains were quite infrequent and light. After a convenient time, with my patient in the usual position, I proceeded to make an examination but was unable to reach the os uteri, it being so far up. I could not with my hand, by any ordinary effort, make a satisfactory examination, but concluded that she was in the initial stage of labor. She remained in much the same condition for the next 24 hours, passing the night comfortably, and I saw no necessity for any interference with the order of things. At the end of 36 hours the pains became more frequent, and on examination I found the os dilating and labor progressing

Fig. 1. Captain and Mrs. M. V. Bates, parents of 30-inch, 23 3/4-lb. infant. (Photograph courtesy Cleveland Health Museum)

favorably. The head engaged; position, second occipito-anterior. Notwithstanding the long interval between pains the head made good speed through the great depth of pelvis. At 4 P.M., on the 18th, while conducting an examination during pain, the membranes gave way spontaneously and the amniotic fluid came pouring out so profusely as to startle everyone. I had my patient very close to the margin of the bed, as was necessary in order to facilitate manipulation on account of her great size.

The bed was well protected with rubber blankets, which carried the waters over the side of the bed, where they were caught in vessels to the amount of five gallons. That lost by absorption and evacuated with succeeding pains, would make the total of water not less than six gallons. This was, undoubtedly, a case of dropsy of the amnion, co-existent with general dropsy, from which she had suffered to some extent during the last months of pregnancy.

Soon after the rupture of membranes, the foetal head was disengaged, and in the soft parts. The mother was in good condition, the foetus seemed strong and healthy, and everything indicated a speedy and successful termination. But here the trouble began. After the escape of the waters all pain ceased. The great abdominal muscles which had been so much distended lay lax over the foetus like the blanket which covered the person of the mother. Inertia was complete. There was no pain except as the result of manipulation. Ten grains of quinine, Squibb's ergot, and brandy was administered. The forceps were resorted to early, but all to no purpose. The forceps could not be successfully applied because of the unusually large head which lay, with the neck, in a vagina that would measure on its posterior aspect 12 inches at least, and from 7 to 9 in its anterior. The safety of the child was my great fear. The head was seemingly almost born, but the shoulders were fast. How to disengage them was the question. The hand could not be passed to reach the shoulder. I had telegraphed for Dr. J. D. Robinson of Wooster, O., who now came to my assistance. He attempted the use of the forceps with but little success. The child could not be so delivered. After further consultation, as it was our desire to deliver if possible without mutilation, we passed a strong bandage over the neck of the child, and while one made downward and lateral traction, the other, after several attempts, succeeded in bring down one arm, and finally after a laborious siege we succeeded in delivering our patient of a male child. It weighed 23 ¾ lbs.; its height, 30 inches; breast measure, 24 inches; breech, 27 inches; head, 19 inches; foot, 5 ½ inches in length. The secundines, which were soon removed, weighed 10 lbs. The mother was considerably exhausted, but is making a good recovery. Mrs. Bates, six years ago, gave birth to a dead child in London, weighing 18 lbs., and 24 inches in height. She was attended at that time by one of the celebrated obstetricians of that city, who encountered the same difficulty in delivery that I had.

To this report of Dr. Beach's, the editor, Dr. Shrady, adds the following editorial note:

> We believe that this is the largest infant at birth of which there is any authenticated record. Cazeaux refers to one that weighed 19 pounds. There is a foetus in the London Hospital Museum 24 inches long. The average length is 20 inches; average circumference of head 13 ½ inches. The placenta usually weighs ⅙ as much as the foetus. In this case, the secundines in all weighed nearly half as much as the child.

There are perhaps a few comments revolving around this case report that should be noted. The Bates home in Seville, Ohio was torn down only a few years ago, which is a shame because it was perfectly proportioned for the tremendous size of its occupants; all doors, windows, and ceiling heights being geared for a housewife who was a little over 7 ½ feet, instead of being approximately 5 ½ feet tall.

A model of the Bates' baby executed from the given measurements is now in the Cleveland Health Museum, where it towers over the models of the average American neonatal and the smallest recorded premature to survive (Fig. 2). Furthermore, one is tempted to speculate as to whether or not the 24-inch fetus in the London Hospital Museum mentioned by Dr.

Fig. 2. Model of Bates baby (largest), average-sized infant (7 ½ lb.) and smallest record-ed surviving premature infant (1 ½ lb.). (Photograph courtesy Cleveland Health Museum)

Shrady in his editor's note is the first Bates' child, mentioned in Dr. Beach's case report, which was born in London and was "24 inches in height."

Finally, the dates should be noted carefully by all those who submit manuscripts to medical journals. Mrs. Bates went into labor on January 15, 1879[,] and the case report saw the light of day on March 15, 1879. In other words, in a space of 60 days Dr. Beach attended this prolonged delivery, thought about the matter "for a few weeks," prepared his manuscript, had it accepted and presumably read proof on it, and saw it published. There were giants on the earth in those days!

Obstet Gynecol 1957;9:237–40.

COMMENTARY

Reports of individual cases have always been an important part of the Green Journal. Charles Hendricks, who was responsible for case reports when he was Associate Editor (1980–1985), used to say there are two types of case reports, "Gee whiz!" and "Oh, my God." This one is a classic example of the former. It was uncovered—by what means is not stated—by Allan Barnes (see biographical infor-mation, page 61).

The American Obstetric Heritage: An Inspiration in Teaching Obstetrics

Herbert Thoms, MD

NOVEMBER 1956

he teaching of the principles of obstetrics is carried on to a greater extent today than ever before. To the increased numbers of students in medical schools and nursing schools must be added a great number of men and women who are attending childbirth-preparation classes and courses on human reproduction given by colleges, public health groups, church groups, and others. The greatest part of all this teaching is being done by doctors and nurses and they are for the most part doing it voluntarily. It should be recognized that they are also doing a fine service for American Medicine.

The teaching of obstetrics outside medical institutions is no less challenging in its problems and it is equally demanding in the quality of its performance. One outstanding characteristic of these lay groups is their eagerness to learn, an enthusiasm which reflects a wide public interest in all phases of human reproduction.

This envisages quite a legion of persons teaching obstetrics in many situations, ranging from classrooms to doctors' offices, from dispensaries to church parlors. I believe that those who teach obstetrics like to do so and that they are interested in improving their methods.

Teachers of obstetrics to American medical students, to nurses, or to lay groups can find effective and inspirational values in the historical background of American obstetrics. The narrative is an exciting one. It is made more so because it is an illustrious part of our American medical tradition and also because the chief characters in the story belong to us. They are *our* men.

The widespread public interest in medical history and biography is another reason why a teacher in any medical field should keep his view at a wide angle. The teacher in obstetrics by knowing something of the background of his subject could avoid discomposure if he is asked, for instance, "How did it come about that a New England poet made the most important contribution to modern obstetrics" Or "Who was Anne Hutchinson?"

We should be reminded that the American public today has an astonishing craving for medical information; "Medic" still is a close runner-up to "I Love Lucy."

HISTORY

The story of American obstetrics begins of course with the midwives who were brought to our shores by the colonists. They were held in high esteem. In the early New Haven colony, Widow Bradley was voted to have a house and lot, rent free. In Manhattan, the midwife Joris, was voted a salary of 100 guilders a year. In the South, midwives were often paid in tobacco, as were the ministers. The most celebrated New England midwife was Anne Hutchinson, who was also something of a revivalist. There is a good deal written about her in both capacities. She was finally banished from the Massachusetts colony and after a continuing stormy career was murdered in an Indian raid on her home in Pelham, New York. Her name is memorialized today in the beautiful Hutchinson River Parkway, which runs through Pelham. There is considerable literature on the subject of our colonial midwives. Good accounts are found in W. B. Blanton's *Medicine in Virginia in the Seventeenth Century*, Richmond, 1930; Henry Viets' *History of Medicine in Massachusetts*, Boston, 1930; J. J. Walsh's *History of Medicine in New York*, New York, 1919. Anne Hutchinson's story is well told in *Unafraid*, by R. K. Rugg, New York, 1930. Excellent contemporary sidelights are to be found in Samuel Sewall's diary, *Transactions of the Massachusetts Historical Society*, vol. V.

The practice of obstetrics in the English colonies was naturally a reflection of the system in use in the mother country. It was only after the invention of the forceps became known that in England the practice of midwifery began to be taken up by male practitioners. One circumstance in the colonies that favored the supplanting of midwives by male practitioners was that there were no institutions available for the systematic training of midwives.

William Shippen

The first public teacher of obstetrics in this country was William Shippen of Philadelphia. His first course was given in 1762 and about the same time John V. B. Tennant [sic] was giving instruction in New York. Shippen went further than teaching and provided "convenient lodgings" for a few poor women. The "lodgings" were practically a lying-in hospital. He is acknowledged as the great pioneer in obstetrics in America.

Shippen had an extraordinary medical education for that day. As a young man he lived in London for a time in the family of John Hunter, who was then assisting his brother William in teaching. The story of his friendship with John Fothergill, the famous London physician, resulted in the famous Fothergill anatomic drawings becoming the pride and property of the Pennsylvania Hospital. Shippen was friendly with other notables in the British capital among whom were William Hewson, Sir John Pringle, Lawrence Sterne, and David Garrick. On occasions, too, he met Fanny Burney, Dr. Samuel Johnson, and James Boswell. This experience in London undoubtedly found reflection later in his ability as a teacher. John Adams who attended one of Shippen's lectures wrote, "He entertained us with a clear, concise, comprehensive lecture upon all parts of the human frame. The entertainment charmed me." And it is not likely that our second president was easily charmed. Shippen had a remarkable career as physician-in-chief to the army of the revolution. He was a great physician, teacher, and patriot. Accounts of William Shippen are to be found in J. T. Flexner's *Doctors on Horseback*, New York, 1937; N. G. Goodman's *Benjamin Rush*, Philadelphia, 1934; and J. M. Toner's *Medical Men of the Revolution*, Philadelphia, 1876.

Samuel Bard

At the start of the nineteenth century scientific obstetrics in America was beginning to come into its own. Obstetric teaching in medical schools was beginning to be put on an equal basis with other branches of medicine. An important contribution was the publication in 1804 of the first work on obstetrics by an American, Samuel Bard of New York. Bard was the son of a famous father, Dr. John Bard, intimate of Franklin and physician to Washington. Samuel Bard, however, became famous in his own right, not only as a physician but as a breeder of sheep and horticulturist. Like Shippen he was sent abroad to complete his medical studies but was interrupted at the start by 5-month imprisonment in France as a prisoner of war. His father's friend Franklin got him released. Bard's little book is worth reading from cover to cover. It served as the subject of Philip F. Williams' presidential address to the American Gynecological Society in 1955 (*Am. J. Obst. & Gynec.*, November, 1955). His accounts of labor, rickets and child-bearing, and preeclampsia and eclampsia show many modern aspects to the thinking of that day. For further information on Bard, I recommend S. D. Gross' *Lives of Eminent American Physicians and Surgeons*, Philadelphia, 1861, and J. McVicker's *Life of Samuel Bard*, New York, 1822.

John Stearns

An important first in American obstetrics was the introduction of ergot into scientific obstetrics by John Stearns, of New York, who had been a pupil of Shippen. The discovery of the oxytocic properties of ergot has been likened in importance to that of vaccination in its benefits to mankind.

Stearns' essay, Observations on the Secale Cornutum, or ergot (*Med. Rec.* 5, 1822) is a masterpiece. Highlights in Stearns' career included a seat in the New York State Senate and his election as the first president of the New York Academy of Medicine.

William P. Dewees

The first *System of Obstetrics* was that of William Potts Dewees of Philadelphia. In looking over the third edition published in Philadelphia in 1828, with plates, one is reminded that even old roads may be sometimes profitably trodden. Much of what is generally considered as modern obstetrics today was anticipated by Dewees—diagnosis and treatment of pelvic contraction, conduct of labor, resuscitation of the newborn, version and extraction, forceps on the aftercoming head, treatment of eclampsia, etc. For reference see S. D. Gross, *American Medical Biography*, Philadelphia, 1861.

Hugh L. Hodge

A truly great text book that warrants attention is *Principles and Practice of Obstetrics*, by Hugh Lenox Hodge, of Philadelphia. This is the work of which J. Whitridge Williams said, "It is undoubtedly the most original work which has appeared in America, and with few modifications is as valuable today as when first written." Hodge's medical education included a trip to India as a ship surgeon and serving there in the cholera hospitals. On his return to Philadelphia he occupied various positions which eventually lead to a professorship in obstetrics at the University of Pennsylvania. This he held until 1863 when he resigned because of failure of vision. It was with this handicap that he wrote his great work, relying on an amanuensis and on editorial work from his son. Hodge's knowledge of pelvic architecture was remarkable. His description of the mechanism of labor ranks with any today. He anticipated the third-stage maneuver which we associate with the name of Credé. His directions for forceps application could be used as a model. William Goodell wrote a memoir of Hodge which was published in Philadelphia in 1874. A descendant by his name wrote a *Family History and Reminiscences* in 1902, Philadelphia. Another work of Hodge's which is notable is *Diseases Peculiar to Women*, Philadelphia, 1860.

Charles D. Meigs

A name often linked with that of Hodge is Charles D. Meigs, and two individuals hardly could have been more unlike. Their names are brought together often in reference because they both opposed [Oliver Wendell] Holmes on the transmission of puerperal sepsis and both opposed the introduction of anesthesia in obstetrics. Hodge's opposition to Holmes was far milder than that of Meigs, as Holmes has testified.

Williams once remarked that Meigs was a great man in spite of the fact that he was so often on the wrong side. Meigs also opposed the operation of ovariotomy. What then was his contribution? It was that of a truly great teacher who elevated the standards of instruction and the practice of obstetrics. Meigs too had a famous father, Josiah Meigs, at one time a professor at Yale and later president of the University of Georgia. Meigs's boyhood experiences include spending some time as a guest of the Cherokee Nation.

At the time of the reorganization of the Jefferson Medical College in 1841, Meigs was elected to the post of Professor of Obstetrics and Diseases of Women and Children. Because of his dramatic style in lecturing he became famous as an orator. Among his notable addresses is *The Augustan Age*, published in Philadelphia, 1841.

Meigs was an interesting if controversial figure. His son says that he was never idle. He was something of an amateur artist and also an early exponent of the do-it-yourself school. He had a complete workshop in his house with a carpenter's bench, lathe, and forge, where he worked in wood and metal.

His active and forceful nature was seen in his violent opposition to medical procedures of the day that he did not believe in. He opposed the use of anesthetics on the ground that it interfered with normal physiology and that it was dangerous. At that time chloroform was being used extensively and not always by experienced hands. Meigs opposed the operation of ovariotomy because he objected to any surgery that was avoidable. He based his opinion on Lee's statistics of all known operations of ovariotomy from 1809 to 1846, 118 in all, with 40 fatalities. His greatest mistake was that concerned with puerperal fever about which he said, "I prefer to attribute them (the cases) to an accident, or Providence, of which I can form some conception."

However, I think that Meigs should be remembered more as the inspiring teacher that he was. Meigs's work is best seen in *Women and Their Diseases—A Series of Letters to His Class*, Philadelphia, 1848, and *Obstetrics, the Science and Art*, Philadelphia, 1849.

Oliver Wendell Holmes

In 1844, the British obstetrician Ramsbotham wrote, "The best paper in any language with which I am acquainted, written to prove the highly contagious nature of puerperal peritonitis, is by Dr. Oliver Holmes.... It is a masterly performance and well worth perusal by any skeptics on the subject." This was 16 years before Semmelweiss made his historic contribution. Holmes's essay entitled, "The Contagiousness of Puerperal Fever," appeared first in April, 1843, in the now forgotten *New England Quarterly Journal of Medicine and Surgery*. It was reprinted in 1855 as "Puerperal Fever as a Private Pestilence," and it is this version that is available in reprintings today. At the time of the first publication Holmes was 35 years old. He had practiced in Boston for 7 years. In 1839 and 1840 he held the chair of Professor of Anatomy at Dartmouth College which obliged him to be there 3 months of the year. Holmes became Professor of Anatomy and Physiology at Harvard in 1847. At the time of the reprinting of his essay in 1855 he used these moving words, "I take no offense, and attempt no retort; no man makes a quarrel with me over the counterpane that covers a mother with her newborn infant at her breast. There is no epithet in the vocabulary of slight and sarcasm that reaches my present sensibilities in such a controversy."

Holmes's essay is still the greatest single heritage which American obstetrics can claim. It should be read in its entirety. The facts of Holmes's literary life are well known. His erudition and charming wit still live in cherished tradition. Oliver Wendell Holmes remains "The most successful combination which the world has ever seen of the physician and the man of letters." An excellent *Life of Holmes* is that of J. T. Morse, Jr., Boston, 1896. Also see Osler's essay in the *Johns Hopkins Bulletin*, 1894, vol. V, no. 42.

James White

In the year 1850 a court trial took place in Buffalo, N. Y.[,] which had an important effect on the teaching of obstetrics. This was the trial of the People versus Horatio N. Loomis, a physician, and the defendant in a libel suit. On January 18, 1850, James P. White[,] the Professor of Midwifery in the newly formed University of Buffalo[,] performed a delivery on a woman named Mary Watson before some senior medical students. It was her second child. She was not married. Previous to her delivery she lived for a time with the janitor and his wife at the medical school. After the event White presented her with ten dollars which she averred at the time was no inducement to go there. Testimony at the trial showed that at no time was she unduly exposed and that the whole procedure was very much like that of a similar clinical demonstration today.

The mass of historical material which is available regarding this demonstration is witness to the wide controversy which it started and which finally ended in a complete victory for White, the champion of "Demonstrative Midwifery." Among the protestants of White's action were 17 fellow physicians who inspired the *Louisville Medical Journal* (June, 1850) to say, "The prudish Miss Nancies of Buffalo have unintentionally, conferred a benefit on the medical profession. ... We can easily imagine an innocent childlike simplicity that would put pantelets upon the legs of a piano and that would screen with a veil everything capable of exciting prurient ideas but we do not like to see this excessive flirtation with modesty, introduced into medical teaching."

White was more than a pioneer in clinical teaching. He was a leader in his field. To him belongs the real credit for first bringing to attention the successful treatment of chronic uterine inversion. His name is also associated with a modification of the obstetric forceps. In 1878, White was elected a first vice-president of the American Medical Association. A further account of White and the famous trial will be found in the *American Journal of Obstetrics and Gynecology*, 1934, vol. 28, p. 287.

Walter Channing

Walter Channing was another Bostonian who became involved with Holmes's chief antagonists from the City of Brotherly Love. This conflict related to anesthesia in obstetrics. At the time ether was introduced at the Massachusetts General Hospital, Channing was Professor of Obstetrics and Medical Jurisprudence at Harvard. He soon became interested in the application of ether to childbirth, and it was through his influence more than any other that its use in obstetrics became known in this country. Two names which must ever be associated with the introduction of anesthetic methods in obstetrics are Sir James Y. Simpson of Edinburgh and Walter Channing of Boston. Channing did for America what Simpson did for Europe.

Channing's important written contribution was called *A Treatise on Etherization in Childbirth*, published in Boston in 1848. Although he was able to present adequate proof of the safety of anesthesia in childbirth his clinical data could not satisfy religious objections. The same objections that Simpson found abroad were equally in evidence in America, and the fight lasted for years.

Channing had a great reputation as a professor at Harvard. He was also an author of considerable note. He wrote a book of poems and his *Physician's Vacation* published in 1856 (Boston) is a gem. In the latter is found a splendid portrayal of Simpson, at whose house he stayed while in Edinburgh, and also a fine account of a trip to the Highlands. Walter Channing was one of three illustrious brothers, the others being William Ellery Channing, the saintly Unitarian clergyman, and Edward T. Channing, Professor of Rhetoric at Harvard.

*   *   *

The limits of space have already been reached but the nineteenth century part of the story could go on to include Thomas C. James, a pioneer in the teaching of obstetrics, Theophilus Parvin, a pioneer in hospital instruction; Marmaduke B. Wright, and cephalic version; Henry Miller and the development of obstetric teaching in the New West; and Nathan C. Keep, who gave first obstetric anesthesia in America. There are others in this period whose contributions are no less noteworthy than those mentioned. They but await rediscovery for there is still gold in the hills.

Obstet Gynecol 1956;8:648–53.

COMMENTARY

Herbert K. Thoms (1885–1972) was a Yale man through and through; except for one year at the Sloane Hospital in New York City, and another at Johns Hopkins University in Baltimore, his entire life was spent in or very near New Haven. He is remembered in obstetrics mainly for his seminal work on pelvimetry; his instrument for measuring the bituberous diameter was standard equipment in any obstetric clinic for many years (although, with the declining interest in pelvic architecture and capacity recently, it would probably be hard to find one now). Thoms was anything but one-dimensional, having been recognized for his artistic abilities, especially painting and etching, and his writing. He was acknowledged as a medical historian, as this article outlining prominent obstetric teachers of the 18th and 19th centuries attests. Walter B. Channing, one of those teachers identified by Thoms, was the subject of a recent biography (Kass AM. Medicine and midwifery in Boston. Boston [MA]: Northeastern University Press; 2002).

A Short History of Eclampsia

Leon C. Chesley, PhD

APRIL 1974

here are several histories of eclampsia in the German literature of the past century and a half, but all too often the
authors have not documented their sources and have made
errors that live on in second-, third-, and nth-hand reviews.
Bernhart[1] wrote that eclampsia was mentioned in the
ancient Egyptian, Chinese, Indian, and Greek medical literature. One of the oldest sources that he cited, without reference, was
the Kahun (Petrie) papyrus dating from about 2200 B.C. His source is likely to have been Menascha.[2] Griffith[3] had translated Prescription No. 33,
on the third page of the papyrus, as: "To prevent (the uterus) of a woman
from itching (?) auit pound ... upon her jaws the day of birth. It cures itching of the womb excellent truly millions of times." Menasha cited the
paper by Griffith but rendered the translation (in German) as: "To prevent a woman from biting her tongue auit pound ... upon her jaws the day
of birth. It is a cure of biting excellent truly millions of times." He suggested that the untranslated word "auit" meant "small wooden stick." In
a later book on the Kahun papyrus, Griffith[4] changed his translation to:
"To prevent a woman from biting (her tongue ?) beans, pound ... upon her
jaws the day of birth." Curiously, Menascha did not cite Griffith's second
translation and included the word "auit" from the first version. Possibly
the ancient scribe had eclampsia in mind, but that interpretation is tenu-
ous at best.

Bernhart also wrote, again without specific references, that both the
Indian Atharva-Veda and the Sushruta, of old but unknown dates, mention
eclampsia. He said that the Atharva-Veda described an amulet to be worn
in late pregnancy to ward off convulsions during childbirth. There are several references to pregnancy in the Atharva-Veda (translated by Whitney).[5]
One is a description of a protective amulet to be put on in the eighth
month of gestation (Book VIII, 6), but there is not the remotest indication
of any specific disorder such as convulsions. The ceremonial verses are
clearly directed toward protecting the woman's genital organs against

demons and rapists, who are characterized by such epithets as "after-snuf-fling," "fore-feeling," and "much-licking" (to name the milder ones).

There are two possible references to eclampsia in the Sushruta (English translation edited by Bhishagratna).[6] In Volume II, Chapter 8, page 58: "A child, moving in the womb of a dead mother, who had just expired (from convulsions etc) ..." should be delivered by cesarean section. The parenthetic "from convulsions etc" was supplied by the Editor, and comparison with the Latin translation (Hessler),[7] indicates that it probably was not in the original text. In Chapter 1, page 11 of Volume II: "An attack of Apatànkah due to excessive hemorrhage, or following closely upon an abortion or miscarriage at pregnancy (difficult labor) or which is incidental to an external blow or injury (traumatic) should be regarded as incurable." Again, the parenthetic words are editorial additions, and the "Apatànkah" (convulsions) might well be those associated with severe hemorrhage. By comparison with the Latin translation, the English version seems to have been embellished, for the Latin version specifies only abortion and hemorrhage. An editorial note (pages 58 to 60 of Volume II) asserts that the ancient Indians delivered living eclamptic women by cesarean section, but the editor provided no documentation whatever.

Bernhart's reference to the old Chinese literature was to Wang Dui Me, whose work was translated into German by Lo.[8] The work, originally published in 1832 AD, was thought to be free of any influence of Western medicine, but even if it were, there is no indication that it recorded only ancient observations; it seems to have been contemporary. For instance, the author described what Lo translated as "Eklampsie" and wrote: "I use recipe No. 232 ..."

Several of the German authors cited Hippocrates as commenting on the susceptibility of pregnant women to convulsions and on their prognosis. None of the quotations appears in *The Genuine Works of Hippocrates* as translated by Adams,[9] or in any of the six other translations into three languages that I have seen. Some of the quotations can be found in other Greek sources. Earlier translators, for instance, had attributed the *Coacae Praenotiones* to Hippocrates, but modern scholars agree that it was written before his time. One such quotation, appearing in several German papers[,] is: "In pregnancy, drowsiness with headache accompanied by heaviness and convulsions, is generally bad." It comes from the *Coacae Praenotiones (Cuan Prognosis)*, XXXI, No. 507. The Greeks of that time recognized preeclampsia, for in the *Coan Prognosis*, XXXI, No. 523, we find: "In pregnancy, the onset of drowsy headaches with heaviness is bad; such cases are perhaps liable to some sort of fits at the same time" (translated by Chadwick and Mann).[10] Hippocrates (Fourth Century BC), in his Aphorisms (Section VI, No. 30), wrote: "It proves fatal to a woman in a state of pregnancy, if she be seized with any of the acute diseases." Galen, in the second century AD, agreed and commented that epilepsy, apoplexy, convulsions, and tetanus are especially lethal (Volume 17, part II, page 820, edited by Kühn).[11] It may be significant that Galen specified convulsive disorders, and perhaps he had in mind what we now call eclampsia, which was not to be differentiated from epilepsy for another 1600 years.

Celsus, in the first century AD, mentioned often fatal convulsions in association with the extraction of dead fetuses (Book VII, Chapter 29, translated by Lee).[12] In the same connection, Aetios, in the Sixth Century AD, wrote: "Those who are seriously ill are oppressed by a stuporous condition ...," "Some are subject to convulsions ...," and "The pulse is strong and swollen" (Chapters 22 and 23, translated by Ricci).[13]

There is a possible reference to eclampsia in Rösslin's *Der Swangern Frawen und Hebammen Rosengarten*, a book that was the standard text of midwifery in Europe and England for almost two centuries. In discussing the maternal prognosis in difficult labor with fetal death, Rösslin listed among the ominous signs, unconsciousness and convulsions (Book I, Chapter 9, page 67).[14] The book was largely based on the older classics and the relevant section is reminiscent of Celsus, Aetios, and, especially, Paul of Aegina. The book was translated into English from a Latin version of what probably was the second edition and appeared in 1540 as *The Byrth of Mankinde*. Raynalde revised and amplified the second edition in 1545 and the text was little altered thereafter, except for the variable and carefree spelling of the time.

Gaebelkhouern[15] (variously, Gabelchoverus, Gabelkover), in 1596, distinguished four sorts of epilepsy in relation to the seats of their causes, which he placed in the head, the stomach, chilled extremities, and the uterus. He further specified that only the pregnant uterus causes convulsions, particularly if it carries a malformed fetus. He wrote that the mothers feel a biting and gnawing in the uterus and diaphragm that leads them to think that something is gnawing on their hearts (epigastric pain? The description of that symptom is usually credited to Chaussier, 228 years later).

Although eclampsia is dramatic, it is not astonishing that there are so few references to it in the older writings, for they covered the whole field of medicine. Moreover, obstetrics was largely in the hands of midwives, and eclampsia had not been differentiated from epilepsy. Even some relatively modern textbooks of obstetrics have barely noticed eclampsia and those of Burton[16] and Exton,[17] published in 1751, made no mention whatever of convulsions. In the first edition of Mauriceau's book,[18] in 1668, the only comment on convulsions relates to those associated with severe hemorrhage.

In later editions of his book, Mauriceau devoted more and more attention to what we now call eclampsia. Hugh Chamberlen published purported translations of Mauriceau's later editions, but they seem to have been impostures and really were reissues of the translation of the first edition. Such fraud befits a family that kept so important an invention as the forceps secret through three generations for personal profit, and befits the man who sold the secret.

In the edition of 1694, and possibly earlier, Mauriceau[19] set forth several aphorisms dealing with eclampsia. Among them were: No. 228, The mortal danger to mother and fetus is greater when the mother does not recover consciousness between convulsions; No. 229, Primigravidas are at far greater risk of convulsions than are multiparas; No. 230, Convulsions during pregnancy are more dangerous than those beginning after delivery; No. 231, Convulsions are more dangerous if the fetus is dead. Mauriceau observed that the convulsions often cease with delivery and he recommended prompt termination of pregnancy as the best treatment. Although Denman[20] attributed the origin of forced delivery to Mauriceau, he (Mauriceau) wrote that if the cervix were closed he resorted to phlebotomy, gentle clysters, and emolient fomentations applied to the cervix. He attributed the convulsions to an excess of heated blood rising from the uterus and stimulating the nervous system, and he thought that irritation of the cervix would aggravate the situation. He also believed that if the fetus were dead, malignant vapors arising from its decomposition might cause convulsions. His assigning convulsions to such specific causes carries the implication that he had distinguished eclampsia from epilepsy.

REFERENCES

1. Bernhart F: Geschichte, Wesen und Behandlung der Eklampsie. Wien Kim Wochenschr 52:1009–1013, 1036–1043, 1939
2. Menaseha I: Die Geburtshilfe bei den alten Ägyptern. Arch Gynaekol 131: 425–461, 1927
3. Griffith FL: A medical papyrus from Egypt. Br Med J 1:1172–1174, 1893
4. Griffith FL: The Petrie Papyrus; Heratic Papyri from Kahun and Gurob. Vol 1. London, Quaritch, 1898, p 11
5. Whitney WD (translator): Atharva–Veda Samhitá. The Harvard Oriental Series. Vols 7, 8. Cambridge, Harvard University, 1905
6. Bishagratna KKL (editor): An English Translation of the Sushruta Samhita. Vol II. Calcutta, Bishagratna, 1911
7. Hessler F (translator): Suśruta. Ayurvedas. Id Est Medicinae Systema a Venerabili d'Hanvantare Demonstratum a Suśruta Discipulo Compositum. Erlangac, Enke, 1864
8. Lo JH (translator): Wang Dui Me: Schou Schen Hsiau Bu. Abhandl Med Faculty Sun Yat Sen Univ 2:19–126, 1930
9. Adams F (translator): The Genuine Works of Hippocrates. London, Sydenham Society, 1849
10. Chadwick J, Mann WN (translators): The Medical Works of Hippocrates. Oxford, Blackwell, 1950

11. Kühn DCG (editor): Galen's Opera Omnia. Vol 17, part II. Leipzig, Cnoblockii, 1829

12. Lee A (translator): Celsus On Medicine. London, Cox, 1831

13. Ricci JV (translator): Aetios of Amida: The Gynecology and Obstetrics of the VIth Century A.D. Philadelphia, Blakiston, 1950

14. Rösslin E: Der Swangern Frawen und Hebammé Rossgarté. (Facsimile) Munich, Kuhn, 1910

15. Gaebelkhouern O: Artzneybuch, darninnen vast für alle des menschlichen Leibs, Anlingen und Gebrechen etc. Tübingen, Gruppenbach, 1596

16. Burton J: An Essay towards a Complete New System of Midwifery, Theoretical and Practical. London, Hodges, 1751

17. Exton B: A New and General System of Midwifery. London, Owen, 1751

18. Mauriceau F: Des Maladies des Femmes Grosses et Achouchées. Paris, Cercle du Livre Précieux, 1668

19. Mauriceau F: Traite des Maladies des Femmes Grosses, et Celles Qui Sont Achouchées. Paris, d'Houry, 1694

20. Denman T: An Introduction to the Practice of Midwifery. New York, Bliss and White, 1821

Obstet Gynecol 1974;43:599–602.

COMMENTARY

Leon Chesley (1908–2000) was universally acknowledged as the world's foremost authority on all aspects of preeclampsia and eclampsia. Although not a clinician— he held a PhD in zoology—he spent virtually his entire professional career working with clinicians and helping them become clinical scientists. He was personally responsible for many of the pathophysiologic studies and epidemiologic observations that underlie the modern conceptual framework of pregnancy hypertension, but his focus was not limited strictly to biology, and he was well qualified to write this history of eclampsia. His genius was wide-ranging and, with his characteristic scholarship, one can be certain that every one of the 30 references cited in this work is quoted fully and accurately, regardless of the language in which it was written.

Vesicovaginal Fistula: An Historical Survey

Henry C. Falk, MD,
and M. Leon Tancer, MD

MARCH 1954

Vesicovaginal fistula is a palpable and particularly obtrusive lesion. The patient, her physician and her social intimates become aware of its presence almost immediately. One would believe that such a disease should be among the first to be described in recorded medical history, and yet it is not. This may be due to one of several factors.

First, there is the possibility that vesicovaginal fistulas did not occur until a relatively late period in the history of medicine. Proponents of this theory believe that dystocia is the primary cause of postpartum fistula and a concomitant of advancing civilization. They postulate that the abnormal pelvis is a result of hybrid marriage, and that a "racially pure" pelvis results in a relatively normal labor. The rachitic pelvis is a relatively new lesion, the first authoritative report on rickets having been made by Glisson in 1650.

However, it is more likely that vesicovaginal fistulas have occurred since the beginning of recorded time. In support of this thesis are the findings in an Egyptian mummy dating back to the year 2000 B.C. Professor Derry of the Faculty of Medicine of Fouad I University of Egypt[19, 20, 35] discovered a large vesicovaginal fistula in the mummy of Henhenit, a lady in the court of Mentuhotep of the Eleventh Dynasty, who reigned about 2050 B.C. Derry described the pelvis as dolichopellic and considerably contracted in the transverse diameter. Mahfouz[19, 20] examined the same mummy, and, in addition to the fistula described by Derry, he described a complete tear of the perineum.

A second factor which may explain the delayed recognition of vesicovaginal fistula as a clinical entity was the position of the woman relative to society in the early medical eras. As a result of the secondary status of women, the practice of obstetrics was left to the care of midwives who contributed little to our scientific knowledge.

A third factor might be the prolonged influence of Arab medicine from 600 to 1600 A.D. The Arabs regarded postmortem examinations as sinful, and the practice of obstetrics and gynecology by men was forbidden by their religion. As late as the seventeenth century, Roderic deCastro in his book on gynecologic pathology, quoted by Freund, concluded that the art of obstetrics was beneath the dignity of man.

It was not until the art of obstetrics was placed in the hands of skilled physicians, who were trained as observers and reporters, that we begin to find mention of this problem. This situation eventually led to the surgical cure of the disease. Thus we must conclude that vesicovaginal fistulas undoubtedly existed early in medical history, and the lack of knowledge of their existence was based on early social and religious mores.

In an attempt to trace the history of vesicovaginal fistula, the earliest periods of recorded medicine were reviewed. Imhotep, an Egyptian, about 2700 B.C., was the earliest known physician. The earliest gynecologic references may be found in the Kahun papyrus,[23] which was translated by F. L. Griffith in 1893, and refers back to the year 2000 B.C. These records contain no reference to vesicovaginal fistula. The Eber's Papyrus[23] about 1500 B.C. and other known writings of the ancient Egyptians make no mention of this lesion. Occasionally there are sentences which are suggestive of the existence of urinary incontinence.

The Talmud, in both its scriptural and interpretive portions, fails to give any evidence that the ancient Hebrew physician was aware of this lesion, although vaginal discharges are mentioned.

Actually the first record of the lesion is to be found in the writings of ancient Hindu medicine. The Vedas and Upavedas were written in 800–600 B.C., and, in discussing lithotomy for bladder calculi in women, it is noted by McKay that "care must be taken not to thrust the knife too far forward, as it will wound the uterus and the urine will pass through the vagina, forming a fistula." It is most interesting to note that the Hindu physician was not inhibited by social or religious custom from the examination and treatment of the female genitalia.

Unfortunately there was no continuity between Hindu medicine and our own so that, by the time the Greek schools of Cnidos and Cos became world leaders in medicine, the meager advance of the Hindus was lost.

Hippocrates, whose real and spurious writings certainly covered all phases of disease, is nowhere credited with mentioning vesicovaginal fistula. Polybos, about 360 B.C., was Hippocrates' son-in-law, and two of Hippocrates' spurious volumes were attributed by Galen to him. These were the first known texts on diseases of women and on infertility. Neither volume contains any reference to vesicovaginal fistula.

There must have been many gynecologists of note in classical times, but unfortunately their writings have not come down to us. Only Soranus of Ephesus,[26] who lived in the second century A.D., wrote a textbook on midwifery and gynecology. Although universally accepted as the ablest member of that specialty in classical times, he makes no mention of vesico-vaginal fistula.

The Byzantine period[23] was noted for its excellent compilations of early Greek and Roman knowledge, but added very little to the original knowledge of the day. Oribasius, about 400 A.D., compiled his *Collectio Medicinalis*, in which the gynecologic section was no more than an abstract of the work of Soranus. Aetius of Amida was the first eminent Christian physician, and his compilations of the Greek and Roman eras stood for 1000 years. Paul of Aegina was the link that brought the classics through the era of compilation into the period of Arab leadership. In none of the works of the famed Byzantine compilers can reference to a vesicovaginal fistula be found.

The Moslem era of medicine extended from the seventh century to the twelfth century. While Arab medical writings in general were volumi-nous, those pertaining to gynecology were either nonexistent or based on Greek and Roman writings handed down through the Byzantines. As said before, social and religious customs impeded any further advance in the knowledge of the female genitalia during this period.

Interestingly, it was a Perso-Arab physician, Avicenna (980–1037), who was the first known writer to mention the occurrence of a vesicovaginal fis-tula. He realized, too, the relationship between such a lesion and labor. Mahfouz[20] quotes from Avicenna's chapter on "Prevention of Pregnancy" as follows, "… the bulk of the fetus may cause a tear in the bladder which results in incontinence of urine." Avicenna's book *Al Kanoun* was famous as the leading gynecologic text through the seventeenth century, and may be found in a place of prominence in Middle Eastern libraries today.

The descent of the Dark Ages had its effect on medicine, as it did on all other phases of art and science, so that we find the problem of vesico-vaginal fistula, almost unknown prior to the Renaissance, awaiting the rebirth of art and science to achieve recognition. In 1597 Israel Spach pub-lished his *Gynecia*. This volume begins with a monograph by Felix Plater, in which 2 cases of vesicovaginal fistulae are described. Both occurred fol-lowing difficult labor, and one in particular is worth quoting. "Following a difficult delivery, her first, the orifice of the bladder of a young country girl was lacerated so that a long and deep opening into the bladder was created. I recognized the lesion and placed a probe into it in order to delineate its extent. From this lesion, the involuntary flow of urine continued and the surrounding parts became eroded and inflamed and bound down in adhe-sions from which issued forth a thick creamy pus."

The *Gynecia* ends with a monograph by Mercato. This eminent Spanish physician is the first to apply the term fistula to the lesion which was previously referred to as a rupture. He devotes an entire chapter to "Fistulae of the Uterus" (sic), from which the following is taken: "What an empty and tragic life is led by the affected victims and how great are their embarrassments; for the bladder and the intestines move at the same time, and the uncontrolled urine and feces run from the fistulae with ease; and even those who because of their natural resistance tend to improve somewhat, may in future deliveries have a recrudescence or even a total breakdown, for the only alleviation results when a fistula tends to become adherent to surrounding tissues, but even here the drawn-out period of recovery is so fraught with thousands of bodily miseries and weaknesses, as to render life very grim." Mercato later proposes a definite operation for the relief of these symptoms, but case reports and results are lacking.

Other men writing in this same era mention further cases of this affliction. Among them are Severinus Pinaeus and Fabricius Hildanus. Thus we see that the late sixteenth and early seventeenth centuries brought with them a genuine awareness of the lesion, and it is extremely difficult to know where credit should fall for the earliest description.

In 1663, Hendrik Von Roonhuysen published his *Medico-Chirurgical Observations about the Infirmities of Women.* Commonly thought of as the first textbook on operative gynecology, this excellent volume was translated into English in 1676. The fourth section of the text is entitled, "Rupture of the Bladder; the Signs, Causes, Prognostics and Cure Thereof." In this chapter, Von Roonhuysen gives a clear description of a vesicovaginal fistula and proposes a scientific method of therapy for this lesion. His innovations include proper exposure by the use of a speculum, marginal denudation exclusive of bladder wall, and approximation of the denuded edges with "stitching needles made of stiff swan's quills." Unfortunately he gives no figures or postoperative results. Johann Fatio, whose work was published posthumously in 1752, refers to 2 cases performed in 1675 by Von Roonhuysen's technic which resulted in a cure. These are the first reported cures by modern surgical technic.

Völter, in 1687, suggested that the sutures be interrupted, and he introduced the use of a retention catheter. During this same period, Pietro DeMarchettis strenuously urged the use of the actual and the potential cautery for these fistulas and obtained a complete cure. In later years Monteggia, Dupuytren,[24] and others again recommended the cautery.

Thus we see a spurt of writing from the late sixteenth through the seventeenth century that consolidated knowledge concerning the existence of vesicovaginal fistulas and early attempts at surgical cures, most of which were unsuccessful. The eighteenth century may be considered an incubation period. Very little was written about vesicovaginal fistula, and the disease seems to have been forgotten. Freund, who wrote a history of the lesion in 1860, states that despite the knowledge of the earlier era "there is a surprisingly complete absence of any description ... in the larger pathologico-anatomical works of Morgagni and Lieutard."

A new era in the surgical cure of vesicovaginal fistula occurred in the nineteenth century. In 1834, Jobert de Lamballe, using a procedure which, according to Freund, was first proposed by Velpeau, obtained several cures. He was the first to realize the need to avoid tension in his repair. His work attracted the attention of the entire continent, and rapid progress was soon to follow. Jobert de Lamballe noted that recently acquired fistulas might be cured by indwelling catheters alone. However, when induration of the edges of the fistula already existed, a cure without surgery was impossible. This point of view is still recognized as correct. Jobert de Lamballe also made attempts to cure fistulas by using pedicle flaps from labia, buttocks, and thigh.

Simon of Darmstadt had worked with Jobert de Lamballe and adopted his methods. He suggested transverse colpocleisis in those cases which defied previous attempts at closure. This procedure was almost universally condemned as it caused transvesical menstruation, stone formation, diverticula of the bladder, and terminated normal sexual life for the patient. However, partial transverse colpocleisis was later adopted with great success by Latzko to cure those fistulas which followed total hysterectomy.

In 1834, Gosset used silver-gilt sutures, the knee-elbow position, and an indwelling catheter. Chelius, who was primarily noted for treatment of fistulas by cautery, according to Agnew, suggested a modification of the knee-chest position. Von Metzler, in 1846, described a speculum similar to that subsequently used by Sims. Unfortunately he made no drawing, so his innovation probably escaped notice. His description is an interesting one, "A silver vaginal dilator consisting of a guttered conical blade 5 ½ inches long, whose lower third is turned outward; and an 8-inch-long steel staff, fastened at a right angle to the lower third, and provided for 5 inches of its length with a large wooden handle."

In 1852, Marion Sims published his monumental work, and while none of Sims' "innovations" were actually new, he deserves immense credit because it was he who removed the cure of vesicovaginal fistula by surgery from the category of probability to that of an established procedure. His personality helped give the treatment of diseases of women a major place in American medicine.

Subsequent to Sims, the only real advance in the treatment of fistulas was the separation of bladder from vaginal mucosa and suturing each as an individual layer. Credit for this usually goes to Mackenrodt. However, in 1857, Collis[3] described the flap-splitting method. It is remarkable that Collis goes unmentioned in English and American texts except that of Lawson Tait in 1889. Mackenrodt in 1894 then developed Collis' idea.

In 1881–1890, Trendelenburg made a radical departure by opening the bladder suprapubically, freeing the bladder wall, and closing the defect. In 1906, Forgue, according to Farsht, was the first to open the peritoneal cavity, detach the bladder from the uterus, and close the fistula in what is now known as the Legueu procedure.

Thus, by the early twentieth century, all approaches and methods of repair are at our disposal, and this disease which may cause so much discomfort has been almost completely conquered.

REFERENCES

1. Agnew, D. H. *Laceration of the Female Perineum and Vesico-Vaginal Fistula.* Philadelphia, Lindsay & Blakiston, 1873.

2. Beatty, T. E. Plastic operations on the female genito-urinary organs. *Dublin Quart. J. 31:*273, 1861.

3. Collis, M. H. Cases of vesico-vaginal fistula. *Dublin Quart. J. 23:*119, 1857.

4. Collis, M. H. Further remarks upon a new and successful mode of treatment for vesicovaginal fistula. *Dublin Quart. J. 31:*302, 1861.

5. Culpeper, N. *A Treatise of the Rickets.* London, England, Streater, 1668.

6. DeMarchettis, P. *Observationum Medico-Chiruricarum Rariorum.* Patavi, 1675.

7. Falk, H. C., and Bunkin, I. A. The management of vesicovaginal fistula following abdominal total hysterectomy. *Surg., Gynec. & Obst. 93:*404, 1951.

8. Farsht, I. J. Suprapubic transvesical repair of vesicovaginal fistulas. *J. Urol. 44:*279, 1940.

9. Fatio, J. *Helvetisch-vernünstige Wehenmutter.* (op. posthum.) Basel, 1752.

10. Freund, A. G. *Defistula Uretero-uterina Conspecto Historico Fistularum Urinarium Mulierum Praemisso.* Czechoslovakia, The Viadrine University Vratislaviae, 1860.

11. Glisson *A Full Review of Diseases Incident to Children.* London, England, Millar, 1742.

12. Gosset, M. Advantages of the gilt-wire suture. *Lancet 1:*345, 1834.

13. Herrgott *Etudes Historiques sur Poperation de la Fistule Vesico-vaginale.* Paris, France, Bailliere, 1864.

14. Hildanus, F. *Opera Observation um et Curationum.* Frankfurt, Germany, J. Beyeri, 1646.

15. Jobert de Lamballe *Traité des Fistulés Vèsico-utérines.* Paris, France, Bailliere, 1852.

16. Latzko, W. Behandlung hochsitzender Blasen und Mastdarmscheiden fisteln nach Uterus Exstirpation mit hohem Scheidenverschluss. *Zentralbl. Gynäk. 38:*906, 1914.

17. McKay, S. *History of Gynecology.* London, England; Bailliere, 1901.

18. Mackenrodt, A. Die operative Heilung grosser Blasenscheiden-fisteln. *Zentralbl. Gynäk. 18:*180, 1894.

19. Mahfouz Urinary and recto-vaginal fistulae in women. *J. Obst. & Gynaec. Brit. Emp. 36:*581, 1929.

20. Mahfouz *Atlas of Mahfouz's Obstetrics and Gynecologic Museum.* Altringham, England, Sherratt, 1949.

21. Monteggia *Maladies Chirurgie 5:*339 (see Freund).[10]

22. Pinaeus, S. *Opusculum physiologum Anatomicum.* Francofurti, 1599.
23. Ricci, J. V. *Genealogy of Gynecology* (Ed. 2). Philadelphia, Blakiston, 1950.
24. Sanson and Bégin *Memoire sur une Manière Nouvelle de Pratiquer l'opera-tion de la Pierre.* Paris, France, Bailliere, 1836.
25. Schuppert, M. *A Treatise on Vesico-vaginal Fistula.* New Orleans, Louisiana, Daily Commercial Bulletin Print., 1866.
26. Sigerist, H. E. *The Great Doctors.* New York, Norton, 1933.
27. Simon, G. *Ueber die Operation der Blasen-Scheidenfisteln.* Rostok, Schmidt, 1862.
28. Sims, J. M. On the treatment of vesico-vaginal fistula. *Am. J. M. Sc. 23* n.s.:59, 1852.
29. Spach, I. *Gynaecorium.* Argentinei, 1597.
30. Tait, R. L. *Diseases of Women and Abdominal Surgery.* Philadelphia, Lea, 1889.
31. Trendelenburg, F. *Über blasenscheiden-fisteloperationen.* Leipzig, Germany, Samml. Klin. Vorträge, 1890, p. 3373.
32. Völter, C. *Neu Erröffnete Hebammen-Schule.* Stuttgart, 1687, see Freund.[10]
33. Von Metzler *Präger Viertel Jahresschrift.* 1846, see Schuppert.[25]
34. Von Roonhuysen, H. *Medico-Chirurgical Observations.* London, England, Moses Pitt at the Angel, 1676.
35. Williams, H. U. Human paleopathology. *Arch. Path.* 7:839, 1929.
36. Winkel, F. *Cyclopedia of Obstetrics and Gynecology.* New York, Wood, 1887.

Obstet Gynecol 1954;3:337–41.

COMMENTARY

Vesicovaginal fistula was important historically, for it was the ability to correct the condition surgically that led to the formation of gynecology as a specialty. The name most associated with the conquest of this terrible complication, of course, is J. Marion Sims. This excellent survey of the history of vesicovaginal fistula, written by two master gynecologic surgeons, indicates that Sims's role was only the last chapter in a story stretching back 3,000–4,000 years.

Dilatation and Curettage:
A Development Covering 3000 Years

George J. D'Angelo, MD

SEPTEMBER 1953

oo frequently we students of medicine carry out diagnostic procedures as mere technicians. We are satisfied with knowledge of an instrument when we become adept in its manipulation. But the purpose and nature of an instrument is the crystallization of a long period of development throughout the history of medicine, and we can only understand the one if we appreciate the other.

The specialty now known as gynecology probably began with the development of the vaginal speculum. This first instrument of our profession is of ancient origin. According to the Talmud, where we find the earliest mention of the speculum, Hebrew women attempted to diagnose vaginal bleeding by means of a lead pipe containing a movable rod.[5] The edges of this pipe were bent in, so that the walls of the vagina would not be injured. At the tip of the rod a small sponge was fixed, with which the women could ascertain where the bleeding originated. If the sponge was stained with blood, bleeding came from the uterus; if the pipe was stained, the bleeding came from the vaginal walls.

Hippocrates mentions the use of an anal dilator as a vaginal speculum. Aretaeus, Galen, and Celsus, who lived in Rome and Greece in the first and second century B.C., spoke of vaginal speculums, and Soranus (98–177 A.D.) devoted a chapter of his book on gynecology to the use of the instrument. By the time of Aetius of Alexandria the speculum—called a dioptra by the Alexandrian school—was well known, and in that writer's works we are offered "the fullest and most reliable evidence concerning"[12] the speculum, dilatation of the cervix, and the use of a sound. The Alexandrian school made no pretense of being the first to use such an instrument, for Paul of Aegina, who succeeded Aetius, "alludes distinctly to the speculum as an instrument in general use before his time."[12]

Documentary evidence, then, would indicate that the vaginal speculum has been in existence about 3000 years. The earliest examples of the instrument so far discovered, however, date from 79 A.D. and were found at Pompeii. Those who are interested to see what these early instruments (of bronze) look like may consult the books by C. J. S. Thompson or J. V. Ricci, or the *Hebammenbuch* of Feyerabendt, which was published in 1580 and is one of the earliest books to illustrate the vaginal speculum. The practice of gynecology continued to flourish at Alexandria until 640 A.D., when the city was sacked by the Saracens. Since Moslem law forbade women to be examined by men, there appeared few writings on the subject of gynecology, in general or the vaginal speculum in particular, with the rare exceptions of casual remarks in the texts of such men as Avicenna (980–1037) and Albucasis in 1085. The latter was one of the last of the great Arab medical school, and, coincident with the coming of the First Crusade, the learning of the Moslem world sank to the level of the rest of the civilization of the Middle Ages.

Although in the sixteenth century Paré illustrated a vaginal speculum in his writings, the instrument remained more or less unused from the subjugation of Alexandria in 640 until 1761, when it was reinvented by Astruc of Paris, only to be forgotten shortly thereafter. It did not remain in oblivion very long after this, however, as J. C. A. Récamier (1774–1852), considered by many to be the founder of gynecology, once again discovered the vaginal speculum in 1801. But "it was not until 1818 that he introduced it into the profession, and gave it its place as a valuable addition to science...."[12] His speculum consisted of a slender tin tube; this underwent many modifications until, in 1825, both he and Mme. Boivin independently introduced a bivalve speculum. Many give credit to Récamier as the discoverer of the speculum, but "the credit which belongs to Récamier is not that of a discoverer, but that which is equally great, of having recognized the value of what was well known, but badly appreciated before his time."[12]

In the hands of Récamier the speculum became a powerful adjunct to investigation of the diseases of women.[9] In comparing the speculum of the ancients with that of Récamier, Triaire stated that the ancient speculum was used only as a dilator to separate the vaginal walls, and did not permit light to penetrate. Triaire makes a valid point. Although the speculum was used in the past to separate the walls of the vagina, there is no description recorded of what was observed and one must surmise that the vaginal walls were probably separated just enough to introduce other instruments, without the physician being able to see what he was doing.

J. Marion Sims introduced a new type of speculum. Its main purpose was to act as an aid during the repair of a vesicovaginal fistula by exposing the anterior vaginal wall through pressure on the perineum.

With the rebirth of the speculum other diagnostic adjuncts in the field of gynecology began to be introduced. Sounds for dilatation of the cervix were known to Hippocrates. Its history follows that of the speculum in that with the fall of Alexandria the practice of gynecology remained virtually nonexistent until well after the Dark Ages. Reference to a uterine probe was made by William Harvey, but it was after his death that, in 1657, the uterine dilator was described by Wierus.

The advantages and usefulness of the uterine dilator were not quickly appreciated, and although in 1828 Samuel Lair proposed the use of a uterine sound—a simple straight tube—he was not heeded. Lair, incidentally, also was the "first to pull the cervix down into the field of vision with the use of a cervical (hooked) instrument."[8] Four years later John Mackintosh of Edinburgh began dilating the cervix, using rectal Bougies, in the treatment of dysmenorrhea.

In spite of the opposition of many leading gynecologists—among them von Scanzoni—the uterine sound became popular. A typical early comment is that of Sir James Young Simpson (1811–1870) of Edinburgh, who stated in 1843, in the course of a series of articles, that, "It is possible by the use of the uterine sound or Bougie introduced into the uterine cavity, to ascertain the exact position and direction of the body and fundus of the organ—to bring these higher parts of the uterus, in most instances, within the reach of tactile examination, and to ascertain various important circumstances regarding the os, cavity, lining membranes...."

Here in the United States the cervical dilator was popularized by J. Marion Sims, T. Gaillard Thomas, and Thomas Addis Emmet. John Ball, a physician from Brooklyn, read a paper entitled "Forcible and Rapid Dilatation of the Cervix Uteri for the Cure of Dysmenorrhea" before the Medical Society of Kings County, New York, in 1873, in which he said, "I commence by introducing a three-bladed, self-retaining speculum, which brings in view the os uteri, which I seize with a double-hooked tenaculum and draw down toward the vulva, when I first introduce a metal bougie as large as the canal will admit, followed in rapid succession by others of larger sizes ... then I introduce the dilator and stretch the cervix in every direction." From this description it can be seen that there were two types of cervical dilators in use during this time—the graduated sound and the bivalved dilator (the latter has fallen into disuse). Many modifications of the sound were devised, including a modification by Sims, who added a curve that followed the normal curve of the uterus.

In spite of these additions to the gynecologist's armamentarium, knowledge of intrauterine pathology had not advanced very much since the school of Alexandria. This lack of knowledge, however, did not prevent physicians from treating diseases of the female genital tract. Diseases of the cervix and uterus were treated in the nineteenth century by cautery, caustics, and, later, by surgery, although by the time that treatment was instituted the disease was usually in its late stages. Among the suggested procedures was the application of leeches to the diseased cervix—an innovation proposed by Girolamo Nigrisoli in 1665 and again in 1826 by J. N. Guilbert.

As Greenblatt has noted, "curettage of a crude form was introduced in Roman times, but whether it was used in uterine bleeding is conjectural." The first successful application of this principle was yet another contribution of Récamier. In 1843 he introduced a small scoop or spoon attached to a long blade, which he called a *curette.* In contrast to his rediscovery of the speculum, this instrument was a completely original development. The word *curette* is found for the first time in the French literature of the eighteenth century, introduced by Rene J. Croissant de Garengeot (1688–1759) in his *Nouveau Traite des Instruments de Chirurgie* (1723). It refers, however, to a surgical instrument to scrape wounds, and has no gynecological connotation.

Although there were many eminent supporters of the new procedure—among them Lisfranc of France, Sir James Simpson of Britain, and J. Marion Sims of the United States—Récamier's *curettage* was not generally accepted, despite his continued advocacy of its use. Later, however, it became more popular, and in 1872 Paul F. Mundé presented a paper advocating the use of the curette for the treatment of cancer of the uterus and crediting Récamier with discovery of the curette in 1858.

The original design of the curette went through many modifications, "the last of which was the flushing principle, i.e., curettes with the shaft hollowed out from the end of the handle to the space within the loop of the scraping end. Curettes of this type were devised by P. V. A. Auvard and C. H. F. Routh."[13]

As we have seen, the development of the simple procedure of dilatation and curettage covers a span of about 3000 years and includes the disappointments, endeavors, and achievements of a score of men.

In conclusion, it would be appropriate to emphasize and repeat a statement by George Sarton found in his *The Life of Science:* "Historical initiation would cure young students of the unfortunate habit of thinking that science began with them."

REFERENCES

1. Astruc, J. A treatise on all the diseases incident to women. English trans., 1743.
2. Ball, J. *New York J. Med. 18*:363, 1873.
3. Greenblatt, R. B. Symposium on specific methods of treatment; management of functional uterine bleeding. *M. Clin. North America 34*:1551, 1950.
4. *Hebammenbuch daraus man alle heimligkeit dess weiblichen geschlechts erlehrnen.* Franckfort am Mayn (S. Feyerabendt), 1580.
5. Leonardo, R. A. *History of Gynecology*, New York, Froben Press, 1944.
6. Mundé, P. The treatment of cancer of the uterus with the sharp-edged scoop or curette. *Am. J. Obst. 5*:309, 1872–73.
7. Récamier, J. C. A. Invention du speculum plein et brise. *Bull. Acad. méd. Paris 8*:661, 1842–43.
8. Ricci, J. V. *The Development of Gynecological Surgery and Instruments*. Philadelphia, Blakiston Company, 1949.

9. Simpson, J. Y. Contributions to the pathology and treatment of diseases of the uterus. *Edinburgh Monthly J. Med. Sc. 3*:547, 701, 1009, 1843.

10. Simpson, Sir J. Y. *Diseases of Women*. vol. III, Edinburgh, A. & C. Black, 1872.

11. Thomas, H. *Classical Contribution to Obstetrics and Gynecology*. Baltimore, Charles C Thomas, 1935.

12. Thomas, T. G. *A Practical Treatise on the Diseases of Women*. (ed. 2), Philadelphia, Henry C. Lea, 1869.

13. Thompson, C. J. S. *The History and Evolution of Surgical Instruments*. New York, Schuman, 1942.

14. Trotula of Salerno. *The Diseases of Women*. English translation by E. Mason-Hohl. California, Ward Ritchie Press, 1940.

15. Triaire, P. *La Chronique Medicale*, Paris, *11*:303, 1904.

Obstet Gynecol 1953;2:322–5.

COMMENTARY

The author of this scholarly and interesting history of gynecologic diagnosis was in the early stage of a surgery residency at Duke Hospital, Durham, North Carolina, when he wrote this article. Subsequently, he completed his residency, including advanced training in cardiothoracic surgery, and entered practice in Erie, Pennsylvania, where he was the first in the area to perform several cardiac procedures. He retired from practice 2 years ago.

Lawson Tait: The Forgotten Gynecologist

Ira M. Golditch, MD

JANUARY 2002

ynecology, as we know it today, is essentially American in origin, with most of the early work in this field being done by southerners such as J. Marion Sims and Ephraim McDowell. However, other surgeons, especially in England, have also had a remarkable influence on the development of gynecology as a specialty. Of the many early physicians who helped forge this embryonic specialty, the importance of Robert Lawson Tait's many innovative contributions to the medical and surgical care of women has been overlooked and underappreciated.

Lawson Tait, who dropped his forename by the time he began his medical writing, was born in Edinburgh, Scotland, in 1845, the second son of Archibald Tait, a cousin of the Archbishop of Canterbury. Because Scotland's system of compulsory birth registration did not exist before 1855, there is no official record of Tait's birth. He was said to have had a marked resemblance to the eminent physician and discoverer of the anesthetic action and use of chloroform, Sir James Young Simpson, and the prevailing opinion at one time was that Tait was the natural son of Simpson. Both Tait and Simpson had big heads and lots of hair, but on close inspection of their photographs, there is little other resemblance.

TAIT—THE PHYSICIAN

Tait won a scholarship to the University of Edinburgh in 1860, at age 15, but abandoned the study of arts after 1 year and never graduated. By 1862, having decided in favor of medicine, he was watching, if not assisting, Sir James Simpson and other notable surgeons of the day. Tait's first appointment, in 1867, was as the only resident in-house surgeon at the district hospital in Wakefield, England, a position he held for 3 years before moving with his wife to Birmingham to enter private practice. By 1870, at age 25, Tait had already performed his first five ovariotomies, quite remarkable in that during his earlier stay in Edinburgh, he had abundant opportunity to see that this operation invariably proved to be fatal in the hands of others. Although ovariotomy was first recorded in the early 1700s and performed successfully by Ephraim McDowell in Kentucky in 1809, it was not until 1872, however, when Tait reported only one death in his first nine ovariotomies,[1] that any substantial reduction in mortality was achieved.

By 1880, Tait had reported a 3% mortality rate in his first 100 ovariotomies, a marked improvement compared with the 25–30% rate reported for other surgeons in England and Scotland. He attributed the improved outcome to the abandonment of use of the standard extraperitoneal clamp on the ovarian pedicle in favor of the intraperitoneal use of short ligatures on the pedicle and complete closure of the abdominal incision. This realization by Tait of the importance of the intraperitoneal treatment of the pedicle opened the gates to surgery of every diseased organ in the abdomen and truly made him a founder of modern abdominal surgery. In one of the most remarkable papers of his career, Tait, in 1886, reported 139 consecutive ovariotomies without a death,[2] reducing the overall mortality of this procedure from 25% associated with the clamp to under 4%, a surgical marvel for which he and his methods of tissue handling, peritoneal irrigation, and meticulous cleanliness were greatly responsible.

In 1870, Tait gave up his general practice, passed the examination for the Fellowship of the Royal College of Surgeons, Edinburgh, and, in 1871, in a radically new concept at the time, announced himself as a consulting surgeon. In the same year, Tait promulgated his desire to become known as a gynecologist and was instrumental in establishing the Birmingham Hospital for Women, devoted to the diseases of women, where for the next 20 years he carried out much of the original work that made his name famous in every country where abdominal surgery was practiced.

In 1872, Tait removed a small ovary which harbored a chronic abscess. In what has become a historic operation, this is believed to be the first recorded instance in which a surgeon deliberately removed a diseased ovary for relief of pelvic pain.[3] Tait performed much of the pioneer work in the surgery of pelvic inflammatory diseases and, subsequently, removal of the adnexae became known, especially in the United States, as the "Tait operation."[4] He was the first to note that small cystic ovaries very often give rise to severe hemorrhage from the uterus, an observation that has been confirmed repeatedly in women with anovulation. Tait was the first, in 1879, to induce menopause by ovariectomy, and his description of this procedure to treat extraovarian dysfunction, particularly in cases of menstrual hemorrhage caused by uterine myomata, was one of the first in the English language. Many of Tait's ovariectomies were performed on normal ovaries, a practice that would not be condoned today, but his persistence and bold approach to surgery laid the foundation for future advances.

Tait was the first surgeon to advocate and perform salpingectomy for the treatment of tubal disease. Although removal of diseased fallopian tubes preceded Tait's initial cases by 6 months, there can be no doubt that it was Tait's appreciation of gonorrhea as a cause of acute adnexal infection, beginning in 1877, which established the role of surgery for inflammatory disease of the fallopian tubes and pelvic abscess. In the first important paper he wrote on pelvic inflammation, Tait, in 1882, described what only a few before him had recognized—that the pelvic masses associated with chronic pelvic pain consisted not only of inflamed ovaries but also of occluded and distended tubes. For many years thereafter, Tait was not only devoted to teaching others the truth of this statement, but he led the movement away from the old-fashioned mechanical school of gynecology, wherein many believed that armed with "the speculum, the sound, the caustic stick and the pessary" (preface, p. x),[5] the practitioner could relieve all female pelvic ailments. In another valuable contribution,[6] Tait reported on the treatment of pelvic abscess by abdominal section and drainage rather than by transvaginal trochar placement, which often resulted in fistulous tracts or incomplete relief of symptoms.

Although not trained in midwifery, Tait made important contributions to the evolving practice of obstetrics. In 1878, he reported successful treatment of chronic inversion of the uterus with an apparatus which exerted continuous elastic pressure on the uterine fundus, and developed a similar device for dilating the uterine cervical canal. For the annual oration to the Southampton Medical Society in 1889, Tait, who had not practiced obstetrics for 20 years, challenged the audience with his discussion of the surgical aspects of impacted labor. As an alternative to applying forceps, performing podalic version or craniotomy, or induction of premature labor in patients whose first labor had been greatly protracted, all of which were associated with maternal mortality rates greater than 15–20% and even higher fetal mortality rates, Tait, well versed in pelvic anatomy and the mechanisms of labor, proposed the principle of amputation of the pregnant uterus introduced by Professor Porro. Tait theorized that the Porro operation, ie, removal of the fetus via an incision in the uterus followed by supracervical hysterectomy, would reduce the 90–95% maternal mortality rate to the point at which ovariotomy had arrived, so that not more than 3–4% of the women subjected to it would die. He also proposed a similar approach for placenta previa, stating he would thereby save the child with certainty and relieve the mother with perfect safety from death by hemorrhage, and was the first, in 1872, to successfully leave the placenta in situ in a case of advanced abdominal pregnancy. Although Tait's recommended modification of Porro's procedure did not prove as successful in reducing mortality as he proposed, his prescient, aggressive approach was at the forefront of the evolutionary changes in the practice of obstetrics which resulted in a marked decrease in maternal and fetal mortality.

In what many consider his greatest achievement and for which he is perhaps best known, Tait was the first to completely elucidate the pathology of ectopic pregnancy and perform salpingectomy in the treatment of ruptured tubal pregnancy. In describing the evolution of this procedure, Tait related that when it was suggested, in 1881, that he "open the abdomen and remove the ruptured tube ... the suggestion staggered me, and I am ashamed to have to say that I did not receive it favorably" (p. 19).[7] A postmortem examination convinced Tait that tying the broad ligament and removing the tube would have spared the patient's life. Two years later, Tait tested his conviction, ligatured the ruptured tube and the broad ligament, and this woman was the first ever to survive operation for the rupture of a tubal pregnancy. In 1884, Tait published his seminal paper on salpingectomy as an emergency life-saving procedure,[8] noting that "These cases all confirm the view of the pathology of extrauterine pregnancy ... that in origin it is always tubal, and that its varieties depend merely on the direction in which rupture occurs." In 1888, Tait reported 42 cases of salpingectomy for tubal pregnancy with only two deaths, a marked improvement over the previously reported mortality of approximately 70% (p. 1251).[7]

The technique of transverse, transperineal repair of low rectovaginal fistulas was brought about by Tait in 1886.[9] Largely forgotten until the early 1900s and currently being used again, this technique, which avoids and saves a properly functioning anal sphincter and allows wide mobilization of tissue around the fistula, may be superior to the episioproctotomy approach to fistula repair, which disrupts the intact perineum and anal sphincter in much the same way as a fourth-degree episioproctotomy would be repaired.

Asepsis was practiced to a degree in the 1850s when mortality from childbed fever approached 20%, but it was not until the publication, in 1867, of Lister's classical article on antiseptic technique that appreciation of the fact that disease and death-causing germs could be transferred from the hands and soiled clothes evolved. Tait incurred the odium of many of his colleagues by challenging and rejecting the fashionable Listerian methods of antisepsis because of the tissue-damaging effects of carbolic acid and the carbolic spray. As an alternative, Tait boiled his instruments and silk sutures and advocated meticulous handwashing, copious wound irrigation, and closure and care of the surgical site with dressings that had been autoclave sterilized instead of the chemical-bearing gauzes of Lister. To Tait goes the credit for having made flushing of the peritoneal cavity a common procedure, one that remains an integral part of abdominal surgery. His scrupulous cleanliness was undoubtedly the forerunner of our modern aseptic methods.

Hospital cross-infection has been of concern since the days of Semmelweis 150 years ago. Tait, as well as Semmelweis and Florence

Nightingale, sought to improve this vexing problem. Between 1871 and 1877, he conducted an exhaustive inquiry into hospital mortality in Great Britain and concluded that "hospital hygiene has not advanced as it might and ought to have done,"[10] but acknowledged that what little diminution there had been in hospital mortality was attributed less to therapeutic discoveries and even surgical improvements than to general hygienic improvements. This controversial attack on hospitals, the means of existence for most surgeons, was medical heresy, antagonizing Tait's contemporaries and bringing him instant notoriety. From Tait's data emerged the apparent relationship between high death rates in hospitals and high bed occupancy rates, especially in hospitals larger than 100 beds, and he, along with Florence Nightingale, was among the first to appreciate the benefits of early hospital discharge.

A formidable figure who pulled no punches in the world of controversy, Tait dispensed with the methods of animal experimentation then becoming fashionable in medical circles. In 1882, Tait delivered a scathing indictment of vivisection to the Birmingham Philosophical Society, a speech that found him in a position adverse to the view adopted by the great majority of his professional brethren. Regarding investigation of the actions of drugs by experiments on animals, Tait's observation that "after we have found out what they do in one animal we find that in another the results are wholly different and the process of investigation has to be repeated in many" (p. 19)[11] was an early perception that certain animal models are inappropriate for investigation of drug effects in humans. Unfortunately, Tait did not appreciate the potential in humans of blood transfusion experiments in animals, and his staunch antivivisectionist stance may have retarded the rate of scientific progress.

The high-water mark of Tait's career came in 1890 when he delivered the Address in Surgery at the Annual Meeting of the British Medical Association and pled for the training of the surgeon as an artist and craftsman.[12] Tait advocated for relief of "that senseless system of biological training" that existed in medical student training and encouraged early direct patient contact to obviate the tendency to turn out "scientific young tyros who know neither patients nor their diseases till they have gone through a second pupilage extending for years after they have left their university." Tait urged restoration of the apprenticeship system to teach students how to deal with patients, a concept that has been incorporated into our current system of early clinical clerkships. He also urged careful classification and publication of surgical results as one of the best methods of improving patient outcomes. The last few years of Tait's life were marked by almost continuous ill health, the consequence of renal calculi and nephritis. He died, childless, of uremic poisoning in 1899 at the relatively young age of 54.

TAIT—THE MAN

Once seen, Tait was not easily forgotten. He was a short, stout man with a large head, thick bull neck, corpulent body, pudgy legs, and small hands and feet. He was described variously as idealistic, dogmatic, bold, fearless but not reckless, opinionated, and often less than tolerant of orthodox thinking. Many of his colleagues portrayed him as coarse, swearing, gluttonous, and a rampaging bully lacking in sympathy. He was a man of great intelligence, insight, reasoning power, force of character, immense vitality, and boundless energy. By his personal magnetism, Napoleonic in many respects, he dominated all he came in contact with. Often with a big cigar in his mouth, his typical long workdays included two to five surgical operations and afternoon consultations at his home. Although he was most kind and generous to the poor and afflicted, often treating and operating on them at no charge, Tait had little respect for individuals and never toadied to the rich or great. He often missed large fees by losing his temper with patients.

Tait's unstinting criticism of other surgeons' views and the exposure of the flawed or imperfect methods with which their names were identified made him many bitter enemies in his later years, but he was quite gracious in affording to others the credit they deserved in enabling him to introduce new surgical techniques. In his textbook on diseases of the ovaries,[6] dedicated to "Dear Dr. Marion Sims," Tait explained what, for many generations of medical students, especially in the United States, was quoted as Tait's Law—"... that in every case of disease in the abdomen or pelvis in which the health is destroyed or life threatened, and in which the condition is not evidently due to malignant disease, an exploration of the cavity should be made" (p. 344).

Although steadfast in his beliefs, Tait was not always correct. He believed that all ectopic gestations are primarily tubal and doubted the occurrence of ovarian pregnancy. He believed that under normal circumstances, ovum impregnation occurred in the uterus and not in the fallopian tubes, and was emphatic that if a tube contained a gestation, it must rupture, not realizing that tubal abortion frequently occurred. He held the bimanual method of examination, an essential part of gynecologic diagnosis, in some contempt. He believed that the presence of multinodular myomata in the uterus delayed the menopause indefinitely, yet was aware that when menopause did occur, myomata were arrested in growth. Regarding menstruation, Tait firmly believed that the fallopian tube was the starting point of the process.

Although Tait made many enemies by his outspoken criticism and uncompromising positions, he also had many admirers on both sides of the Atlantic. In 1884, Tait joined with others in founding the British

Gynecological Society and served as its president in 1886. In 1888, he was elected the first professor of gynecology at Queens College, Birmingham, and, in 1891, was elected honorary president of the Obstetrical and Gynecological Society of Glasgow.

In 1884, Tait's visit to Canada and the United States, including lectures and surgery in Boston, Philadelphia, and New York, led to rapid development of abdominal and pelvic surgery in these countries. He was awarded honorary fellowship in the American Gynecological Society and the American Association of Obstetricians and Gynecologists and received honorary medical degrees from St. Louis College of Physicians and Surgeons and the University of the State of New York.

Tait was held in the highest regard by most who knew him, and was recognized as "a giant among giants in the very age of giants, in the world of surgery" (p. 7).[11] Joseph Price, a brilliant American surgeon who looked upon Tait as his master and teacher, noted that "... in pelvic surgery Tait stood first—taught us the best we know" (p. 138).[4] William Mayo stated that "the cavities of the body were a sealed book until the father of modern abdominal surgery, Lawson Tait, and our own Joseph Price, carried the sense of sight into the abdominal cavity" (p. 604).[13] Tait, a superb surgeon and a gifted teacher, primarily of American surgeons, including Kelly and Cushing, correctly claimed that "the evolution of abdominal surgery has proceeded from the necessities of the special diseases of women" and was instrumental in advancing the status "when the treatment of pelvic and abdominal disease, so prevalent amongst women and relatively so rare amongst men, was regarded as a mere appendix to the work of the accoucher [sic]" (preface, p. x).[5] His efforts promoted the separation of obstetrics and gynecology, and this division of labor resulted in enormous advances for both.

In an era when surgeons were considered a low form of paramedical life, when every effort was made to see that obstetric physicians did not trespass upon the jealously guarded province of surgery, and when few members of the Obstetrical Society were allowed by their hospitals to practice operative obstetrics or gynecology, Lawson Tait emerged as an assertive, domineering figure whose work achieved great prominence. His publications were prolific and varied, including at least 151 articles, 33 letters, ten pamphlets, and three books. To be sure, Tait was a man of contradictions whose life passed in conflict. He did, however, make pelvic surgery a separate discipline and did more than any other single individual to create a gynecologic specialty and to inspire the great generation of abdominal surgeons that followed. Robert Lawson Tait deserves greater recognition within our specialty.

REFERENCES

1. Tait L. Statistics of ovariotomy. Brit Med J 1872;1:581–2.

2. Tait L. One-hundred and thirty-nine consecutive ovariotomies performed between January 1, 1884 and December 31, 1885 without a death. Brit Med J 1886;1:921–4.

3. Tait L. The pathology and treatment of diseases of the ovaries. 4th ed. Birmingham: Cornish Brothers, 1883.

4. McKay JWS. Lawson Tait: His life and work. New York: William Wood, 1922.

5. Tait L. Diseases of women and abdominal surgery, Vol. 1. Leicester: Richardson & Co. 1889.

6. Tait L. Diseases of the ovaries. 4th ed. Birmingham: Cornish Brothers, 1883.

7. Tait L. Lectures on ectopic pregnancy and pelvic haematocoele. Birmingham: The "Journal" Printing Works, 1888.

8. Tait L. Five cases of extra-uterine pregnancy operated upon at the time of rupture. Brit Med J 1884;1:1250–1.

9. Tait L. Tait's flap-splitting operation on the perineum. Brit Med J 1897;2:1298.

10. Tait L. Hospital mortality: A statistical examination of the returns of the hospitals of Great Britain for fifteen years. London: Churchill, 1877.

11. Risdon W. Robert Lawson Tait. London: Anti-Vivisection Society, 1967.

12. Tait L. Surgical training, surgical practice, surgical results. Brit Med J 1890; 2:267–73.

13. Mayo W. The influence of European surgery on American practice. St. Paul Med J 1914;16:601–5.

Obstet Gynecol 2002;99:152–6.

COMMENTARY

This article makes a compelling argument that Lawson Tait played a critical role in the early development of gynecology as a surgical discipline. The author, Ira Golditch, served for many years as the director of obstetrics and gynecology at the Kaiser Permanente Hospital in San Francisco and was a member of the Green Journal Editorial Board (1994–1997). He now lives in retirement in Santa Rosa, California.

Peseshet: The First Female Physician?

W. Benson Harer Jr, MD, and
Zenab el-Dawakhly, MA

DECEMBER 1989

s women increasingly fill the ranks of physicians and approach parity in the specialty of obstetrics and gynecology, it is appropriate to honor Peseshet, who was probably the world's first known female physician. This remarkable woman lived in Egypt during the Fourth Dynasty, roughly 2500 BC, the time of construction of the great pyramids at Giza.

Everything we know about her comes from a single inscription found at Giza in the mastaba tomb of her son Akhet-Hetep, excavated by the Egyptian archaeologist Selim Hassan[1] in 1929. This inscription (Figure 1) leaves little doubt regarding her status. The title "Lady Overseer [of the] Lady Physicians" is repeated three times in this space, and the implication is that she was a physician who supervised female physicians and possibly male physicians as well.

The inscription at the top tells us that she "lived to a good old age" and "possessed honor before the king." She is identified as a priestess of the king's mother and as an overseer of the priestesses who served her *ka* (spirit). Finally, she is recognized as one who was "concerned with the king's affairs" and as one "known to the king." This title "acquaintance of the king" was the highest honor that could be accorded a woman at that time.[2, 3]

The inscription is a "false door," an entrance by which the spirit (*ka*) of Peseshet might enter or leave the tomb. Peseshet is depicted twice standing and wearing a long close-fitting gown. In the center she is shown seated opposite a man named Ra Nefer, probably her husband. He also is identified as an intimate of the king.

The space between the seated figures originally depicted a table of offerings. The inscription above this space indicates that it held "purifying water, natron, incense, linen cloth, and mascara." The last was ground-up malachite and was used by both men and women. Contemporary devotees of such cosmetics can rest assured they are following an ancient model.

The tomb was constructed primarily for Akhet-Hetep, the son of Peseshet. He was an important official who followed the pattern of the top

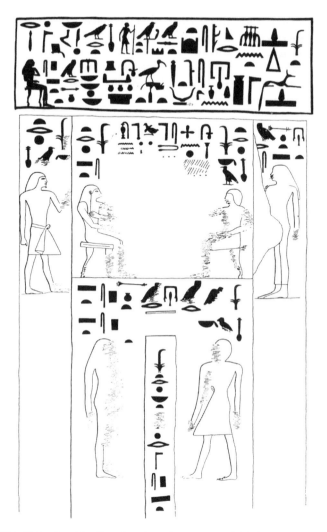

Fig. 1. This "false door" for Peseshet shows her name and title in the lower left corner of the upper block (lintel). They are repeated over both of her standing figures.

officials of his time by constructing an extensive tomb in the royal necropolis not only for himself but also for his family. Clearly these were powerful aristocrats. It is not surprising, therefore, that Peseshet shared the tomb or that she should bear important titles. There is no indication, however, that her medical practice was in any way specialized or limited to women. Her title as Overseer [of] Women Physicians does indicate clearly the existence of a cadre of other female doctors. However, there is no evidence of any specialized midwives or practitioners involved specifically in obstetrics at any time in Pharaonic Egypt.

The first known male physician was Hesy Re, an important official in the Third Dynasty, about 200 years earlier, when the Step Pyramid was constructed at Saqqara. The architect of that pyramid, which started the massive pyramid craze, was Imhotep. By tradition he was accorded the title physician, but there is actually no contemporary evidence to support his role in medicine.

Peseshet is portrayed in size equal to her husband, reflecting the equal social status of the sexes during that time. This is confirmed by the important titles she held and by evidence from other known doctors that the medical profession was held in high esteem.

Even at that early time, medicine had evolved as a science despite the system of beliefs underpinning it, which to modern eyes looks quite bizarre. Specialization was common in the Old Kingdom, and we know of clearly defined ophthalmologists, dentists, proctologists, internists, and surgeons. The Edwin Smith Surgical Papyrus,[4] which dates to the Old Kingdom, portrays a strikingly modern approach to patient evaluation. Each case provides history, physical findings, diagnosis, prognosis, and therapy. Furthermore, the physicians recognized that there were cases beyond their ability to treat successfully.

The progress of late 20th-century medicine has been so dazzling that we tend to lose perspective, but it is probably true that around 2500 bc [sic] Peseshet and her female colleagues practiced medicine as well as anywhere else in the world, until the last century.

REFERENCES

1. Hassan S. Excavation at Giza, 1929–1930. Vol I. Oxford: Oxford University Press, 1932.
2. Ghalioungui P. The physicians of pharaonic Egypt. Cairo: Al Abram Center for Scientific Translations, 1983.
3. Ghalioungui P, el Dawakhly Z. Health and healing in ancient Egypt. Cairo: The Egyptian Organization for Authorship and Translation, 1965.
4. Breasted HJ. The Edwin Smith Surgical Papyrus. Vol I. Chicago: University of Chicago Press, 1930.

Obstet Gynecol 1989;74:960–1.

COMMENTARY

W. Benson Harer, an author of this and the next article, has served ACOG in several different and important capacities extending over the past 15 years; he was Chair of District IX, then Secretary of the College for two 3-year terms, and ultimately President during 2000–2001. He is also an Egyptologist of considerable repute, having published extensively in the field and holding relevant academic appointments. His Egyptology credentials are evident in these two pieces of historical scholarship, one identifying the world's earliest known woman physician and the other describing an instrument used 7,000 years ago to cut the umbilical cord.

Peseshkef: The First Special-Purpose Surgical Instrument

W. Benson Harer Jr, MD

JUNE 1994

*S*ir William E. Flinders Petrie,[1] the father of Egyptology, excavated some bizarrely shaped flint knives in 1894–1895 in burials at Ballas and Nagada. They were dubbed "forked lances" and "fish tail" knives (Figure 1), and Petrie speculated that they were used for hunting despite their fragile nature. They are the most exquisitely worked class of flints known, with blunt pointed ends and razor-sharp, broad fish tail surfaces.

As knowledge of ancient Egypt advanced, these enigmatic flints were identified with the Peseshkef, an essential instrument in the "opening of the mouth" funerary ceremony for mummies. This procedure, carried out on the embalmed mummy, would magically permit the deceased to take nourishment in the afterlife.

The ancient Egyptians believed literally in rebirth after death. This is nicely depicted in the famous papyrus of Ani, a royal scribe who lived in Thebes (modern Luxor) circa 1500 BC. His "Book of the Dead" (British Museum 10470) was a sort of handbook of the afterlife. A critical moment is shown when Ani's heart is weighed against the feather of truth (Figure 2) to prove his worthiness. The monster Ammit waits to devour the heart, thus dooming him to oblivion if he fails this test. Present to observe and

Fig. 1. Functional flint Peseshkef with sharp fish tail end to cut the umbilical cord. Instrument retains a trace of red ochre and is dated circa 4000 BC. (Harer Family Trust Collection.)

Fig. 2. Weighing of the heart from the papyrus of Ani. (British Museum 10470.)

assure success are two important goddesses associated with birth and fate—Meskhenet, the birth goddess, and Renenutet, the goddess of lactation and nourishment. Presumably, both attended his original birth and are again present for his rebirth.

Because there was no substitute for human milk, a baby's survival depended absolutely on the mother's lactation. Literal rebirth would require the mummy to take nourishment, too. This led to the important magical process to permit the mummy to open its mouth.

Although details of the "opening of the mouth" ceremony are unknown, the appropriate equipment has been amply documented. By the time the ancient Egyptian empire reached its apogee around 1500 BC, the Peseshkef in stylized form was a standard instrument for the ceremony. It was usually on a tray accompanied by small vessels (Figure 3). The application of this tray of instruments is unknown, but a stylized adze was touched to the mummy's mouth. The blunt model Peseshkef may have symbolically severed a phantom umbilical cord. No actual cuffing was done, so both adze and Peseshkef were blunt.

The goddess of birth, Meskhenet, is identified by her name in hieroglyphs and by her unique headdress, the Peseshkef (Figure 4). The gods of the Egyptian pantheon are usually identifiable by their headdresses bearing unique symbols. In this instance, the knife to cut the cord symbolized the goddess of childbirth.

Roth[2] collected numerous references to childbearing in the ancient Egyptian literature and tomb scenes. She analyzed the hieroglyphic signs

Fig. 3. Instrument tray, used for the opening of the mouth ceremony, contains stylized magical Peseshkef in right lower corner. (Museum of Fine Arts, Boston.)

and their potential relations as both homonyms and actual representations. She further analyzed funerary practices and their depictions, as well as actual artifacts involved. Birth and rebirth after death were dangerous processes. The Peseshkef played important roles in both. Roth forcefully synthesized data, such as presented here, to show that it was used specifically to sever the umbilical cord. The name Peseshkef comes from ancient Egyptian words: *kef* for "flint" and *pesesh* or "that which divides." The Peseshkef may have originated as a knife whose sharp fish tail readily adapted to cut any cord, but because of its religious significance it became restricted to cutting the umbilical cord. This action separated the baby from the mother and thus separated its fate from that of the mother.

Until the advent of modern health care, childbirth carried serious risks: about 1% maternal mortality and up to 30% neonatal mortality. In the absence of modern sanitary and health practices, these statistics still hold true today. It is clear that the first surgical procedure was cutting the umbilical cord. This could be done with almost anything, but with the ancient religion so focused on birth and rebirth, the climactic cutting of the cord was readily invested with magic, which justified a special instrument used exclusively for that purpose.

The astonishing skills of the advanced artisans of the Neolithic period have never been surpassed, and are exemplified by the flint Peseshkef shown in Figure 1. The sharpness of a flint knife is comparable to that of a broken glass fragment. This example is typical. It is 17 cm long and 3 mm thick. The blunt end is a bit thicker, at 0.5 cm, and may have fit into a wooden handle. The sharp inverted cutting edge shows masterful craftsmanship, with smaller than 1-mm facets along the 5-cm width. This example and others show traces of red ochre, which probably was applied to symbolize blood. In many undisturbed predynastic burial sites, the Peseshkef was found broken in two even though all other grave contents were intact. This suggests that a ritual was performed with the burial, and the flint knife was broken to prevent its reuse.

During the Bronze Age, new technology displaced the advanced craftsmanship of the Neolithic period. The prehistoric flint Peseshkef, dating circa 4000–5000 BC, was transformed over the millennia into the highly stylized model with a curved "fish tail," as shown on Meskhenet's head and on the instrument tray for the opening of the mouth. Because it worked by magic rather than actual cutting in the funerary ritual, a rounded blunt Peseshkef was suitable. Flint was replaced by limestone, alabaster, and other materials. King Tutankhamen's Peseshkef was bronze. The functional knife became a magical icon.

At the time of construction of the pyramids, circa 2500 BC, mummification was limited to the king and royal family. Over following centuries,

Fig. 4. Meskhenet, goddess of birth, with stylized Peseshkef crown. (Budge EAW. The gods of the Egyptians. London: Methuen, 1904.)

as the cult of Osiris promised rebirth for all who believed, mummification became available to anyone who could afford it. The ancient religion deteriorated under Roman rule. After Christianity became the state religion, mummification passed out of vogue. By the fifth century AD, the Peseshkef was already an historical artifact.

Every year we are presented with new special-purpose surgical instruments, often with the innovator's name attached in a bid for immortality. The name of the inventor of the Peseshkef has been lost for over 7000 years, but the hope for immortality lingers.

REFERENCES

1. Petrie WEF. Nagada and Ballas. London: Bernard Quaritch, 1896:50–8.
2. Roth AM. The PSS.KF and the opening of the mouth ceremony: A ritual of birth and rebirth. J Egypt Archaeol 1992;78:113–47.

Obstet Gynecol 1994;83:1053–5.

The Sewing Machine Problem, As Seen Through the Pages of *The American Journal of Obstetrics and Diseases of Women and Children*, 1868–1873

Charles H. Hendricks, MD

SEPTEMBER 1965

he sewing machine was presented as a sinister threat to American womanhood at an 1868 meeting of the New York Obstetrical Society. Chamberlain reported that he had recently been treating a patient who had "enlargement and prolapse of the right ovary, attended by general debility, which was evidently caused by operating on a sewing machine." When he asked the experiences of others "on the effect of the use of sewing machines on menstruation and on the condition of the uterus and ovaries," his worst fears appear to have been confirmed. Perry had known "two or three cases of severe uterine disease, in one of which death occurred, that were due to the use of the sewing machine." Peaslee had more information (1:158, 1869), obtained from one of his patients who was forewoman of 50 female sewing machine operators. Most of these unfortunate workers suffered from dysmenorrhea and leukorrhea, and the "derangement of the menstrual function" was so great that they were generally obliged to be absent during the menses. It had recently been observed also that "the motion of the limbs in working the machines occasions a sexual excitement."

Two years later, Decaisne reported to the French Academy of Medicine concerning the "Effect of the Sewing Machine on the Health of Female Operators" (3:362, 1871), based on the study of 661 female operators of sewing machines. He concluded that the effects upon the muscular system did not differ from those produced by any other muscular labor. He could find no ill effect on the digestive apparatus, nor upon the respiratory system. He found that women soon became accustomed to the noise of the machines, so that their nervous systems were not harmed. The women could not be demonstrated to be unusually subject to abnormal menstruation, abortion, peritonitis, or leukorrhea. He said that: "Without stating positively that the sewing machine is not the cause of certain genital excitements, I have been induced to assert that the remarks published upon this subject, and the conclusions deduced therefrom, have no value. In this case, too, as I have shown in my work, the evil is very rarely the effect of the sewing machine and I have almost always found the cause of the excitements of which I speak in previous habits ..." He did caution, "As regards the machines with the women as motive agent, those with isochronous pedals should be preferred to those with alternate pedals; in this way the operator is guarded from any excitation." He concluded: "... we think that the sewing machine with woman as motive agent when it is used within reasonable limits has no more ill effects upon the health than has sewing by hand."

The matter was not permitted to rest there. It was considered a final time in the March 1873 meeting of the Philadelphia Obstetrical Society. Harris said that "reference has been made by *French* physicians to the evil effects of sewing machines. This applied to the French machines only which were worked by double treadle, and necessarily with alternate action of the feet. On the other hand, the *American* machines were worked with a single treadle on which both feet were placed" (6:295, 1873). This seemed to settle the matter, by the implication that it was really a French health concern and one which should not be of any great concern to the operator of any real American sewing machine. There the matter rested. In the short space of about four years during which the sewing machine problem appeared in the American medical literature, at least one death was reported as having been due to the operation of a sewing machine, and the matter was conveniently "exported" to France—apparently being considered by American physicians as a peculiarly "French" problem.

What are the Sewing Machine Problems of 1965? How will they look 100 years from now?

Obstet Gynecol 1965;26:453–4.

COMMENTARY

Charles Hendricks, who served on the Editorial Board (1975–1978) and was Associate Editor (1980–1985), wrote this provocative article about the various gynecologic and sexual complications suspected a century earlier of being caused by operating a sewing machine. The association is laughable today, but Hendricks asks rhetorically (and provocatively) what we are doing that is accepted today but will look ludicrous a hundred years hence.

Eponyms

Gabrielle Faloppio, 1523–1562. Professor of Anatomy in the University of Padua, 1551–1562. (De Lint JG. Atlas of the history of medicine. I. Anatomy. New York: Paul B. Hoeber Inc.; 1931.)

Between 1955 and 1958, eight articles by Harold Speert concerning eponyms important in obstetrics and gynecology, extending from Falloppio in the 16th century to Couvelaire in the 20th, appeared in After Office Hours. Seven of the eight are reprinted in this section. Without exception, they are richly illustrated and represent models of historical scholarship.

Following military service in World War II, Harold Speert settled in New York, where he spent the next 40 years teaching and practicing at Columbia–Presbyterian Medical Center. He made several important research contributions and developed a reputation as a clinician–teacher, but he is best known for his interest in medical history. Characterizing him as having "interest" in medical history vastly understates the case, for he is unquestionably among the world's leading authorities on the history of medicine as it relates to obstetrics and gynecology. He has written numerous articles and several books on history and now resides in Keene, New York.

Gabriele Falloppio and the Fallopian Tubes

Harold Speert, MD

OCTOBER 1955

he uterine tubes, or oviducts, are inseparably linked with one of the most famous of all medical eponyms. The term *fallopian tube* has been incorporated into the nontechnical vocabulary of practically all modern languages; and in medical and anatomic literature it is usually spelled with a small f, the acme of eponymic acceptance.

The writings of Galen suggest that the uterine tubes were known to Herophilus (335–280 B.C.), but none of the latter's works remain extant. Ruphus of Ephesus, of later date (end of the first century A.D.), described briefly the oviducts of the ewe, picturing them as varicose and tortuous vessels passing from the testes, as the ovaries were then called, to the cavity of the uterus, and comparing them to the spermatic ducts. Ruphus also noted the presence of the tubes in women but made no reference to their function and seems to have regarded the tubes, like the round ligaments, as suspensory structures.

THE DARK AGES OF ANATOMY

Very little advance in anatomic knowledge was made between the second and sixteenth centuries, for corpses for dissection were hard to obtain and the conditions for anatomic dissection and demonstration were rigidly prescribed by the civil authorities. In Bologna it was the students' responsibility both to procure the cadavers and to stand the expense of the demonstrations, until 1442, when the city assumed this burden. Even then, however, only the bodies of executed criminals who had been born at least thirty miles distant could be used. As a result, only one or two dissections were performed each year, and dissections of female cadavers were very rare. There is little if any evidence to support the commonly stated charge that dissection of the human body was prohibited in Italy by religious prejudice.[1] On the rare occasions when dissections were carried out in conjunction with courses in anatomy at the universities, the professor read aloud from Galen, whose authority remained beyond question, while assistants performed the dissections. For fifteen hundred years the grossest errors were thus perpetuated, until the anatomic renaissance ushered in by the famous quintet of the sixteenth century: Sylvius, Vesalius, Fabricius, Eustachius, and Gabriele Falloppio.[4]

FALLOPPIO'S DESCRIPTION OF THE OVIDUCT

The first accurate description of the human oviduct was made by Falloppio in his *Observationes Anatomicae* (Figure 2), published in Venice in 1561. In this work he calls the tube the *uteri tuba*, or trumpet of the uterus:

> That slender and narrow seminal duct rises, fibrous and pale, from the horns of the uterus itself; becomes when it has gone a little bit away, appreciably broader, and curls like a branch until it comes near the end, then losing the horn-like curl, and becomes very broad, has a distinct extremity which appears fibrous and fleshy through its red color, and its end is torn and ragged like the fringe of well-worn garments, and it has a wide orifice which lies always closed through the ends of the fringe falling together; and if these be carefully separated and opened out, they resemble the orifice of a brass trumpet. Wherefore since the seminal duct from its beginning to its end has a likeness to the bent-parts of this classic instrument, separate or attached, therefore it has been called by me the Uteri Tuba. These are present not only in the human body, but also in the sheep, cows and all other animals which I have dissected.[7]

It was not long before the oviducts became known universally as the fallopian tubes.

THE LIFE AND WORK OF FALLOPPIO

Gabriele Falloppio, descended from a noble Italian family,* was born in Modena, Italy, about 1523, there being some question as to his precise date of birth, certain historians giving a date 33 years earlier.[5]

Before he undertook the study of medicine, Falloppio held an ecclesiastical appointment in the cathedral of his native town,[2] but the details of his early life remain unknown.

He later studied medicine at Ferrara, under Antonio Musa Brasarola, and soon achieved renown as a surgeon. As a pupil of Vesalius, some of whose erroneous views he subsequently corrected, Falloppio attained, through his anatomic discoveries, the most illustrious name in Italian medicine. In 1548 he was appointed Professor of Anatomy at the University of Pisa, at the instance of Cosimo I de' Medici, the Grand Duke of Tuscany,

*The origin of the family name is shown in its coat of arms, which contains 3 falloppe, or imperfect silk cocoons. The original Italian spelling of the name was probably Falloppia; the Latin, Falloppius or Falloppius. It has since been written in several other forms: Falloppio, Fallopio, and Faloppio.[3]

Fig. 1. Title page of *Observationes Anatomicae.* (Second printing, 1562)

Meatus ueró ifte feminarius gra-
cilis & anguftus admodum oritur
nerueus ac candidus à cornu ipfius
uteri, cumque parum recefferit ab
eo latior fenfim redditur, & capreo
li modo crifpat fe donec ueniat pro
pè finem, tunc dimiffis capreolari-
bus rugis, atque ualde latus reditus
finit in extremum quodam, quo d
membranofum carneumque ob co
lorem rubrum videtur, extremum-
que lacerum ualde & attritum eft,
ueluti funt pannorum attritorum
fimbriæ, & foramen amplum habet,
quod femper claufum iacet conci-
dêtibus fimbriis illis extremis, quæ
tamen fi diligenter aperiantur, ac di
latentur tubæ cuiufdam æneæ extre
mum orificium exprimunt. Quare
cum huius claffici organi demptis
capreolis, uel etiam iifdem additis
meatus feminarius à principio ufq;
ad extremum fpeciem gerat, ideò à
me uteri tuba uocatus eft. Ita fe hæc
habent in omnibus non folùm hu-
manis, fed etiam ouinis, ac uacinis
cadaueribus, reliquifque brutorum
omnium, quæ ego fecui.

Fig. 2. Excerpt from Falloppio's description of the human oviduct. From *Observationes Anatomicae.*

but relinquished this post 3 years later in response to a call by the Senate of Venice to the chair of surgery, anatomy, and botany at Padua, where he succeeded Vesalius and Realdus Columbus. Here Falloppio remained, conducting his most important researches, until his death from pleurisy, October 9, 1562. An attempt was thereupon made by the Venetian Senate to recall Vesalius from his pilgrimage to the Holy Land to the chair he had previously held at Padua. His return voyage was rough and prolonged, however, resulting finally in shipwreck on the desolate island of Zante, where Vesalius is believed to have died of typhus in October, 1564.[8] The chair at Padua was then filled by Falloppio's favorite pupil, Fabricius ab Aquapendente.

The collected works of Falloppio, published in Venice in 1606 in 3 folio volumes, embrace 24 treatises containing a total of more than 1500 pages. Because of the variations in style, however, some authorities maintain that these works, with the exception of the *Observationes Anatomicae*, were not published from Falloppio's manuscripts, but rather from the notes of the students who attended his lectures.

CONTRIBUTIONS TO ANATOMY

Although best known for the uterine tubes, with which his name has since been associated, Falloppio made many other important contributions to the knowledge of anatomy. He gave the first precise description of the clitoris, the skeletal system of the fetus, and the epiphyses of the long bones, introduced the anatomic use of the word *vagina*, and was the first to use the word *luteum* in describing the ovary.[11] Falloppio is credited by some historians with having originated the name *placenta*, but this term also appears in the writing of Realdus Columbus, and there is some question as to who actually invented it. Falloppio first described the villi conniventes of the small intestine, the ileocecal valve, and the inguinal ligament, later erroneously named after Poupart. He introduced the terms *hard* and *soft palate*, and first described the muscles of the latter. His description of the ear was more minute than any previously published, calling attention for the first time to the semicircular canals, the chorda tympani, the fenestrae rotunda and ovalis, and the communication of the mastoid cells with the tympanic cavity. He was also the first to describe the ethmoid and sphenoid bones; the trigeminal, auditory, and glossopharyngeal nerves; and the canal (which bears his name) for the facial nerve.[10]

INTEREST IN HORTICULTURE

In addition to his anatomic researches, Falloppio maintained an active interest in horticulture and for several years served as superintendent of the Botanical Gardens at Padua, in recognition of which a genus of plants (*Fallopia*) was named after him. Little wonder that he has been referred to as the "Aesculapius of his century."[13]

REFERENCES

1. Alston, M. N. The attitude of the church toward dissection before 1500. *Bull. Hist. Med. 16:*221, 1944.

2. Baily, H., and Bishop, W. J. *Notable Names in Medicine and Surgery.* London, Lewis, 1946.

3. Castiglioni, A. "Fallopius and Vesalius." In Cushing, H.: *A Bio-Bibliography of Andreas Vesalius.* New York, Schuman, 1943.

4. Effler, L. K. *The Eponyms of Anatomy.* Toledo, Ohio, McManus-Troup Co., 1935.

5. Fisher, G. J. Historical and biographical notes: V. Gabriello Fallopio, 1523–1562. *Ann. Anat. & Surg. Soc. 2:*200, 1880.

6. Gnudi, M. T., and Webster, J. P. *The Life and Times of Gaspare Tagliacozzi.* New York, Reichner, 1950.

7. Graham, H. *Eternal Eve.* New York, Doubleday, 1951.

8. Leonardo, R. A. *A History of Gynecology.* New York, Froben, 1944.

9. Marx, K. F. H. *Herophilus: Ein Beitrag zur Geschichte der Medicin.* Carlsruhe and Baden, 1838.

10. Mettler, C. C., and Mettler, F. A. *History of Medicine.* Philadelphia, Blakiston, 1947.

11. Ricci, J. V. *The Genealogy of Gynecology.* Philadelphia, Blakiston, 1943.

12. Ruphus of Ephesus *Oeuvres de Ruphus d'Éphèse.* Ch. Daremberg and Ch. Emile Ruelle, Eds. Paris, 1879.

13. Sampson, J. A. Little biographies: VII. Fallopius, 1523–1563. *Albany Med. Ann. 27:*496, 1906.

Obstet Gynecol 1955;6:467–70.

Thomas Wharton and the Jelly of the Umbilical Cord

Harold Speert, MD

SEPTEMBER 1956

he lifeline of the fetus, the umbilical cord, contains a unique type of mucoid matrix, Wharton's jelly, in which are embedded the umbilical vessels and which imparts to the cord its soft, ropelike character. Because of its gelatinous consistency Wharton's jelly is admirably adapted as a medium and casing, as well as a cushion, for the fetal vessels, easily accommodating to the pulsatile changes in the arteries during the intrauterine life of the fetus and permitting the rapid constriction of the vessels that occurs immediately after its birth. Bathed in its normal environment of amniotic fluid, the cord remains soft and pliable; exposed to the desiccating effect of the atmosphere, Wharton's jelly rapidly shrivels, allowing the umbilical stump to wither and drop off.

DESCRIPTION OF UMBILICAL-CORD JELLY

Exactly 300 years have elapsed since Thomas Wharton's description of the umbilical-cord jelly and the expression of his views concerning its origin. In his famous *Adenographia* (Fig. 1), published in 1656, Wharton wrote (Figs. 2 and 3):

> Although we are not able, in truth, to follow their rivulets all the way to the placenta, we can nevertheless discern a certain copious jelly in the umbilical cord itself that covers all the other vessels. In the cow's fetus this jelly clearly has the same odor as the tense amniotic fluid and it is very likely that this fluid emanates from the same copious source. On the other hand, something else is also true: that this jelly is in a space in the vessels or in the trunk of the vessels, through which the amniotic fluid is supplied. And further, this jelly ends unevenly in innumerable tiny papillae encircling and extending along the whole length of the cord. But notice, the fetus does not supply the umbilical cord. It is certain, therefore, that this jelly takes its origin from the placenta and turns around to flow into the umbilical cord. Indeed, it cannot come from the fetus, not only because the jelly is separated from the vessel in the umbilical cord itself, but also because none of this kind of material is found next to the umbilicus, and also

151

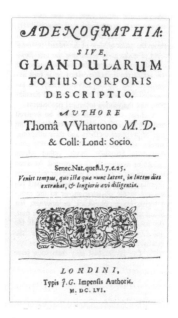

Fig. 1. Title page of Wharton's *Adenographia*.

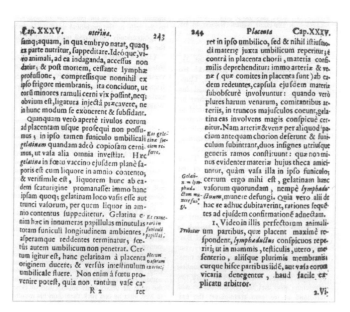

Figs. 2 and 3. Pages from Wharton's *Adenographia* containing his discussion of the jelly of the umbilical cord.

because very similar material is found in the chorion of the placenta. On the other hand, the arteries and veins (which are companions in the placenta), returning from the same source, are enveloped and obscured by a covering of the same material. Thus when several of these veins, with the accompanying arteries, come together into great trunks, the jelly enveloping them may be seen more easily. For the arteries and veins lead away from the chorion by a separate path and pass out of view into the funis, constituting two prominent branches of one sort or another; it being no less evident that they are encased in a covering of this material than are the vessels in the cord themselves. I am positive that this particular jelly of the vessels is secreted as a function of the lymph ducts. Even though some may doubt what I say here, they need only follow my reasoning in the same logical fashion to be convinced.

LIFE OF THOMAS WHARTON

Thomas Wharton was born August 31, 1614, in Winston-on-Tees, England.[1] He was admitted to Pembroke College, Cambridge, in 1638 but later continued his studies at Trinity College, Oxford, where he also served as a tutor. In 1642 he went to Bolton for 3 additional years of preparation before embarking on the study of medicine under John Bathurst in London. Returning to Oxford in 1646, Wharton received his M. D. degree there on May 7, 1647. Three years later he was made a Fellow of the Royal College of Physicians, which body he served as a Censor for 6 annual terms, between 1658 and 1673. In 1659 Wharton was appointed Physician to St. Thomas Hospital, a post he held until his death on November 15, 1673. He was buried in London in the church of St. Michael Bassishaw, which was dismantled in 1897, but his tomb received special care at that time.

During the outbreak of plague in London in 1665, Wharton was one of the very few physicians who met his responsibilities and remained at his post throughout the epidemic. In recognition of this devoted service he received a promise, which was never fulfilled, of appointment as physician-in-ordinary to the king. When the awaited vacancy occurred it was filled by another aspirant, despite Wharton's petition. In an obvious attempt to mollify him, and to assuage his disappointment, a grant was made of honorable augmentation to his paternal arms, for which he had to pay Sir William Dugdale the sum of 10 pounds.

Wharton is known today primarily as an anatomist, the *Adenographia* being his most outstanding contribution. His descriptions of the glands of the body, more accurate and detailed than any previous, were based on his own dissections and experiments. Particularly noteworthy was his study of the minute anatomy of the pancreas. In addition to the jelly of the umbil-

ical cord, his name is eponymically associated with the duct of the sub-
maxillary salivary gland.

Little is known of Wharton's nonprofessional interests. He composed
a few English verses, as a prefix to a book by one of his friends. His enthusiasm for fishing is suggested by the following note in Izaak Walton's
Compleat Angler:

... and yet I will venture to tell you a real truth concerning one [fish] lately
dissected by Dr. Wharton, a man of great learning and experience, and of
equal freedom to communicate it; one that loves me and my art; one to
whom I have been beholden for many of the choicest observations that I
have imparted to you. This good man, that dares do any thing rather than
tell an untruth, did, I say, tell me he lately dissected one strange fish and
he thus described it to me.

"The fish was almost a yard broad, and twice that length; his mouth
wide enough to receive or take into it the head of a man; his stomach seven
or eight inches broad. He is of a slow motion, and usually lies or lurks close
in the mud, and has a moveable string on his head about a span, or near
unto a quarter of a yard long, by the moving of which, which is his natural
bait; when he lies close and unseen in the mud, he draws other smaller fish
so close to him, that he can suck them into his mouth, and so devours and
digests them."

REFERENCES

1. Lee, S. (Ed.) *Dictionary of National Biography*. New York, Macmillan, 1909,
   Vol. 20.
2. Walton, I. *The Compleat Angler, or the Contemplative Man's Recreation*.
   London, 1653. Part 1, Chapter 19.
3. Wharton, T. *Adenographia: sive, Glandularum Totius Corporis Descriptio*.
   London, England, 1656.

Obstet Gynecol 1956;8:380–2.

François Mauriceau and His Maneuver in Breech Delivery

Harold Speert, MD

*U*ntil the popularization of the obstetric forceps and before cesarean section on the living woman became an acceptable operation, version and extraction was the accoucheur's sole device for delivery of a living child in labors complicated by mechanical difficulties, as well as the principal method of dealing with a variety of other obstetric complications. Operative obstetrics considered in large part, therefore, of breech delivery, and then, as now, its bête noire was the aftercoming head.

HISTORY OF VERSION AND EXTRACTION

Version and extraction on a dead infant was first described by Celsus, about 13 A.D., but it was not until almost a hundred years later that Soranus performed this operation on a living fetus. Version then fell into disuse until its revival by Ambroise Paré in the sixteenth century, remaining an important part of the obstetrician's repertoire from that time until the most recent years.

An important manual technic for delivery of the aftercoming head, whether the infant was turned in utero or presented initially by the breech, is identified with the name of François Mauriceau. This procedure, the *Mauriceau maneuver*, was subsequently modified by a number of later obstetricians, including Levret, Gifford, Lachapelle, Veit, Wigand, Martin, and von Winckel, whose names have also been associated with the technic for extraction of the aftercoming head. Its principal features consist in turning the infant so that it faces posteriorly (away from the pubic symphysis) and inserting one or two fingers into its mouth, to aid flexion of the head and provide gentle traction for its delivery.

Jacques and Charles Guillemeau

Long overlooked by obstetric historians as the probable originator of what is now called the Mauriceau maneuver, but antedating Mauriceau, was Jacques Guillemeau. This distinguished French obstetrician was born in

Orléans in 1550 and died in Paris, in 1609 according to some authorities, and in 1612 according to others.[2,4] Guillemeau, a pupil of Paré, from whom he had learned the technic of podalic version, was probably the first to advocate it in the treatment of placenta previa. Unlike his master, Guillemeau had also studied the humanities and, being well versed in the classics, was able to read the writings of Hippocrates. In the latter's *De superfoetatione*, dating back to about 400 B.C., Guillemeau had read the recommendation to insert a finger into the mouth of a dead fetus to assist in its delivery in cephalic presentations. Applying this principle to the aftercoming head, Guillemeau wrote in his textbook, *De la Grossesse et Accouchement des Femmes:*

> One would have to turn the body of the infant upside down gently, placing it face downward.... Working the head loose by moving it up and down in this situation, and holding the infant with one hand, and with the index finger of the other hand placed in the infant's mouth, it will be easy to extract [the head] with the body.

These lines were probably written, as a matter of fact, by Charles Guillemeau, son of Jacques, after the latter's death. The first edition of the book, which appeared in 1609, the probable year of Jacques' death, contains a chapter on breech delivery, but in a very rare copy of the 1612 English translation that I was able to examine, the above passage does not appear, the author merely mentioning the importance of having the infant's back toward the symphysis to prevent impaction of the chin. It is in the second edition, "corrected and enlarged by Charles Guillemeau," and published in 1621, after Jacques' death, that this technic for delivery of the aftercoming head is first described.

It is obvious that Mauriceau was familiar with the writings of the Guillemeaus, for although no acknowledgment of their priority in this technic is made, striking similarities are to be found in their respective chapters on breech delivery.

MAURICEAU'S INSTRUCTIONS FOR BREECH DELIVERY

Mauriceau's celebrated text, *Traité des Maladies des Femmes Grosses,*[6] was published initially in 1668 but the early editions and their English translations by Hugh Chamberlen did not contain the famous chapter on breech delivery. The earliest edition of Mauriceau's book in which I have succeeded in finding his instructions for breech delivery is the third (Figs. 1 and 2) published in 1681, from which the following excerpt is taken (Chap. XIII, pp. 271–6):

> Now as soon as the Surgeon will have recognized that the infant is presenting in this position, and that the uterus is sufficiently dilated to allow the passage of his hand (otherwise he brings about gradual dilatation, lubri-

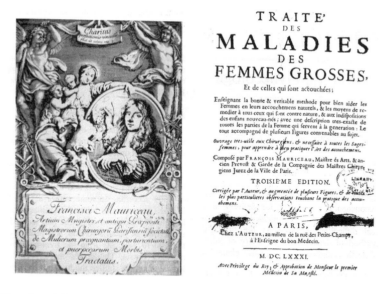

Figs. 1 and 2. Frontispiece and title page in *Traité des Maladies des Femmes Grosses*.

cating its entire passage with oil or fresh butter, also using his fingers for this purpose, spreading them apart after having introduced his hand with the fingers together, and continuing to do so until it [the cervix] is sufficiently dilated) and having his nails cut short, his fingers without any rings and his whole hand anointed with oil or fresh butter, he will introduce it gently into the entrance of the uterus where, finding the feet of the infant, he will extract it in this position, in the manner that we are about to describe. But if only one of the feet presents itself, he must determine which it is, whether right or left, and in which position it is presenting; for these points will help him determine on which side the other foot lies. Having noted this, he will go after it and having found it, he will extract it very gently together with the first foot. Before doing this, he must be very careful that the second foot is not that of another child; because if it were so, he would burst the mother and infants before extracting them thus. This he will recognize easily if, having slid his hand along the leg and thigh of the first infant up to the groin, he finds that the two thighs are part of one and the same body. This is also an easy means of finding the other foot, when only one presents at first.

Several authors recommend that for fear of losing hold of the first foot, one tie it with a ribbon with a slip knot, in order not to have to search for it again after having found the other foot; but this is not often necessary; for ordinarily when one has hold of one foot the other is not very hard to find. Nevertheless let him who wishes take this precaution, which does no harm except that it prolongs the time of the operation. Now as soon as the Surgeon will have found both of the infant's feet, he will extract them. Then taking them by both hands, above the malleoli, and holding them close together, he will pull evenly in this manner, until the thighs and hips of the infant are extracted. For this purpose he will grasp the thighs firmly above the knees as soon as he is able to, being careful to wrap these parts in an ordinary cloth, which should be dry, so that his hands, which are already greasy, will not slide on the body of the infant, which is very slippery because of the mucoid material with which it is covered and which would prevent him from being able to hold firmly. This done, and always holding the infant by both feet, or above the knees, he will extract it to the top of the chest in this manner, after which he will with his hand bring down both arms of the infant alongside its body. The arms he will then find easily, being careful to hold them near the wrists rather than at any other point, and to disengage them skillfully one at a time, without using too much force, for fear of breaking them, as those who operate unmethodically often do; and being very careful then to hold the abdomen and face directly downward, to prevent the head, if facing upward, from getting caught by the chin on the os pubis. This is why, if it were not so turned, one would have to put it in this position, which one can easily do if, as soon as one starts to pull the infant by the feet, one lowers them while turning them gradually, proportionately to the amount of extraction, until the heels directly face the mother's abdomen. And if they are not in exactly this position when one has extracted the infant to the upper part of its thighs, before extracting it any farther the Surgeon must slide one of his flattened hands up to the infant's pubis and hold both its feet with the other hand, in order to turn its body at the same time to the side more favorable to a good position, until it is as it should be, that is to say, with the chest and face downward. Having thus guided it to the top of the shoulders, it is then necessary to take one's time (urging the patient to bear down now) in order to make sure that by pulling on it, the head can take the shoulders' place at the same time, and by so doing, will not be arrested in the birth canal. Several authors recommend, in order to prevent this mishap, bringing down only one of the infant's arms, and leaving the other up [in the uterus]; so that the other may serve as a splint for its neck, the uterus not being able to close before the infant's head is completely delivered. But if the Surgeon is able to take his time without losing his head, he will not need this precaution to prevent this accident, which would be more likely to occur if he left one arm of the child up [in the uterus]; for besides occupying by its size a part of the birth passage which is not too large anyway, by inclining the head more to one side than to the other, it would result in its surely being arrested where the infant's neck is not thus splinted. When I have sometimes wished to try to leave one arm up [in the uterus] in this manner while extracting infants by the feet, I have always been obliged to bring both arms down, after which I have completed my operation much more easily.

There are nevertheless some infants with a head so large that it remains caught in the passage after the body is completely out, in spite of all the precautions one can take to prevent this. In this case one must not fool around simply pulling the infant by the shoulders; for sometimes one would do better to quit and separate the neck than to continue thusly. But while some other person will pull unskillfully on the infant's body, holding it by both feet or above the knees, the Surgeon will disengage the head gradually from the bones of the pelvis. This he will do by gently sliding one or two fingers of his left hand into the infant's mouth, in order to release the chin first, and with his right hand he will grasp the back of the infant's neck, above the shoulders, with the help of one of the fingers of his left hand placed in the infant's mouth, as I have just said, to disengage the chin; for it is chiefly this part that causes the head to be held up in the pelvis, out of which one cannot extract it until the chin is completely disengaged. One must take care to do this as promptly as possible, for fear that the infant may suffocate, as would doubtlessly occur if it were to remain thus caught and arrested for a long time. This is because the umbilical cord that is outside, being cold and tightly compressed by the body or by the infant's head which remains too long in the birth canal, can then no longer keep the infant alive by the mother's blood, the movement of which is arrested in the cord, as much by its cooling, which makes it clot in it, as by its compression, which prevents its circulation, in the absence of which the child should breathe immediately. This it cannot do until its head is completely out of the uterus. This is the reason why after one has begun to extract the infant, he must try to deliver it completely as soon as he can; this being properly done, one will immediately deliver the woman of the afterbirth, in the manner that we have already described.

MAURICEAU'S REPORT ON USE OF THE MANEUVER

The next (fourth) edition of Mauriceau's *Traité* ... in 1694, was published together with a companion work, *Observations sur la Grossesse et l'Accouchement des Femmes*[7] (Fig. 3), which consisted of illustrative case reports to document his teachings. Three of these case reports relate his use of the Mauriceau maneuver for the aftercoming head, the following one serving also to air his attitude toward the Hippocratic belief, then still popular, that an infant born after 7 months' gestation has a better chance for survival than one born after 8 months:

> On the 2nd of October, 1672, I delivered a young woman who, being 7 months pregnant with her first child, was injured the day before while taking a rough carriage ride to Versailles. When I was called to help her I found

Fig. 3. Title page in *Observations sur la Grossesse et l'Accouchement des Femmes*. (1738 edition; the first edition appeared in 1694 as a companion to the fourth edition of the *Traité*.)

that the midwife, having attempted to deliver her of the child, which was presenting by the feet, had extracted the body well, but the head was still in the birth passage, the midwife being unable to deliver it. This I did the very moment I arrived, after disengaging the chin from the passage with the help of my finger introduced into the mouth of the little infant, whose heart was still beating after I had extracted it. After I had thus completed the delivery of this woman, she told me that when she felt the first pains of labor she consoled herself with the common belief that, being pregnant 7 months, her child could survive. But she was quite disillusioned of this common opinion by her own experience, for her child was so small, as are all children at this stage, that it could never have survived even if she had delivered it without any accident at this stage of 7 months, when the deliveries, which are always premature, ought to be called abortions rather than true deliveries, as they are mistakenly called.

LIFE AND WORK OF FRANÇOIS MAURICEAU

François Mauriceau was born in Paris in 1637.[1, 5] Although not a doctor of medicine but rather an "ordinary surgeon," belonging to the community of surgeons of Saint-Côme, he became the most accomplished obstetrician of his day in France and the dominant figure in obstetrics of the seventeenth century. He acquired his early obstetric experience at the Hôtel-Dieu before entering private practice in Paris, but the record of this stage of his career is not entirely clear. According to the books of the Hôtel-Dieu, a young surgeon named François Mauriot on November 19, 1660, applied for permission, which was subsequently granted, to perform obstetric deliveries in that institution. He was expelled from the obstetric service on January 28, 1661, following a maternal death for which he was held responsible, and also because the allotted time of his appointment had expired. One of Mauriceau's biographers[5] concluded that François Mauriot and François Mauriceau were the same person, because (1) Mauriot and Mauriceau would both have been young men in 1660, (2) there are records indicating that Mauriceau was working in the maternity division of the Hôtel-Dieu at the end of 1660, and (3) no other record can be found of a seventeenth-century surgeon named Mauriot.

The publication of Mauriceau's text in 1668 was a milestone in the history of obstetrics, providing a tremendous impetus toward its establishment and recognition as a specialty. This book was soon translated into English, German, Dutch, Italian, Latin, and Flemish, and enjoyed the popularity of many editions. Much in the treatise, as in practically all textbooks, parroted the erroneous teachings of previous generations, but it also contained much that was original and important. In the former category was Mauriceau's perpetuation of the glaring anatomic error that regarded the ovarian ligaments as ejaculatory vessels leading from the ovaries to the uterus for the transmission of the female semen. Consistent with this view was his steadfast refusal to accept the concept of tubal pregnancy, and his rigid adherence to the Galenic doctrine that impregnation occurs in the uterine cavity by mixture of the male and female semens. Mauriceau attributed hydatidiform moles to excessive frequency of intercourse.

Contributions to Obstetrics

Among the significant new features of Mauriceau's work was his detailed analysis of the mechanism of labor and his description, probably the first, of brow presentation. He drew sharp distinction between the uterine forces during labor and the passive role of the fetus. Earlier generations of accoucheurs had delivered their patients in the squatting position or on the birth-stool; it was Mauriceau who introduced the practice of delivering women in bed. His book contains the earliest account of the prevention of congenital syphilis by antisyphilitic treatment during pregnancy. Rupture of the membranes had been employed for about 75 years for the induction of labor, but Mauriceau was the first to treat placenta previa by this method. In cases of ruptured perineum associated with childbirth he pioneered in advocating primary repair, recommending "cleansing the womb from such excrements as may be there, with red wine, then applying 3 or 4 stitches." He remained immovable in his opposition to cesarean section, which was almost invariably fatal to the mother, and stated that the few cases of reported success existed only in the imagination of the authors.

Mauriceau described the main differences between the male and female pelvis, but discredited Paré's observation of pubic separation in a woman who had been hanged 2 weeks after giving birth:

> I will not in this case accuse him of imposture, for I have too much respect for him, and esteem him too sincere for it; but I indeed believe that he was mistaken in this separation; for there is no likelihood that, being so at the time of her labor, it would remain so a fortnight at the breadth of half a finger, for then they should have been obliged to carry this woman to her execution; for she would not have been able to have supported herself to climb the ladder of the gibbet and to keep herself on her legs ... because the body is only supported by the stability of these bones: Wherefore we must rather believe ... that such a disjunction and separation was caused either by the falling of this woman's corpse from the high gibbet to the ground after execution, or rather by some impetuous blow on that place received from some hard or solid thing.

In further support of his argument, Mauriceau informed his readers of his practice of having his hospital patients walk from the birth room back to their bedroom immediately after delivery, perhaps the first record of early ambulation in organized obstetrics.

Gynecologic Observations

In 1694 Mauriceau published his *Aphorismes Touchant la Grossesse, l'Accouchement, les Maladies et les autres Indispositions des Femmes*, in which he demonstrated a familiarity with gynecologic problems as well. Among his numerous observations he gave the first clear reference to membranous dysmenorrhea and called attention to the significance of postmenopausal bleeding as a probable sign of genital cancer.

With Mauriceau's constantly growing fame came an ever-increasing demand for his services as a consultant, leading him finally to the decision to abandon his lucrative practice and retire to the country, where he enjoyed several years of leisure before his death, October 17, 1709.

REFERENCES

1. Bayle and Thillaye *Biographie Médicale*. Paris, France, Adolphe Delahays, 1855.
2. Fasbender, H. *Geschichte der Geburtshülfe*. Jena, Germany, Fischer, 1906.
3. Guillemeau, J. *De la Grossesse et Accouchement des Femmes*. Paris, France, Abraham Pacard, 1609 (Ed. 2, 1621). Translated by A. Hatfield: *Childbirth, or the Happy Deliverie of Women*. London, England, 1612.

4. Klein, G. Zur Geschichte der Extraktion und Expression des nachfolgenden Kopfes. *München med. Wchnschr.* 49:1307, 1902.
5. Le Prieur, E. *Étude sur l'oeuvre de François Mauriceau.* Thesis. Paris, France, 1902.
6. Mauriceau, F. *Traité des Maladies des Femmes Grosses, et de Celles Qui Sont Accouchées.* Paris, France, 1668. Translated by H. Chamberlen: *The Diseases of Women with Child and in Child-bed.* London, B. Billingsley, 1673.
7. Mauriceau, F. *Observations sur la Grossesse et l'Accouchement des Femmes.* Paris, France, 1694.
8. Robb, H. *The writings of Mauriceau.* Bull. *Johns Hopkins Hosp.* 6:51, 1895.

Obstet Gynecol 1957;9:371–6.

Reinier de Graaf and the Graafian Follicles

Harold Speert, MD

MAY 1956

he *graafian follicle*, like *fallopian tube*, belongs to that select group of eponymics which, through long usage and universal acceptance, are no longer capitalized in spelling. The story of the graafian follicle comprises an exciting chapter in man's long search for the mammalian egg, an effort that engaged his attention for two millennia. The highlights of this search have been narrated with charm and authority by George Corner in one of his delightful essays on the history of medicine.[1]

According to the views of Aristotle, long accepted by succeeding generations, the mammalian egg was formed in the uterus as the result of activation of the menstrual blood by the male semen. This theory was seriously disputed for the first time by Galen, who thought that the female semen, like the male semen, was made in the blood vessels supplying the gonad, in which organ the semen was strained and purified. The semen elaborated by the ovary, according to Galen, was then transmitted via the tubes to the uterus, where admixture with the male semen produced a coagulum from which the embryo evolved.

The presence of vesicles in the female testes was mentioned in the sixteenth-century writings of Vesalius and his disciple, Falloppio, but these Paduan anatomists had no thought of the true function of the fluid-filled structures. Falloppio's successor, Fabricius ab Aquapendente, described the hen's ovary and even gave it the name *ovarium*, recognizing it as the organ of egg formation. But so strongly entrenched was the Aristotelian teaching that the egg was formed in the uterus that Fabricius naturally believed the ovary to be simply a part of the brood chamber. According to La Torre, Gian Matteo de Gradi of Milan, also known as Ferrari d'Agrate (died 1480), had long before applied the name *ovary* to the female testis and, by analogy with the hen, assumed its egg-producing function in other species.[4]

The latter part of the seventeenth century witnessed a resurgence of the idea that the mammalian female testes, like the ovaries of birds, are the site of egg formation. Swammerdam and Van Horne, working together in Leyden in 1666, and the Danish anatomist Stensen in 1667, independently developed this theory in relation to the human and exchanged letters concerning their views. Stensen, "for friendship's sake," acceded to Swammerdam's brazen request that he and Van Horne be permitted to publish a proposed book on the subject, in preparation by Van Horne, before Stensen; but Van Horne never completed it and died in 1670, the book remaining unpublished.

Two years later there appeared a brilliant volume by Reinier de Graaf, his third, entitled *De Mulierum organis generationi inservientibus* (Figs. 1 and 2), Chapter XII of which was devoted to the female testes. Here, with due credit to Van Horne, de Graaf advanced the evidence that this organ is indeed an ovary and in it he described the follicles which have ever since been associated with his name.

After describing the gross morphologic characteristics and anatomic relations of the female testes and contrasting them with the male, de Graaf proceeded to the internal structure of the organ, illustrating the chapter

Fig. 1. Frontispiece from *De Mulierum organis.*

Fig. 2. Title page of *De Mulierum organis.*

with drawings of the bisected ovaries of the cow, sheep, and human (Fig. 3). Of the follicles, he wrote:

> The normal structures, regularly found in the membranous substance of the testicles just described, are vesicles full of liquor, nerves, and nutritive vessels, which run to the testes in almost the same way as in males ... and course throughout the whole of their substance, and enter the vesicles, within whose tunics many branches end after free division, in just the same way as we have seen happening in the ovaries of fowls composed of clustered egg yolks....

These vesicles have been described under various names by Vesalius, Fallopius ... and others, whose accounts it would be too tedious to repeat here in full. ... Some call these vesicles hydatids, but the celebrated Dr. Van Horne in his *Prodromum* preferred to call them *ova*, a term which, since it seems to me more convenient than the others, we shall in the future use, and we shall call these vesicles *ova* as does that distinguished man, on account of the exact similitude which they exhibit to the eggs contained in the ovaries of birds; for these, while they are still small, contain nothing but a thin liquor like albumen. That albumen is actually contained in the ova of women will be beautifully demonstrated if the ova are boiled, for the liquor contained in the ova of the testicles acquires upon cooking the same color, the same taste and consistence as the albumen contained in the eggs of birds.

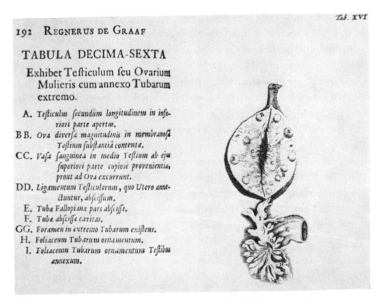

Fig. 3. Illustration of bisected human ovary from *De Mulierum organis*.

It is of no importance that the ova of women are not, like those of fowls, enveloped in a hard shell, for the latter are incubated outside the body in order to hatch the chickens, but the former remain within the female body during development, and are protected as thoroughly from all external injuries by the uterus as by a shell....

These ova arise and are developed in the testes in exactly the same way as the eggs in the ovaries of birds, inasmuch as the blood flowing to the testes through the nutritive arteries deposits in their membranous substance materials suitable for the formation and nourishment of the ova, and the residual humors are carried back to the heart through the nutritive veins or lymphatic vessels....

Thus, the general function of the female testicles is to generate the ova, to nourish them, and to bring them to maturity, so that they serve the same purpose in women as the ovaries of birds. Hence, they should rather be called ovaries than testes because they show no similarity, either in form or contents, with the male testes....*

De Graaf's great mistake, now obvious, but one which can scarcely fail to arouse our sympathy as a natural conclusion in a premicroscopic era, was his assumption that the entire follicle was the ovum. We can only surmise how many troubled hours he must have spent in an unsuccessful effort to reconcile this concept with his observations on early rabbit embryos. Examining the contents of the doe's genital tract at different time intervals after mating, he recovered nothing in animals killed during the first 2 days; on the third day after coitus he found only tiny spherical masses in the fallopian tubes, and only slightly larger spheres in the uterus on the following day. De Graaf had unwittingly made the first discovery of tubal ova and supplied the potential, crucial evidence that the embryo begins to develop before reaching the uterus.

Only a few weeks after the publication of de Graaf's book the irate Swammerdam, whose priority of publication had been thwarted by the procrastination of his erstwhile collaborator, Van Horne, issued a bitterly worded pamphlet impugning de Graaf's personal integrity as well as the scientific accuracy of his observations and claiming for himself the credit for discovery of the ovarian function of the female testis. Diemerbroeck, Professor of Anatomy at Utrecht, who knew both contestants, remarked that Swammerdam had "smeared the ovary, not with honey, but with the bitterest gall." Swammerdam had made his bid too late; and de Graaf was rewarded with eponymic immortality.

Excerpts from the English translation of Chapter XII of De Mulierum organis *by G. W. Corner.[2] An earlier translation, by R. Knox, is to be found in* The British Record of Obstetric Medicine and Surgery, Vol. I, 1848.

More original than his thoughts concerning the ovarian follicles were de Graaf's observations on the corpus luteum, of which he gave the first detailed description, calling it the *substantia glandulosa*. He believed that each egg (follicle) was surrounded by this glandular substance which, as it ripened and moved toward the surface of the ovary, forced the egg out. His erroneous assumption that the presence of a corpus luteum implies impregnation was doubtless based on his study of rabbits, in which species ovulation normally occurs only after coital stimulation. He wrote:

> These structures [corpora lutea] which, though normal, are only at certain times found in the testes of women, are globular bodies in the form of conglomerate glandulae which are composed of many particles, extending from the center to the circumference in straight rows, and are enveloped by a special membrane. We assert that these globules do not exist at all times in the testicles of females; on the contrary, they are only detected in them after coitus [being one], or more in number, according as the animal brings forth one or more foetuses from that congress. Nor are these always of the same nature in all animals, or in the same kind of animal; for in cows they exhibit a yellow color, in sheep red, in others ashen; because a few days after coitus they are composed of a thinner substance and contain in their interior a limpid liquor enclosed in a membrane, which when ejected with the membrane leaves only a small space within the body which gradually disappears, so that in the latter months of gestation they seem to be composed of a solid substance; but when the foetus is delivered these globular bodies again diminish and finally disappear.

De Graaf and his contemporary scientific world thought that the mammalian ovum and its ovarian origin had been demonstrated; yet a century and a half later, in 1821, a contest was sponsored by the Göttingen Academy of Sciences offering a prize for the discovery of its site of formation. The prize was awarded, 3 years later, to the author of a paper proving that the ovum is formed in the uterus!

Our story concludes about the first of May, 1827. Karl Ernst von Baer, studying the embryology of the dog, had departed slightly from the usual procedure of examining the embryos in sequential stages of development and was working backward instead, taking the later stages first. After he had studied the free blastocysts in the fallopian tubes, as others had done before him in other species, he stated:

> The next step was to learn the state of the ova in the ovary, for it is very clear that such minute eggs cannot be the graafian follicles themselves expelled from the ovary, nor does it seem likely that such solid corpuscles as we find the tubal ova to be are formed by coagulation of the follicular fluid. Examining the ovaries before making any incision I saw plainly in almost every follicle a yellowish-white point.... Led by curiosity rather than

by any thought that I had seen the ovules in the ovaries through all the layers of the graafian follicle, I opened one of the follicles and took up the minute object on the point of my knife, finding that I could see it very distinctly and that it was surrounded by mucus. When I placed it under the microscope I was utterly astonished, for I saw an ovule just as I had already seen them in the tubes, and so clearly that a blind man could hardly deny it. It is truly wonderful and surprising to be able to demonstrate to the eye, by so simple a procedure, a thing which has been sought so persistently, and discussed *ad nauseam* in every text-book of physiology, as insoluble!

Reinier de Graaf* was born in Schoonhaven, Holland, July 30, 1641. After completing his early studies in Delft, he continued his training in France under de la Boë, then returned to Delft where he entered the private practice of medicine. When only 23 years old, and while still a student, he published his famous *De natura et usu succi pancreatici*, which reported his pancreatic fistula experiments and established the digestive function of the pancreatic juice. He subsequently studied the functions of the bile by the same method. Four years later, in 1668, his *De virorum organis generationi inservientibus* appeared, dealing with the anatomy of the male genital organs and giving especially good descriptions of the vasa deferentia and the spermatic tubules of the testicle.

It was his *De mulierum organis*, however, published in 1672, which achieved for de Graaf his greatest renown. This volume contains a full and remarkably accurate account of the female reproductive organs, including certain gynecologic disorders, and is beautifully illustrated with detailed drawings (Fig. 4). In it he described the pelvic blood supply, the lymphatic system of the uterus, and the crura of the clitoris, in addition to the ovaries and their function. He also reported on prolapse, myoma, and closure of the fallopian tubes, illustrating the last condition with excellent drawings (Fig. 5), probably the first recorded of this common affliction, with the titles *Oviductus extremum Testibus Naturam agglutinatum* and *Oviductus extremitas praeter Naturam clausa*. Gonorrhea was not mentioned by de Graaf as the cause of tubal closure, but he clearly recognized the paraurethral ducts as a focus of this disease.

De Graaf had been deeply aggrieved by Swammerdam's reckless and damaging charges against him; and although de Graaf published a pamphlet in his own defense which convincingly absolved him of all taint of plagiarism or dishonor, he continued to brood over the affair. Some believe that his continuing preoccupation with this unpleasant incident was a factor in his premature death on August 17, 1673, at the age of only 32 years.

The first name is variously spelled Regner, Regnier, Reinier, *and* Reijnier, *and on the title page of his publications, written in Latin,* Regnerus.

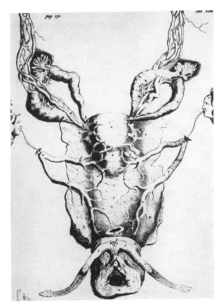

Fig. 4. One of the anatomic drawings of the female generative organs in *De Mulierum organis*.

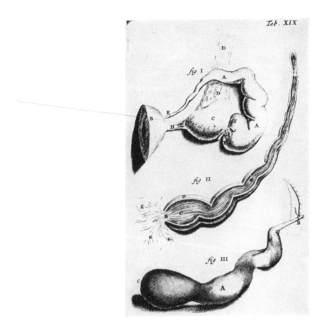

Fig. 5. Probably the first illustration of closure of the fallopian tubes, from *De Mulierum organis*.

REFERENCES

1. Corner, G. W. "The discovery of the mammalian ovum." In *Lectures on the History of Medicine: A Series of Lectures at the Mayo Foundation*, 1926–1932. Philadelphia, Saunders, 1933.

2. Corner, G. W. "On the female testes or ovaries. By Regner de Graaf." In *Essays in Biology, in Honor of Herbert M. Evans*. Berkeley, Calif., Univ. California Press, 1943, pp. 121–37.

3. De Graaf, R. *De mulierum organis generationi inservientibus*. Leyden, Holland, 1672.

4. Leonardo, R. A. *History of Gynecology*. New York, Froben, 1944.

5. von Baer, K. E. *Di ovi mammalium et hominis genesi*. Leipsig, Germany, 1827.

Obstet Gynecol 1956;7:582–8.

Carl Siegmund Franz Credé, Placental Expression, and the Prevention of Neonatal Ophthalmia

Harold Speert, MD

September 1957

xpulsion of the placenta, the denouement to the birth act, varies like the latter from a simple, rapid process to a tedious, delayed effort that may tax the skill and judgment of the obstetrician and the patience of the parturient and her family. Harried by the fear of uterine bleeding that may result from retention of the afterbirth, doctors and midwives alike have resorted to a variety of technics, often forceful, to expedite the delivery of that organ. Most textbooks of the early nineteenth century advocated a waiting period of five to ten minutes after the birth of the infant, for separation of the placenta. Combined external and internal palpation then disclosed its location; if already in the vagina it was delivered with the assistance of the intravaginal fingers and traction on the cord. This method, while simple enough when carried out by the expert, was dangerous in the hands of the inexperienced or the impatient, leading occasionally to avulsion of the cord, laceration and incomplete removal of the placenta, injuries to the cervix and lower uterine segment, and even inversion of the uterus.

Expression of the Placenta

Carl Credé sought to eliminate these hazards in 1854, substituting for vaginal extraction of the placenta its abdominal expression by a method[2] with which his name has since been associated. Credé pointed out the dangers of a prolonged third stage and outlined his method of placental expression in the following words:

> In most cases the placenta is expressed from the uterus by spontaneous postpartum contractions after about a quarter-hour. Even if the third stage lasts a long time it is not necessarily harmful to the parturient.... However, hemorrhage can occur at any moment; and the longer time elapsed after birth of the child the more difficult is artificial removal of the placenta from the uterine cavity, should this become necessary.... In order not to leave the parturient too long in an agitated state of worry over the final stage of labor, and at the same time not to keep the physician needlessly

Fig. 1. Title page of Credé's textbook, in which his method of placental expression is first described.

from other important professional duties ... it is quite proper and legitimate to expedite artificially the desultory process of nature. The intervention necessary to bring forth the separated placenta from the maternal birth canal is so slight that it is inconsequential in comparison to the hazards of delayed spontaneous expulsion. The simplest and most natural means of artificial delivery of the placenta consists in the stimulation and augmentation of the lazy uterine contractions. A single vigorous contraction of the uterus brings the whole process to a speedy termination. In a countless number of cases without exception, I have succeeded in producing an artificial and strong contraction a quarter- to half-hour after birth of the child, by means of massage of the fundus and body of the uterus through the abdominal wall, gently at first and then progressively more vigorously. As soon as it reached the peak of its contraction, I grasped the whole uterus with my entire hand, so that the fundus lay in my palm with my five fingers surrounding the corpus, and then exerted gentle pressure. Under my fingers I always felt the placenta glide out of the uterus, and indeed this usually occurred with such force that the placenta appeared immediately at the external genitalia, or at least in the lower vagina. The patient experienced no more discomfort from the manual grasp than from the pain that accompanies the firm uterine contraction. Moreover it is unnecessary to disturb her by inserting the finger or hand into the sensitive genital organs in order to remove the placenta by forceful pulling and tugging.

In his subsequent teaching,[3] Credé emphasized the importance of selecting the proper moment for the application of pressure, only at the height of a contraction, and the futility of pressure on the relaxed organ.

Apparently unbeknown to Credé was the fact that a similar method of placental expression had been used many years earlier by Samuel Bard and by John Harvie. Bard, author of the first textbook of obstetrics published in America, wrote in 1807, in his instructions to the midwife for delivering the placenta:

> If, on the contrary, she cannot reach the root of the string, let her examine the patient's belly; she probably will find the womb soft and flaccid, resting on the lower side, or perhaps hanging a little over the pubes; by taking it in the hollow of her hand, compressing it moderately, raising it up towards its natural position, and at the same time rubbing the surface briskly with the hand, she will soon perceive the womb to contract in size, and to assume the form of a ball of considerable firmness; after this, a very few pains will probably deliver the placenta.

Even earlier, in 1767, John Harvie, a nephew by marriage of William Smellie, had written:

> There is another safe method of assisting nature in the delivery of the *placenta*, and which, for these five or six years last past, I have found to answer generally very well in practice. As soon as the child is committed to the care of the nurse, let the accoucheur apply his hand upon the belly of the woman, which is then very loose, and he will readily feel the contracting *uterus*: then having placed the flat of the hand over it, let him, by a light and gentle pressure, bring it downwards, or towards the *pubes*, and he will feel the uterus sensibly contracting, and often will feel it so reduced in size, as to be certain that the *placenta* is expelled. By this method we will seldom have anything to do afterwards, but to help it through the *os externum*, if even so much remains undone.

Historians have not overlooked Harvie's and Bard's priority in advocating abdominal expression of the placenta by means of the contracted uterus, but the procedure still retains its popular designation as the *Credé maneuver*.

PREVENTION OF OPHTHALMIA NEONATORUM

The name of Credé is also associated eponymically with one of the most important advances in obstetric practice of the nineteenth century, the prevention of gonococcal ophthalmia in the newborn. As early as 1854 Credé had recognized inflammatory lesions of the mother's lower genital tract as the source of this scourge, the commonest cause of blindness in infants, for in his *Klinische Vorträge*[2] he wrote:

At the same time, the effect on the fetus must not be overlooked; for during the act of birth the infant's eyelids are coated with the corrosive mucus, which then becomes continuous with the conjunctiva and thus becomes the most frequent cause of blennorrhea.

It was not until a quarter-century later, however, that Credé hit upon an effective method of prophylaxis, his first definitive paper on the subject appearing in 1881.[4] The following quotations are taken from it:

> Eye inflammations in the newborn in general occur less often in the upper classes, most often in the proletariat; in the lying-in hospitals they are associated with a rapidly progressive and very serious disturbance. Therefore, in order to test further the method of prophylaxis recommended by me, I direct my attention at the very outset to those colleagues who work in lying-in hospitals or obstetrical clinics and, like me, frequently see diseases.
>
> Probably shared by most obstetricians will be my view that the exceedingly common catarrhal conditions and inflammations of the vagina result from gonorrhea, and that the infectiousness of the discharge continues long after the specific gonorrheal manifestations have disappeared; indeed that infection is still present in the maternal vagina, even in cases where almost no discharge is any longer to be found, if an eye inflammation develops within the first few days after birth.

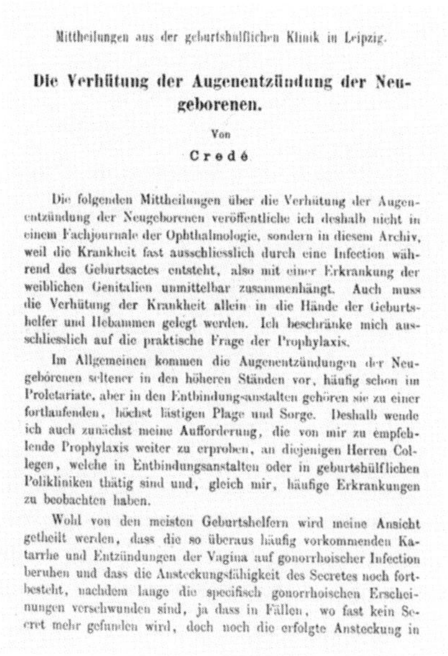

Mittheilungen aus der geburtshülflichen Klinik in Leipzig.

Die Verhütung der Augenentzündung der Neugeborenen.

Von

Credé

Die folgenden Mittheilungen über die Verhütung der Augenentzündung der Neugeborenen veröffentliche ich deshalb nicht in einem Fachjournale der Ophthalmologie, sondern in diesem Archiv, weil die Krankheit fast ausschliesslich durch eine Infection während des Geburtsactes entsteht, also mit einer Erkrankung der weiblichen Genitalien unmittelbar zusammenhängt. Auch muss die Verhütung der Krankheit allein in die Hände der Geburtshelfer und Hebammen gelegt werden. Ich beschränke mich ausschliesslich auf die praktische Frage der Prophylaxis.

Im Allgemeinen kommen die Augenentzündungen der Neugeborenen seltener in den höheren Ständen vor, häufig schon im Proletariate, aber in den Entbindungsanstalten gehören sie zu einer fortlaufenden, höchst lästigen Plage und Sorge. Deshalb wende ich auch zunächst meine Aufforderung, die von mir zu empfehlende Prophylaxis weiter zu erproben, an diejenigen Herren Collegen, welche in Entbindungsanstalten oder in geburtshülflichen Polikliniken thätig sind und, gleich mir, häufige Erkrankungen zu beobachten haben.

Wohl von den meisten Geburtshelfern wird meine Ansicht getheilt werden, dass die so überaus häufig vorkommenden Katarrhe und Entzündungen der Vagina auf gonorrhoischer Infection beruhen und dass die Ansteckungsfähigkeit des Secretes noch fortbesteht, nachdem lange die specifisch gonorrhoischen Erscheinungen verschwunden sind, ja dass in Fällen, wo fast kein Secret mehr gefunden wird, doch noch die erfolgte Ansteckung in

Fig. 2. Title page of Credé's first paper describing his method of prophylaxis against ophthalmia of the newborn.

In the Leipzig Lying-in Hospital the possibility of transmission of infectious material from another infant with infected eyes can be completely excluded, for every child with infected eyes is removed with its mother to the infirmary, which is completely isolated from the section for postpartum patients. Furthermore, the puerperae can scarcely infect the infants by means of their fingers, which might be contaminated with lochia, because the infants always lie so far away from the mothers in their beds that the mothers cannot reach them, only coming in contact with the infants when they are put to the breast by the attendants.

I thus came to the conclusion ... that, almost without exception, the affected infants in my institution become infected only through direct transfer of the vaginal discharge into their eyes during the act of birth....

For a long time I occupied myself with the important problem of finding ways and means for preventing the illness ruinous to so many eyes, for best getting at the infecting discharge.

My first efforts included the most meticulous management and as thorough a cleansing as possible of the vagina of the pregnant and parturient patients. The results, however, were meager, not satisfactory. The eye infections declined in number, but they did not disappear. I then began disinfecting the infant's eyes themselves, and henceforth the results became surprisingly favorable....

In October, 1879 I made the first experiment with prophylactic instillations into the eyes of the newborn immediately after birth, using a solution of borax (1:60), which I considered the mildest, least caustic agent. At first this was done only to the infants of affected mothers, in whom vaginal irrigations had also been carried out during the entire labor. But this procedure too did not lead to the desired goal; and from December, 1879 instead of the borax I used solutions of silver nitrate (1:40), which was squirted into the eyes immediately after birth. Before the instillation the eyes were carefully washed with a solution of salicylic acid (2:100). The infants of affected mothers treated in this manner remained well; while other infants who had not been treated prophylactically because we did not consider their mothers to be affected, continue to get sick....

From June 1, 1880 on, all eyes without exception were disinfected immediately after birth with a weak solution of silver nitrate (1:50). However, the solution was no longer squirted in, but only a few drops of it were instilled, by means of a small glass tube, into each eye, previously cleansed as before and gently held open by an assistant. The eyes were then soothed for 24 hours with linen compresses soaked in salicylic solution (2:100). The repeated vaginal douches were then given up entirely.... All the infants treated in this manner remained spared from eye inflammations, even of the slightest degree, although many of the mothers showed vaginal blenorrhea and trachomatous proliferations....

Credé closed his case with the following tabular presentation of the incidence of ophthalmia neonatorum in his hospital during the recent years preceding and in the 6 months following the routine application of his new method of prophylaxis:

Years	No. of births	Cases of ophthalmia	Percent
1874	323	45	13.6
1875	287	37	12.9
1876	367	29	9.1
1877	360	30	8.3
1878	353	35	9.8
1879	389	36	9.2
1880 to May 31	187	14	7.6
1880 June 1 to Dec. 8	200	1*	0.5

*In this case the eyes were not disinfected; therefore the true incidence should be considered 0.0%.

Later in the same year (1881), Credé published a supplementary report[5] of 400 new cases, 300 of which were treated by a simplified technic, again without a single case of ophthalmia resulting. His final paragraph concluded with the prophetic words:

A goal long striven for has been attained. Now all infants born in lying-in hospitals are sure to be protected ... this prophylactic measure cannot fail to blaze a trail for itself in private practice. May this soon come about!

LIFE OF CARL CREDÉ

Carl Siegmund Franz Credé was born on December 23, 1819, in Berlin, Germany, where his father, a French immigrant, held a high position in the ministry of health and education.[6, 8, 9] After attending the Friedrich-Wilhelm Gymnasium, young Credé entered the study of medicine at the University of Berlin, but spent one semester in Heidelberg, where he met the illustrious Naegele. Graduation at age 22 was followed by visits to the clinics in Belgium, Paris, Vienna, and Italy, after which Credé returned to Berlin with the hope of obtaining a position in the surgical clinic. Finding no opening at the time, he accepted an assistantship in obstetrics under Professor von Busch and remained at this post for the next five years.

In 1849 Credé qualified as an independent lecturer in obstetrics. His first class began with only four students but rapidly increased in size as his teaching ability became recognized. Three years later, in 1852, he was appointed Director of the School for Midwives in Berlin and Chief Physician to the Charité Hospital. Here he established a gynecologic department, the first separate and exclusive department of its kind in continental Europe. In 1856 Credé was called to Leipzig to fill the chair of obstetrics vacated by the death of Jörg. Remaining here for the rest of his professional life, he continued to demonstrate an unusual talent for organization and administration until poor health forced his retirement in 1887. His illness proved painful and lingering, and he finally died of prostatic cancer on March 14, 1892.

With von Busch, von Ritgen, and von Siebold, Credé served as coeditor of the *Monatsschrift für Geburtskunde*, and when this was succeeded by the *Archiv für Gynäkologie*, Credé served as its editor for 39 years, initially as coeditor with Spiegelberg, and alone after the latter's death. Among the distinguished obstetricians trained by Credé were Ahlfeld, Fehling, Leopold, and Sänger. Credé was the first to introduce the cephalotribe into Germany, but this was soon replaced by the cranioclast. His principle literary works were his three books: the 2-volume *Klinische Vorträge über Geburtshülfe* (1854); his *Lehrbuch der Hebammenkunst* (1875), which went through five editions; and his *Gesunde und Kranke Wöchnerinnen* (1886), which warned against unnecessary internal examinations as a cause of puerperal infection. Credé's most enduring contribution to posterity was his method of eradicating gonococcal ophthalmia, the commonest cause of blindness in children.

REFERENCES

1. Bard, S. *A Compendium of the Theory and Practice of Midwifery, Containing Practical Instructions for the Management of Women During Pregnancy, in Labor, and in Child-Bed; Calculated to Correct the Errors, and to Improve the Practice, of Midwives; As well as to Serve as an Introduction to the Study of this Art, for Students and Young Practitioners.* New York, Collins and Perkins, 1807.

2. Credé, C. S. F. *Klinische Vorträge über Geburtshülfe.* Berlin, Germany, Hirschwald, 1854.

3. Credé, C. S. F. *In* Versammlung deutscher Naturforscher und Aerzte in Königsberg im Jahre 1860. Verhandlungen der Section für Gynäkologie. Sept. 17 meeting. *Monatsschr. Geburtsk. u. Frauenk.* pp. 337–342, 1860.

4. Credé, C. S. F. Die Verhütung der Augenentzündung der Neugeborenen. *Arch. f. Gynäk. 17:*50, 1881.

5. Credé, C. S. F. Die Verhütung der Augenentzündung der Neugeborenen. *Arch. f. Gynäk. 18:*367, 1881.

6. Findley, P. *Priests of Lucina: The Story of Obstetrics.* Boston, Little, 1939.

7. Harvie, J. *Practical Directions, Shewing a Method of Preserving the Perinaeum in Birth, and Delivering the Placenta Without Violence.* London, D. Wilson and G. Nicol, 1767.

8. Leopold, G. Carl Siegmund Franz Credé. Gedächtnissrede gesprochen in der gynäkologischen Gesellschaft in Dresden am 14 April 1892. *Arch. f. Gynäk.* *42*:193, 1892.

9. Simpson, A. R. Presidential address. *Tr. Edinburgh Obst. Soc. 18*:5, 1893.

Obstet Gynecol 1957;10:335–9.

Alfred Hegar: Hegar's Sign and Dilators

Harold Speert, MD

DECEMBER 1955

cientific discoveries and inventions, although built upon the earlier labors of others, are usually credited to him who first proclaims his findings to the world or records his work in the published press. Yet medical history contains numerous instances of misplaced credit for priority in original observations. It has been pointed out in an earlier essay, for example, that the inguinal ligament, although commonly associated with the name of Poupart, was described many years earlier by Falloppio. Another possible inequity in obstetric terminology may be embodied in Hegar's sign, universally recognized as an early indication of pregnancy.

HEGAR'S SIGN

Hegar's sign, a selective softening of the uterus in the region of the lower segment, resulting in an increased mobility between the cervix and the corpus, was actually described first by C. Reinl, one of Hegar's assistants, who published this observation (Fig. 1) in 1884 as a new and certain diagnostic sign of pregnancy:

> Apart from the general disturbances in the sense of well-being, amenorrhea, changes in the breasts and external genitalia, alterations in the consistency of the enlarging uterine corpus and the cervix, we have no further diagnostic signs for the early months of pregnancy.
>
> The discovery of a new sign should therefore be of particular value, since some of the above-mentioned local changes are often absent or are only present in slight degree, or, in multiparas, are not always reliable.
>
> Last winter, in Professor Hegar's gynecological clinic, I had the opportunity of acquainting myself with a new and excellent sign of the early months of pregnancy.
>
> This consists in the demonstration of an unusual softness, flexibility, and thinning of the lower uterine segment, that is, of the part directly above the insertion of the uterosacral ligaments.

Fig. 1. The initial description of Hegar's sign, by C. Reinl, in June, 1884.

This finding is not only demonstrable when the rest of the uterus feels firm, as is often the case, but also very definitely when it is soft and elastic. Also, in the latter case it is always possible to compress the lower uterine segment, to actually thin it out with the finger, and so to differentiate it from the upper part of the uterus, while it still clearly differs in consistency from the cervix below. The pliability and laxness of these parts can be so extensive that one may be in doubt as to whether any connection exists between the cervix and the larger abdominal or pelvic mass.

We know of no condition which can produce findings similar to pregnancy; solid tumors certainly do not, and hemato- and hydro-metra present no diagnostic difficulties. Our sign can therefore be used with confidence for the differential diagnosis of pregnancy.

This remarkable development results from the fact that the lower uterine segment becomes the most attenuated and elastic part of the entire uterus during pregnancy; therefore, as one can easily demonstrate, it is possible, after displacing the uterus upward, to grasp the lower segment between the finger of the vaginal and abdominal hands, compress it, and completely thin it out.

Absence of this sign does not, however, exclude pregnancy by any means, for one can easily imagine that with chronic infarction of the lower uterine segment pregnancy could occur without this change being demonstrable.

It is not clear, from this account, whether Reinl discovered this sign of pregnancy himself or whether it was pointed out to him by Hegar. It was the latter, however, who taught and publicized it until it eventually came to bear his name, while Reinl's possible role in the discovery has been completely overshadowed by the celebrated name of his master. Hegar's own paper[1] on the subject, with illustrative diagrams, did not appear until 1895, 11 years after Reinl's. In it he acknowledged Reinl's priority of publication, but strongly implied that recognition of the significance of the pregnancy change in the lower segment was his (Hegar's):

> Fortunately we have still another diagnostic aid, which is based on the compressibility of the lower uterine segment. I was led to this while reading an article by A. Martin in which he describes an hypertrophy of the cervix, as a result of which the connection between the soft lower uterine segment and the cervix can only be demonstrated with difficulty.

Martin, whose paper was published in 1881, had reported 7 cases, regarding them as unusual, in which he observed a peculiar hypertrophy of the supravaginal part of the cervix during pregnancy. He discussed the possible diagnostic significance of this change when present but seemed uncertain of its practical clinical value.

Credit for Hegar's sign should therefore probably be divided among three men: Martin, who first called attention to the selective pregnancy change in the lower uterine segment; Reinl, who stressed the specificity of this change and its value for the early diagnosis of pregnancy, and first published on it; and Hegar, who later popularized it.

HEGAR'S CERVICAL DILATORS

Hegar is also identified today with the curved metal cervical dilators (Fig. 2) which bear his name. The development of this type of instrument represented a great advance over the laminaria tents formerly used to dilate the cervix, often with severe parametritis resulting. The first recorded reference to Hegar's dilators appeared in 1879 in an article by Tchoudowski, who had seen the dilators in use while visiting Hegar's clinic in the summer of that year. Hegar's own description of the dilators was published for the first time in the second edition of his textbook on operative gynecology, published with Kaltenbach as coauthor in 1881:

> We have used this method of dilatation many times in recent years and found it to be very satisfactory. That it has not been generally adopted as yet is probably due in large measure to unsatisfactory technique and imperfect instruments. One must have a large number of dilators at hand, each one of which that is introduced having only a slightly greater diameter than the previous one. This is essential at least for difficult cases. We have therefore had solid, cylindrical dilators made out of ebonite with conically

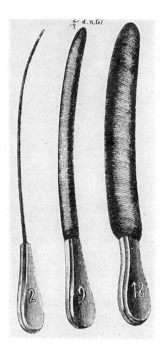

Fig. 2. Hegar's original dilators, as illustrated in his *Operative Gynäkologie*, published in 1881.

tapering ends. They are about 12–14 cm. long, in addition to a flattened handle, which is about 5 cm. long. The smallest dilator is 2 mm. in diameter. The rest are graduated in diameters which increase progressively only 1 mm. at a time. The increase in circumference is therefore about 3 mm. It is even better to order dilators which increase only 0.5 mm. at a time. At least the dilatation will then be easier in difficult cases. For gynecological purposes, namely for manipulation of the uterus, a dilator with a 16–17 mm. diameter, suffices. Even the first phalanx of a thick index finger can then be inserted into the uterine cavity. Even more marked dilatation can easily be achieved with larger dilators, which we have provided for up to a diameter of 26 mm. for gynecological purposes. For obstetrical purposes, for example for use with placenta previa, larger dilators are sometimes necessary. For injections into the uterine cavity, cauterizations with silver nitrate or nitric acid, use of the curette, introduction of a small polyp forceps, etc., 6–12 mm. dilators suffice. Likewise for cervical stenosis or with the view of stretching the canal to somewhat more than its usual lumen.

In the notes accompanying this description of the dilators, reference is made to graduated metal dilators previously described by others, the earliest description of similar instruments being attributed to Peaslee.

Peaslee, while Professor of Diseases of Women in Dartmouth College, had published in 1870 a description of his set of 5 steel dilators, ranging from ⅛ to ⁵⁄₁₆ inch in diameter. Each dilator had a bulb 1 ¾ inch from its uterine end, to prevent "needless intrusion into the uterine cavity." This author, in turn, had called attention to a description by Kammerer in the previous year of a similar type of dilator. We see, therefore, that the principle of progressive cervical dilatation by graduated metal sounds had been described in the literature 10 years before Tchoudowski's publication first announcing Hegar's dilators.*

THE LIFE AND ACHIEVEMENTS OF ALFRED HEGAR

Alfred Hegar was born in Darmstadt, Germany, January 6, 1830, the son of a general practitioner. He studied in Giessen, Heidelberg, Berlin, and Vienna, receiving his medical degree in 1852. After a brief stint as a military surgeon he returned to practice in his home town, where he soon established himself as a busy obstetrician. He began to write on the pathology of pregnancy in the early 1860's, and his studies on early abortion were so well received that they led to his appointment, in 1864, as Spiegelberg's successor as Professor of Obstetrics and Gynecology at Freiburg, where he remained for 40 years until his retirement in 1904. During this period he helped establish the *Oberrheinische Gesellschaft für Geburtshilfe und Gynäkologie*, and in 1898 he founded and served as editor of the *Beiträge zur Geburtshilfe und Gynäkologie*. When the Universitäts-Frauenklinik was opened in Freiburg in 1868, Hegar was made its first chief. He had the reputation of working himself, as well as his assistants, very hard, often starting his schedule of operations as early as 5 A.M. He died on August 5, 1914, at age 85.[9]

In addition to the early sign of pregnancy and the cervical dilators with which his name is associated, Hegar distinguished himself in several other spheres. He achieved renown for his diagnostic prowess and was said to possess an unusually well developed tactile sense. He was an ardent disciple of Semmelweis and was one of the first to implement the latter's principles of antisepsis. Hegar was a pioneer in the early studies on genital tuberculosis in women. He was probably best known among his contemporaries for his work in operative gynecology. Early in his career his reputation for the successful repair of urinary fistulas became widespread, and women from all parts of Europe sought him out for the correction of this

---

*Graduated dilators of tin or lead, hollow at one end and mounted on long wooden handles, were actually described long before, in the writings of Hippocrates; these dilators being used principally to permit the introduction of various medicaments into the uterine cavity (Ricci, J. R. The Development of Gynecological Surgery and Instruments. *Philadelphia, Blakiston, 1949, p. 13).*

affliction. He devised a perineorrhaphy operation which also bears his name, and was the first in Germany to perform myomectomy. In the treatment of uterine fibroids, however, he is better known for his ovariectomies and for his demonstration that this operation resulted in shrinkage of the tumors and cessation of bleeding. Although McDowell of Kentucky had performed ovariectomy many years before (1809), Hegar (July, 1872) was probably the first to remove normal ovaries to create an artificial menopause, an operation he resorted to frequently in the treatment of dysmenorrhea as well as bleeding uterine fibroids.

A bibliography of Hegar's writings, compiled by his son, was published in 1915,[4] and in 1930 there appeared a *Festschrift*[2] in commemoration of the hundredth anniversary of his birth.

REFERENCES

1. Hegar, A. Diagnose der frühesten Schwangerschaftsperiode. *Deutsche med. Wchnschr. 21*:565, 1895.

2. Hegar, A. *Zum Gedächtnis*. Speyer & Kaerner, Universitäts-Buchhandlung, Freiburg, I. B., 1930.

3. Hegar, A., and Kaltenbach, R. *Die Operative Gynäkologie* (ed. 2). Erlangen, Enke, 1881.

4. Hegar, K. Bibliographie von Alfred Hegar. *Monatsschr. Geburtsh. u. Gynäk. 42:* 543, 1915.

5. Kammerer, J. On the treatment of uterine catarrh. *Am. J. Obst. 2*:185, 1869.

6. Martin, A. Zur Kenntniss der Hypertrophia colli uteri supravaginalis. *Ztschr. f. Geburtsh. u. Gynäkol. 6*:101, 1881.

7. Peaslee, E. R. Intra-uterine medication: Its uses, limitations, and methods. *New York State J. Med. 11*:465, 1870.

8. Reinl, C. Ein neues sicheres diagnostischen Zeichen der Schwangerschaft in den ersten Monaten. *Prag. med. Wchnschr. 9*:253, 1884.

9. Sonntag, B. Alfred Hegar. *Arch. f. Gynäk. 103*:II Heft, 1914.

10. Tchoudowski, M. De la dilatation du canal cervical (d'après Hegar). *Arch. Tocol. 6*:737, 1879. (Reprinted from Gaz. méd. de Strasbourg, 1879.)

Obstet Gynecol 1955;6:679–83.

Alexandre Couvelaire and Uteroplacental Apoplexy

Harold Speert, MD

June 1957

The writer of one of Alexandre Couvelaire's obituaries,[4] in order to emphasize the originality of his subject's observations, stated that even in Germany one would someday speak of the "maladie de Couvelaire." These lines, written about a French patriot shortly after World War II, were intended to stress the importance of Couvelaire's studies on premature separation of the placenta and the universality of the term *Couvelaire uterus.*

In one of his papers on uteroplacental apoplexy,[2] Couvelaire refers to a few previous authors who had already noted, at cesarean section or autopsy, subserosal ecchymoses in the uteri of patients with premature separation of the placenta. The characteristics of the Couvelaire uterus remained unrecognized, however, although this condition was undoubtedly responsible for many of the secondary hemorrhages requiring postpartum hysterectomy in patients with placental abruption. The cataclysmic and extensive hemorrhage into the myometrium, ovaries, broad ligaments, and pelvic peritoneum which occasionally accompany this accident were described for the first time in a detailed case report by Couvelaire in 1911[1] (Fig. 1).

COUVELAIRE'S REPORT ON SURGICAL TREATMENT OF UTEROPLACENTAL HEMORRHAGE

The patient was a 26-year-old primigravida with toxemia of pregnancy who developed signs of retroplacental hemorrhage in the eighth month. Despite artificial rupture of the membranes her condition worsened. The cervix failed to dilate; the uterus, ligneous in consistency, continued to enlarge, and shock rapidly ensued. Although the fetus was known to be dead, as judged by the absence of its heart sounds, Couvelaire undertook to empty the uterus by cesarean section in order to control the retroplacental bleeding. The placenta was found completely separated, the uterine cavity full of blood. Not only was the surface of the uterus covered with subserosal hemorrhages but the myometrium itself, the broad ligaments, and the adnexa appeared to be completely infiltrated with blood. Because

186

TRAITEMENT CHIRURGICAL DES HÉMORRAGIES UTÉRO-PLACENTAIRES AVEC DÉCOLLEMENT DU PLACENTA NORMALEMENT INSÉRÉ

Par A. COUVELAIRE.

A propos d'une observation personnelle d'opération de Porro pour hémorragie utéro-placentaire grave chez une femme enceinte de 8 mois environ, albuminurique et azotémique, je désirerais présenter quelques considérations sur les particularités anatomo-cliniques, de cette observation, et esquisser l'étude du traitement chirurgical des hémorragies rétro-placentaires survenant à la fin de la grossesse ou au cours de l'accouchement.

I. — Observation (1).

1° Partie clinique.

Le 14 décembre 1910, j'étais appelé à la clinique Baudelocque par les chefs de clinique, MM. Lacasse et Pottet, auprès d'une femme albuminurique qui présentait des symptômes d'une hémorragie rétro-placentaire et dont l'état s'aggravait rapidement.

Cette femme, enceinte pour la première fois, est âgée de 26 ans. Elle a été réglée à 18 ans irrégulièrement. Dans ses antécédents pathologiques on ne relève qu'une scarlatine à l'âge de 13 ans.

Les dernières règles dataient du 8 au 16 avril 1910. Dès le début de la grossesse elle avait présenté des céphalées et des vomissements. Vers le 3° mois ces symptômes avaient disparu. A aucun moment elle ne fut examinée.

Elle est venue à la clinique parce qu'elle ressentait des douleurs dans le ventre.

Elle entre dans le service à 2 heures après midi.

Son facies est pâle, toutes les muqueuses sont décolorées. Léger œdème des membres inférieurs. Céphalée. Troubles de la vision (sensation de brouillard devant les yeux). Le pouls est à 90, tendu, régulier.

Le fond de l'utérus remonte à 27 centimètres au-dessus du pubis. Les parois utérines ont une consistance dure et telle que les contractions la modi-

(1) Observation communiquée à la Société obstétricale de France (5-7 octobre 1911).

Fig. 1. Title page of Couvelaire's original paper on uteroplacental apoplexy.[1]

of this, Couvelaire elected to perform hysterectomy and bilateral salpingo-oophorectomy. The patient recovered. Couvelaire's description of the specimen employed the term *uteroplacental apoplexy* for the first time and accurately pictured the hemorrhagic extravasations which have been recognized ever since as the characteristic lesion of the Couvelaire uterus.

The lesions observed during the course of the operation and later on histologic examination could not be exactly characterized by the classic term retroplacental hematoma.

The bloody infiltration was not localized at the placenta and decidua serotina. The whole utero-ovarian apparatus seemed covered with blackish splotches. The uterine wall, in the zone of membranous insertion as well as the zone of placental insertion, was the site of a tremendous bloody infiltration separating the muscle bundles and dissociating some of them fiber from fiber (Fig. 2). The ovaries were peppered with a punctiform bloody suffusion. The broad ligaments were infiltrated with blood.

This was indeed a true case of *uteroplacental apoplexy*. One could do no better than to compare the appearance of these lesions with that of ovarian cysts with a twisted pedicle. However, no analogous position of the pregnant uterus was observed during the operation. The uterus was tilted slightly to the right and dextro-rotated, as is usual during pregnancy.

Histologic examination did not reveal any lesion in the walls of the blood vessels to explain their bursting.

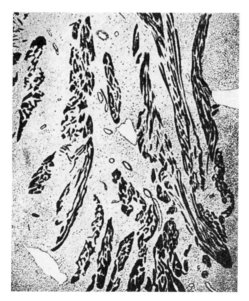

Fig. 2. Illustration from Couvelaire's paper.[1] Section of uterus, showing dissociation of muscle bundles by hemorrhage into myometrium.

These lesions made it extremely unwise to conserve the uterus and suf-
ficed in themselves to justify hysterectomy.

Couvelaire concludes his paper with these recommendations:

1. The anatomical state of the uterine wall alone can make hysterectomy
   necessary.
2. A desire to preserve reproductive function cannot in itself serve as an a
   priori argument in favor of conservative surgery.
3. Surgery must be rapid and provide the maximum degree of security
   with respect to hemostasis during and after the operation.

For all these reasons, it seems to me that for the severe cases in which
uteroplacental hemorrhage clearly dictates surgical treatment, it is wisest to
operate by the abdominal route; it is most prudent to perform a Porro
cesarean section, an operation which is absolutely indicated when the uterine walls are infiltrated with blood.

For four decades Couvelaire's therapeutic recommendations occupied
a prominent place in obstetric practice. In the light of modern knowledge
of blood coagulation, however, and with the present-day availability of
blood for transfusion, blood substitutes, and fibrinogen, they seem unnecessarily radical. Certain it is that Couvelaire's teachings have saved many
maternal lives; it is equally certain that they have been responsible for the
needless removal of many uteri.

THE LIFE OF ALEXANDRE COUVELAIRE

Alexandre Couvelaire was born in Bourg, France, in 1873, the son of a professor.[6] Early in his professional life he came under the influence of Varnier
and later was accepted as an assistant to Pinard. Each of these distinguished French obstetricians exerted a characteristic and permanent
influence on the sensitive, impressionable Couvelaire. From Varnier he
obtained an appreciation of scientific method and precision of thought;
from Pinard, a feeling for the social, humanitarian, and public-health
aspects of obstetrics.

Couvelaire spent his entire professional life in the Baudelocque
Clinic, where he was made chief of clinic in 1901 and from which he did
not retire until October 1, 1943. In 1914 he was appointed Professor in the
University of Paris and was later elected president of the Société
d'Obstétrique et de Gynécologie.

In addition to his studies on placental abruption, Couvelaire is best
known for the special dispensary he organized, together with Marcel
Pinard, for the antisyphilitic treatment of pregnant patients, and for his
establishment of a special pavilion for tuberculous women in his obstetric
clinic, each of these units long serving as a model. Couvelaire was especially accomplished in obstetric surgery and in 1913 published a magnifi-

cently illustrated book, *Introduction à Chirurgie Utérine Obstétricale,*[3] in which his obstetric teachings are set forth. In addition to his radical therapy for premature separation of the placenta, Couvelaire was one of the pioneers in the use of cesarean section for certain cases of placenta previa. Couvelaire went into seclusion following the German occupation of France, and after a long illness, died on March 14, 1948.[5] During his active career he was probably the dominant figure in French obstetrics.

REFERENCES

1. Couvelaire, A. Traitement chirurgical des hémorrhagies utéro-placentaires avec décollement du placenta normalement inséré. *Ann. de Gynéc.* *8*:591,1911.

2. Couvelaire, A. Deux nouvelles observations d'apopléxie utéro-placentaire (hémorrhagies rétro-placentaires avec infiltration sanguine de la paroi musculaire de l'utérus). *Ann. de Gynéc.* *9*:486, 1912.

3. Couvelaire, A. *Introduction à la Chirurgie Utérine Obstétricale.* Paris, G. Steinheil, 1913.

4. Lacomme, M. Alexandre Couvelaire (1873–1948). *Gynéc. et Obst.* *47*:603, 1948.

5. Lepage, F. Alexandre Couvelaire (1873–1948). *Paris méd.* *38*:181, 1948.

6. Portes, W. Alexandre Couvelaire. *Bull. Acad. nat. méd.* *132*:341, 1948.

Obstet Gynecol 1957;9:740–3.

Academia and Medical Education

Albert the Great. Print. National Library, Paris, France. Photo © National Library, Paris.

As obstetrics and gynecology emerged as a specialty, it acquired the academic infrastructure to promote research and education. With this growth came the inevitable pains and eventual rewards as talented physicians joined the specialty. Although the academic component is only a small segment, it usually provides the voice that articulates concerns.

Obstetrics, Cinderella of Medicine

Sam. Gordon Berkow, MD

February 1954

The emergence of obstetrics from a lowly state is almost entirely a phenomenon of the second quarter of the twentieth century. We are very close to the transformation. To appraise it properly we need a yardstick and elbowroom. For perspective, a peep through the keyhole of history is essential. The comparative status of medicine and surgery provides a satisfactory frame of reference.

Long ago, before medicine and surgery splintered into a score of specialties, before surgery left the barber shop and set up its own establishment, and while the medicine man still dealt in witchcraft and incantations, there was the midwife. Even in the Stone Age this progenitor of the obstetrician must have squatted in her patient's cave, tended her fire, and waited for her to give birth.

The witch doctor and the wound healer held this oldest of specialists in contempt. They were better favored than the ancient crone. Their social position and emoluments were superior, for they trafficked in mystery, with the sinister and malign powers of disease, whereas the midwife's services were in connection with a natural phenomenon, commonplace long before the sons of Noah knew their wives and begot.

This disparity continued throughout the ages. When the witch doctor doffed his fearsome mask and donned the chaster vestments of the priest-physician, the sick and the troubled came reverently to his gold and marble temples, bringing rich votive and thank offerings. The surgeon's place, lacking the powerful aids of demonology and theurgy, was less exalted. His prestige had to be won on the battlefields. From the Peloponnesian to the Franco-Prussian Wars, his fortunes vacillated, but were never so low as those of the midwife. She still toiled, actually among the cinders, watching pots of boiling water, snatching her food and rest when she could, waiting for women to have their babies.

After the Franco-Prussian War, during which Lister's principles were first tested on a considerable scale and emerged triumphant, surgery, for the first time in history, overtook and surpassed medicine in popular and professional esteem. But it was not until the first quarter of the present [20th] century that it took a commanding lead. The rapid growth in membership in and influence of surgical organizations, such as the American College of Surgeons, is an instance of this world-wide trend.

Meanwhile, what of obstetrics, with its equal interest in anesthesia and a prior concern with asepsis—the twin discoveries which had made surgery great? Remarking on conditions prevailing at the turn of the century, the White House Conference on Child Health and Protection (1932) reported, "Obstetrics, then commonly termed midwifery, was not attractive. The tedious hours of attendance on confinement, with small fees, did not invite men whose prestige commanded large fees. The general surgeon or the gynecologist did the few cesarean sections which were done. During these years, the obstetrician occupied a menial place, entirely unenviable, in the medical school and hospital, and received scant respect from the public at large."

During the first quarter of this [20th] century these conditions had not improved commensurately with progress in surgery or in clinical or preventive medicine. Midwives and "others," with no training at all, still attended about one-fifth of all births in the United States. In most European countries, the proportion was reversed—midwives attended over 80 per cent of all births. Yet childbed death rates in the United States exceeded those of every European country. To make matters worse, competent authorities estimated that at least two-thirds of such deaths were preventable.

Statistics compiled by Louis I. Dublin show that even as late as 1930, maternal deaths in this country stood at 6.7 per 1000 live births, "only slightly less than the maximum of earlier years." But "after that year mortality from puerperal causes had declined, at first slowly and later more rapidly and without interruption." Remarking on this survey, in 1939, De Lee declared, "It appears ... that the movement for maternal welfare has finally come into its own."

Cinderella had emerged from the kitchen.

The fairy godmother was not plasma or blood transfusion, nor was it the sulfa drugs or antibiotics. These are in the wand which the fairy wielded. They were instrumental, as were advances in obstetric technic. The fairy godmother role was played by the dedicated men, Joseph B. De Lee, Fred L. Adair, and Joseph L. Baer in Chicago, John O. Polak in Brooklyn, Jennings C. Litzenberg in Minnesota, J. Whitridge Williams in Baltimore, Reuben Peterson in Ann Arbor, Walter T. Dannreuther and George W. Kosmak in New York, Edward Schumann in Philadelphia, to name but a few. These men were more than teachers of obstetrics. They were imbued with an evangelic fervor. They were crusaders.

Chiefly through their efforts, the American Board of Obstetrics and Gynecology was organized. Its purpose was "to elevate the standards and advance the cause of obstetrics and gynecology," to encourage and induce potential specialists to prepare themselves thoroughly, to obtain adequate undergraduate facilities for clinical instruction in obstetrics in medical schools, and to persuade both medical schools and hospitals to extend and improve their facilities for graduate training in obstetrics.

So Cinderella got rid of her grime and donned a new dress. But someone must still get her to the ball. For this purpose local arrangements had to be made in each state and/or in each community. In New Jersey, for example, these began with a one-man campaign by Arthur W. Bingham. His efforts resulted in The New Jersey Maternal Welfare Committee. Fortunately, this was placed in the Bureau of Maternal and Child Health, then headed by Julius Levy, which offered sympathetic guidance with no bureaucratic interference. The Committee published minimal standards of obstetric procedure, prescribed consultations in difficult and prolonged labors, and undertook the systematic investigation of maternal deaths by its field physicians. Many of the original appointees are still serving in this capacity, and with exemplary devotion.

Nor was this all. Day and night, in all weathers, Dr. Bingham traveled up and down the State to address hospital and County Society meetings. Whenever the occasion for a sermon on "lessons from a death certificate" presented itself, this apostle of better obstetrics arose to preach, to accuse if necessary, and to point the way.

Similar movements had their champions in nearly every city and in most of the states. American obstetrics had been called "a national disgrace," and all over this country doctors, young and middle-aged, responded to the summons to erase this stigma. The inertia of centuries and millenniums yielded at last to the persistence of these champions of a cause.

Public health nursing organizations wrote a brilliant chapter in this story. It should also be recorded that the movement for better obstetrics gained momentum from informative articles which appeared in such national publications as *The Ladies' Home Journal, Good Housekeeping, Woman's Home Companion,* and *The Reader's Digest.*

Symptomatic of the change, as well as contributing to it, is the present emphasis on obstetric teaching in medical schools, the increased number of obstetric specialists and general practitioners especially interested in obstetrics, the improved position of obstetricians on hospital staffs, and the increased proportion of obstetric patients in total hospital admissions. Speaking of this trend, a surgeon in a general hospital said recently, "We are fast becoming a maternity hospital, with the other departments as adjuncts."

Best of all, the maternal death rate in the United States has plummeted to 0.72 per thousand live births for 1950, about one-tenth of the 1925 figure! And it is still decreasing.

But there is a danger implicit in the Cinderella story. If the magic is not sustained, the splendor must fade. The price of good obstetrics, like the price of liberty, is everlasting vigilance.

Obstet Gynecol 1954;3:222–4.

COMMENTARY

Sam. Berkow made a number of contributions to After Office Hours, including the 24 "Berkow Visits" mentioned in the Preface. In this article, Berkow traces the remarkable history of obstetrics during the period from roughly 1925 to 1950, when it became a full-fledged, respectable branch of medicine. His writing was always incredibly rich and poetic in its imagery.

The Alphabet of Academic Medicine

Steven G. Gabbe, MD

September 1996

or the past 2 years, the Society of Perinatal Obstetricians has sponsored a retreat for fellows in maternal-fetal medicine. I was invited to address the fellows on the keys for a successful career in academic medicine. In considering how I might organize this discussion, I thought it would be helpful to present an alphabet of academic medicine, incorporating the important lessons I have learned along the way. Although many of the guidelines apply primarily to a career in an academic setting, others relate to the profession of medicine in general.

THE ALPHABET

A—Abstracts: Publish each good one. When I review someone's curriculum vitae, I examine the number of abstracts he or she has published and compare it with the number of papers. If the abstract was good enough to present at a meeting, why hasn't a full report on the subject been completed? Maybe the research wasn't that important, or perhaps the author did not see the project through to completion.

B—Book chapters: Limit their number. Writing an authoritative chapter on an important subject in a widely read textbook can help advance one's academic career. However, if a faculty member is not careful, he or she may spend too much time writing chapters or review articles and not enough time seeking new knowledge.

C—Committees: Avoid them! At the start of one's academic career, it is best to limit the time spent serving on committees. Committees that help a junior faculty member understand how a medical school, department, or hospital is organized can be valuable. On the other hand, working on a committee to decide on the logo for a new obstetrics service might best be left to others.

Course: Chart yours. During a job interview, many of us have been asked where we want to be in the next 5 or 10 years. It is important to know where you want to go, or you may never get there. On occasion, when I have asked this question, the resident or faculty applicant will respond, "I'd like to have your job." Such an answer clearly convinces me they have poor judgment!

D—Divisions: Avoid those with only two faculty members. For a junior faculty person to join a division with only one other member means that he or she will have little time for academic pursuits. In addition, should that senior person leave, the junior faculty member will be alone, without a colleague or collaborator.

E—Expert: Be an authority in one area. In academic medicine, it is essential to select an important area of investigation and pursue it, becoming recognized as a national and international expert on that subject.

Expectations: What are yours? What are your division director's? What are your chairperson's? When looking at a new position, it is essential that the junior faculty member decide what he or she would like to do and make certain those objectives are in line with the thoughts of the division director and chairperson. For example, if the junior faculty member is seeking a position that emphasizes research but the department's leadership wants to recruit someone whose primary interests are teaching and clinical care, a mismatch will result.

F—Family and friends: They must come first. When my son, Daniel, now a college senior, was 6 years old, he wrote me a note: "Dear Dad, I love you. I hope you will be back from work soon. I wish you did not have to go to work. I love you." I kept that note and framed it. It is the first thing I see when I come to work in the morning.

G—Good people: Bad things do happen to them, but not very often. Likewise, good things do happen to bad people, but not very often. Certainly, life is not fair, nor is it a meritocracy. But things generally work out the way they should.

H—Hallways: Don't stand in them. Nothing good happens in a hallway. People talk too much, rumors get started, and time is wasted.

I—Inconsequential: Keep things in perspective. Many years ago, when I was going through a difficult time, the late Val Davajan, a wonderful clinician, investigator, and teacher at Los Angeles County–Women's Hospital, took me aside and gave me these words of advice: "Know what the mosquitoes are and what the elephants are." He explained that some problems were inconsequential and, like mosquitoes, could be easily swatted away. Others were like elephants and sat right on your shoulder, weighing you down. Even though I was carrying around an elephant, it was helpful to know he recognized my problems and wanted to help.

I: Use this letter with caution in your academic alphabet. If the junior faculty member is speaking with administrators in the department, medical school, or hospital, it is important to emphasize the "we." How can we make things better? If you approach a hospital administrator with the statement, "*I* want this done because it is important to *me*," you are much less likely to gain support than when you say, "How can *we* work together to accomplish this because it will be best for all of *us?*"

J—Justice: Be fair and know the facts. Before making a decision about who is right or who is wrong in a dispute, it is important to take time to find out what really happened.

K—Know your limits: Don't be embarrassed. When you need help, seek it. Always assume there are people smarter than you. One of the great benefits of working in an academic environment is the accessibility of senior faculty and experienced clinicians. Although it may be difficult to say, "I don't know," it is important to do so.

L—Listen: Do this about ten times more than you talk, and *really listen!* What is the other person saying? How are they saying it? Is what they are telling you the real message? As academicians, we like to lecture much more than we like to listen. Thus, in a conversation, our temptation is to think about our response rather than what the other person is saying.

M—Managed care: Understand it nationally, statewide, and locally. For those of us in academic medicine, the change in health care brought about by managed care organizations demands that we understand how this system will influence support for our academic programs.

Mentors: Find a good one. Be a good one. Each of us can remember the importance of advice from a senior faculty member and how that helped us through our career. In turn, we have a responsibility to provide that counsel for medical students, house officers, fellows, and junior faculty.

N—Never: Open your mouth without knowing the politics of your department.

Never: Complain about the people or place you have just left. Too often, a junior faculty member will offer unsolicited comments about the problems or deficiencies where he or she worked. Perhaps they think this will enhance their position with their new colleagues. It doesn't!

Never: Get angry in public. It is okay to throw books, stamp your foot, and yell and scream behind closed doors. But if one gets angry in public, he or she may be labeled a hothead and his or her ability to influence change and process in the academic setting will be impaired.

O—Opportunity: Take chances now. It will be more difficult later. It is always easier to try something new early in your career rather than later.

P—Promotion and tenure: Understand the process. There's no hurry if you're good. It is essential that a new faculty member have a thorough understanding of the promotion and tenure process. Having chaired two college of medicine promotion and tenure committees, I know how different the process may be from institution to institution. What are the guidelines for awarding tenure and for being promoted? The junior faculty person should also be extremely cautious before seeking an accelerated promotion. Most committees are reluctant to grant early promotion or tenure. A negative decision will lead to disappointment and may be difficult for a young academician to accept.

Prestige: You can't eat it, but you can't buy it. Having a national or international reputation for academic excellence may not translate into a larger paycheck. But that's not what academic medicine is about.

Q—Quilligan: "Let me think about that." Ted Quilligan, the chairperson of the department in which I had my first faculty appointment, said this many times, emphasizing the need for thoughtfulness and consideration before making a decision.

R—Research: Do it early, often, and always. The foundation of a successful academic career is continued participation in basic and/or clinical research.

S—Slides: Don't pack them! How many times have I heard about a young faculty member who packed his or her slides in a suitcase on the way to an important presentation? When their luggage was lost.... Well, you know the rest of the story.

T—Time and trust: Precious commodities. Time is our most valuable resource. Trust is the key to any successful relationship.

Teach: Remember your medical student and residency training. It is a privilege to give back.

U—Understand: Understand yourself; sometimes you are ugly. Recognize the situations in which you are likely to exercise poor judgment, and try to avoid them. If you do make a mistake, admit you were wrong.

V—Voracious: Be a voracious reader. Like research, reading and more reading are essential parts of a successful academic career.

W—Writing: Get it in *writing!* Yes, trust is important. But when accepting a new position, it is best for all parties to have the important points defined in writing, before that job offer is accepted.

X—Xenophobia: Avoid it. Be open-minded. Xenophobia is simply a dislike of what is foreign or different. As an academician, one must be open to new ideas.

Y—Yourself: Take care of yourself. Today, we live life in the fast lane. It is essential to take time for family, a hobby, exercise, and relaxation.

Z—Zuspan: "Thank you ever so much for sending us this patient." Fred Zuspan, who chaired the Department of Obstetrics and Gynecology at the Ohio State University College of Medicine before my appointment to that position in 1987, frequently gave me important advice. He emphasized that we must rely on the support of our colleagues in our community and throughout our region. Treating them with respect and providing feedback on patients they referred is essential.

CONCLUSION

Here, then, is the alphabet of academic medicine. I hope those who read it will find it helpful. Some may want to change it or add their own letters. In closing, I would add one last lesson for success, something my father told me over and over when I was growing up: "Do good and don't complain."

Obstet Gynecol 1996;88:479–81.

COMMENTARY

This and the subsequent article used the alphabet to list rules for success. The purpose is slightly different—academic medicine in one case and professionalism in the other—but the degree of overlap is striking. The authors are each eminently qualified to offer advice. Steven Gabbe chaired two excellent departments, at Ohio State University and the University of Washington, and is now Dean of the School of Medicine at Vanderbilt University. Patrick Duff had a distinguished career in the U.S. Army and then moved to the University of Florida about 15 years ago, where he has developed an enviable reputation as an outstanding clinician–teacher. Gabbe and Duff served on the Green Journal Editorial Board in 1984–1987 and 1988–1991, respectively.

Professionalism in Medicine: An A–Z Primer

Patrick Duff, MD

June 2002

 have practiced medicine for 27 years, first as a resident and fellow, then as a student clerkship director, division chief, residency director, and finally an associate dean of students. In my experience, I have observed that very few physicians falter because of a lack of intellect or a major deficit in technical skills. Rather, the few that are not successful in their practice have difficulty because of poor professional behavior. Medicine demands an exceptionally high standard of professionalism, and this high standard can be achieved by virtually all of us if we simply remember that, to be good physicians, we first must be good people. I offer the following A–Z primer as a reminder of the simple rules of good behavior in medical practice.

A is for *arrogance*. We must avoid it at all costs. There is no other trait that puts others off as much as arrogance. It severely tarnishes the brightest intellect and the most superb technical skills. For all of our formal education and rigorous training, we are no better or worse than anyone else engaged in an honest endeavor.

B is for *benevolence*. We must treat everyone with kindness and not let anger and malice have any role in our professional interactions.

C is for *compassion*. We must strive to display it in full measure when interacting with patients. Compassion is particularly important in situations when cure of disease is impossible and when we struggle simply to sustain the human spirit and provide comfort for an ailing body.

D is for *dogma*. We should eschew it and practice on the basis of the best available medical evidence, not in accordance with strongly voiced opinions or comfortable old habits.

E is for an *even temperament*. We must work hard to cultivate one. Our responses to different situations should be predictable and consistent. Our patients, students, and colleagues should not have to walk on eggshells because we are in a bad frame of mind.

F is for *fair minded*. We must be consistently equitable in our interactions with others. We always must strive to put the interest of our patient first and to do what is right and just, not what is expedient or financially profitable.

G is for *good humor.* We must try to display one consistently. We must not take ourselves too seriously, and we must be willing to laugh at our foibles and avoid a pattern of defensiveness.

H is for *honesty* and *humility*. These may, in fact, be the most important of all personal traits. The former is the rock upon which we build our professional reputation; the latter enhances our achievements with the soft light of graciousness.

I is for *insight*. We must recognize not only our strengths, but also our limitations. We must not let ego interfere with good patient care. No matter what our level of training or breadth of experience, we never should hesitate to ask for assistance when confronted by unfamiliar situations.

J is for *judgment*. We must avoid the rush to it—in making a diagnosis or adopting a new therapy. We must acknowledge that most serious mistakes in medicine result more from haste than lack of expertise. Therefore, we must strive to be calm, logical, and deliberate in our approach to patient care.

K is for *knowledge*. We must stay informed of the facts by making a lifetime commitment to self-education. We must remain abreast of the scientific literature, read avidly and critically, and be conservative in evaluating apparent startling new developments. We should neither be the first to adopt the new nor the last to abandon the old.

L is for *listen*. We learn the most by listening to our colleagues and our patients, not by talking. Sometimes the best medicine is no medicine at all, but rather a soft shoulder, a kind heart, and a receptive ear.

M is for *modesty*, a trait that complements humility. Our counseling of patients, students, residents, and coworkers is far more likely to be heeded if we are well regarded by others rather than being perceived as demanding, abrasive, and insensitive.

N is for *negativism*. We must avoid it at all costs. We must remain free of the company of angry, negative people, for they will be like anchors that weigh us down. We must strive to be part of the solution to a problem, not part of the problem itself.

O is for *open mindedness*. We must be tolerant of others. Many patients will have lifestyles that are quite different from our own. In fact, many of their illnesses may be the direct result of their unhealthy patterns of behavior. Nevertheless, they are deserving of our respect, sympathy, and expertise.

P is for *promptness*. We must be respectful of other individuals' time, particularly our patients. We should not overschedule ourselves so that we are unable to accord patients the time they deserve for assessment of their medical problem.

Q is for *quizzical.* We continually must ask new questions to expand our fund of knowledge and enhance our efficiency. We must be willing to think outside the box in creating new ways to deliver compassionate, expert, and cost-efficient care to patients.

R is for *reliable.* We must be steady and dependable. Colleagues and patients should feel secure in depending on us to complete assignments and honor deadlines. We must learn to say "no" politely but firmly when our plate is too full. When we promise to do something, we need to do it right and on time. R is also for respect. We must earn it, from both our colleagues and our patients by our conscientious, dutiful actions.

S is for *sensitivity.* We must display this trait in full measure in our interactions with patients and colleagues.

T is for *tact.* We must be able to give constructive criticism to students and colleagues without crushing their self-esteem. Similarly, we must be able to provide realistic assessments to patients without taking away their hope or belittling their judgment.

U is for *user friendly.* We must be willing to change outdated methods of doing business and make traditional practices (eg, admission to the hospital, scheduling of appointments, hospital room assignments, laboratory tests) convenient, dignified, and culturally sensitive for our patients.

V is for *vigor.* We must avoid the phenomenon of burn-out and remain passionate and positive in our approach to our personal and professional lives.

W is for *work ethic.* Ours must be impeccable. We must strive for the endurance and consistency of the long-distance runner over the flash of the sprinter. Slow and steady wins the race to excellence in patient care. *W* is also for *well organized.* Good organization is the key to efficiency and productivity in any profession, but particularly medicine where the demands on our time are intense and so often unpredictable.

X is for *eXacting standards.* We should set the bar of performance at a lofty height, but not impossibly high. We should strive consistently for excellence but not perfection. A standard of perfection will always be unrealistic and elusive and invariably will lead to disappointment and loss of self-esteem.

Y is for *yourself.* We must be ever attentive to the proper balance between our professional and personal lives. We must nourish our mind, spirit, and body so that we are able to care properly for our loved ones and our patients.

Z is for *zero tolerance.* This is the type of personal and corporate policy that we should have toward sexism, boorishness, and ethnic, racial, age, or gender discrimination.

I conclude with several simple suggestions for how professionalism might be taught during medical school and residency training. First, faculty members must model desirable professional behaviors so that students and residents have excellent examples to emulate. Second, professional behavior can be taught in the context of small group seminars where students are presented with difficult scenarios (eg, the noncompliant and hostile patient, suspected drug abuse by a colleague, suspected financial improprieties by a partner, need for correction of inappropriate behavior by a student or resident during rounds). Third, students and residents may be assigned readings on the subject of professionalism and be required to attend lectures or seminars that discuss ethical and professional behavior. Residents and students should be evaluated by patients, ancillary staff, and faculty concerning their behavior. Finally, as is now mandated by the Accreditation Council on Graduate Medical Education and the Residency Review Committee for Obstetrics and Gynecology, professional behavior should be brought to the forefront of the curriculum and made one of the major criteria for student or resident promotion and graduation.

Obstet Gynecol 2002;99:1127–8.

Faculty Assessment and Review

Warren H. Pearse, MD

JULY 1973

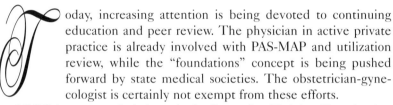 oday, increasing attention is being devoted to continuing education and peer review. The physician in active private practice is already involved with PAS-MAP and utilization review, while the "foundations" concept is being pushed forward by state medical societies. The obstetrician-gynecologist is certainly not exempt from these efforts.

AGOG has responded through the In-service Training Examination devised by the Council on Resident Education in Obstetrics-Gynecology. The Self-Assessment Test type examination for the practicing physician has been available at the last three Annual Clinical Meetings of the College. Due care and concern is directed for (indeed at) the practicing physician. But what of the academic faculty member? What about his continuing education and peer review? While he maintains his affiliations with the SGI, the Admiral's Club, the Ambassador Club and Piedmont Airlines 6 ½ Mile Club, is he keeping up with his chosen piece of the specialty? It seems to me high time that an in-service examination was devised for the academic obstetrician-gynecologist.

To spur such a worthy development, and indeed prepare the laggard full-time faculty member for his first exam, a sample of carefully constructed multiple choice questions is provided. Parenthetically there is no doubt that the multiple choice question is the appropriate vehicle—after all, haven't you opened a speculum many times and seen a multiple choice question?

From the files of FARP, the Faculty Assessment and Review Program, the following questions have been selected:

Select the best answer.

1. The airport serving The Homestead is named:

   a) Dulles International

   b) Ingalls Field

   c) Roanoke International

   d) No matter what anybody says, you can't fly to The Homestead

2. Your medical school installs a giant new computer which calculates in pico-seconds. You can expect the following benefits:

   a) Your payroll check wins the Times fiction award of the year.

   b) Your last grant accounting is 14 months old. Since then all supplies have been charged to the morgue, and you are paying three instructors in the Ancient History Department.

   c) Three years of fetal heart recordings are erased by mistake.

   d) You receive a detailed monthly student grade report for Occupational Therapy (OT). OB student grades are lost.

3. The Zip Code for Bethesda, Maryland, is:

   a) 20014

   b) 60601

   c) 23298

   d) 68105

This question, which has been very important in the past, has been deleted as irrelevant for the future.

4. The least expensive transportation from O'Hare International to the Drake Hotel is:

   a) Airport limousine to Palmer House, taxi to the Drake.

   b) Taxi from O'Hare to the Drake.

   c) Gold Coast airport limousine to the Drake (wait one hour).

   d) Your last NIH grant was approved, but not funded. Stay at the LaSalle Hotel instead.

5. Your U.S. Congressman, who helped you secure a federal contract, calls concerning entering his son into medical school. The following are likely to be true ($P > .05$):

   a) The son is a cretin.

   b) The son is on parole for drug pushing.

   c) The Congressman's brother is on your Board of Regents.

   d) All of the above.

6. It is 5:35 pm and your office phone rings. Select your first priority from among the following messages:

   a) Your wife says that the first guests are arriving for the cocktail party.

b) The Dean has called an emergency meeting about the faculty pay plan.

c) The nurses can't irrigate the catheter on the patient with this morning's vesicovaginal fistula repair.

d) Two students are occupying the office until you answer their protest about question six on the last exam.

7. The baggage claim area at LaGuardia Airport is:

a) On the lower level straight ahead from the gates.

b) Down the escalator and to the right.

c) On the upper level near the ticket counter.

d) Of no importance. Your bag (including slides) has been sent to Boise.

8. Desperate for teaching assistance since you now admit 258 medical students each year instead of 75, you seek an Assistant Professor of Obstetrics-Gynecology.

Which of the following is most likely:

a) The Dean has allocated all new faculty positions to the School of Nursing.

b) Faculty funds have been transferred to the Physicians Assistant program.

c) Obstetrics-Gynecology is made an elective subject, with the time saved awarded to Experimental Biophysiology. Therefore, no new faculty lines are provided.

d) Your prize chief resident, who agreed to join your faculty for $14,000 per year, is offered a $62,000 salary plus bonuses to work a 30-hour week in LaJolla.

9. Your hospital admitting privileges have been revoked simultaneously by the Medical Records, Utilization, Peer Review, Disaster, and Second-Year Medical Curriculum Committees. This problem arose from a patient admitted for a diagnostic curettage, on whose record (select the most likely):

a) The physician's order for a general diet was illegibly signed by a resident.

b) The word "curettage" was misspelled on page 16 of the student's history and physical.

c) The patient's hospital discharge was delayed four hours by a broken elevator, thus creating a stay of 2.2 days, exceeding usual and customary.

d) The operative report indicated a student was first assistant.

10. Your carefully conducted study on cyclic AMP levels in dividing paramecia may be difficult to publish because of a question about adequately matched controls. You can assure success by:

a) Addressing the journal editor as, "Dear Dick."

b) Submitting simultaneously to three journals.

c) Reducing the number of listed authors to eleven.

d) Sending the manuscript to the Northern Michigan Journal of Obstetrics and Gynecology.

e) "Leaking" the manuscript to a "throw-away" medical paper, complete with your personal photograph.

No answers need be provided; they are all too evident. A word of caution: the author achieved a perfect score on a prototype examination utilizing the Official Airline Guide for an open book test, and was promptly made a Dean. Unfortunately, only intuition is required for such a post, and prior study went for naught.

This sample, if carefully studied by you, should show the way to a suitable corrected raw score with an adequate standard score, validity and discrimination. Regression may follow. The rewards for successful completion are continued appointment, eventual tenure, depiction as a money vulture by HR-1, accusation as a poor provider by your wife, and identification as a valued customer in the friendly skies. Godspeed!

Obstet Gynecol 1973;42:146–8.

COMMENTARY

Warren Pearse has enjoyed remarkable success in everything he undertook—department chair, dean, and for 20 years executive officer of ACOG. No doubt this reflected a combination of great ability and hard work, but all who know him would agree that his success also was due, in no small measure, to a highly developed sense of humor. This comes across in this quiz. The topic may be a little dated in some instances—after all, it was written 30 years ago—but the whole thing is still uproariously funny. Pearse, incidentally, holds the distinction of the shortest tenure of any Editorial Board member; he began his term on January 1, 1975, and resigned the next month when he was appointed Executive Director of ACOG.

Hospital Hazards

Roger P. Smith, MD

ospitals are not good for your health. As a society, we have become more aware of our environment, and a greater emphasis has been placed on environmental hazards in the workplace. The Occupational Safety and Health Administration (OSHA—the folks who brought us horse-shoe-shaped toilet seats) has been preaching safety for many years. Only recently have people viewed OSHA's work as anything other than the federal equivalent of underwear that rides up. However, OSHA's diligence has identified many previously unknown risks to those of us who must labor in the vineyard of disease. Now we find that those hallowed hospital halls are actually dangerous to our health. To assist colleagues who may not have had the benefit of an on-site inspection, the following is a list of syndromes, conditions, and complaints indigenous to hospital staff. Proceed with caution.

Beeperlinthitis—A vertigo-like state induced by rapid back and forth movement of the head made in an attempt to hear and interpret sounds coming from a pocket pager.

Borborygamortis—Hunger pains that occur at 2 AM and threaten to kill you.

Housestaff knees—A pre-patellar bursitis resulting from periodic and forceful genuflection at the feet of attending physicians.

Hallowedtoesis—Attending physician's feet.

Chart cart farts—The expulsion (sometimes explosive) of gastrointestinal gas due to the intense Valsalva maneuver required to move a chart rack with only one functional wheel. Usually result in only minor injuries, but have led to a need for Environmental Protection Agency waivers in some metropolitan centers.

Dysadmenorrhea—Painful administration.

Schizophrenic—A learned ability to use the diaphragm to both inhale and continue presenting a case at the same time. Found most commonly in interns. A leading cause of *inspirational aspiration*, in which your best thoughts are choked off.

Radiolunacy—An acute psychotic state induced by ineffective attempts to obtain copies of imaging studies from the clutches of the radiology clerk.

Chaparoaming—The glazed look in the eye and sense of wanderlust that occur while looking for an attendant to assist with a pelvic examination.

Dermatographia pigmentosa (Japonica)—A semipermanent discoloration of the hands induced by using writing devices bearing brand names (usually of antibiotics).

Acute otis-itis media—Traumatic inflammation of the middle or index finger arising from repeated rapid (and ineffectual) pushing of the elevator call button.

Acquired or contagious vertigo—That uneasy feeling engendered by dealing with dizzy members of the health care team.

CTDTs—Intense facial twitching accompanied by palmar cramping occurring when informed that computed tomography is not available and that an actual pelvic examination must be performed.

Glove and shocking paresthesia—The tingling sensation experienced in the hand immediately following the performance of a pelvic examination necessitated by CTDTs.

Primal stream—The primitive, but very real, sense of relief offered by finding a rest room after a very long surgical case.

Delirium tremendous—The semistuporous state seen acutely during 2 AM telephone calls (seen chronically in interns).

Dyspepsia—A panic state and form of caffeine withdrawal seen when the labor-delivery room vending machine is out of your favorite cola product.

Allergic lionitis—The plaintive bellowing sound heard when a sneeze sends hot coffee toward your lap. An excessively large spill may lead to irritation and pain in the gluteal region, known as hot cross buns.

Even a trip to the rest room is filled with danger:

Acute roll reversal—The abrasion of the thumb and first finger that results when the previous occupant places a roll of toilet paper backwards on the holder and leaves the end pasted down.

Gender deassignment—An uneasy sense of foreboding and guilt that occurs when using a "unisex" bathroom.

Acute pile-itis—We've all used the paper. Enough said.

Obstet Gynecol 1992;80:138–9.

COMMENTARY

A few people are gifted with the ability to find humor in nearly everything, and Roger Smith is surely one of them. This and the next three articles, plus one in a later section (see page 252), demonstrate this clearly. No one who has become ingrained with the culture of hospitals or sat through soporific teaching conferences or waded through tedious descriptions of statistics can read them without at least a chuckle. Smith's piquant sense of humor enlivened Editorial Board meetings during his tenure as a member (1996–1999). His career has taken him from private practice in Illinois to faculty positions at the Medical College of Georgia in Augusta and more recently the University of Missouri at Kansas City.

Hospital Physicals

Roger P. Smith, MD

FEBRUARY 1989

*I*f you are like many professionals, you may think such things as crossword puzzles and card games are forms of aerobic exercise. (No, taking the garbage out to the curb once a week does not qualify as cardiac training.) To combat this trend toward sedentary staff and corpulent consultants, some have suggested that hospitals take a tip from those popular fitness trails found in shopping malls. Someday, in trendier hospitals, one might combine rounds with a fitness program geared to the busy professional. Here is a brief description of some of the "fitness stations" being considered.

Beeper Lateral Neck Stretch. At the sound of the beeper, you bend your head to the horizontal (or beyond) in an effort to understand the unintelligible transmission. This should be repeated six times. To avoid asymmetrical muscle development, remember to alternate sides.

Elevator Wind Sprints. This station (found mainly in VA hospitals) begins at the elevator with the push of the button. You are given several minutes of Zen-like rest and contemplation. This is followed by a leisurely stroll away from the elevator once you have figured out that today must be a little-known national holiday on which no elevator runs. At the sound of the bell, you sprint toward the closing door in an effort to avoid the stairs. The use of a black bag or button-pushing accomplice to delay the doors is considered akin to adding sugar to Gatorade, inconsistent with the spirit of competition. This station not only allows for psychological conditioning and meditation, but also improves agility.

Hallway Hamper Hop. In this exercise, the long-awaited telephone call from the consultant comes to the phone at the end of the hall. At the sound of the bell, you must sprint down the hall, under, over, around, or through the linen hampers, food service carts, chart racks, wheelchairs, medicine carts, and housekeeper's mops to reach the phone before the fourth and final ring. Agility is the key. You will lose points if you lose your pen, flashlight, or stethoscope, but extra points are available for creative excuses.

Patient Powerlift. A patient weighing more than your current automobile must be moved from the bed to a specially reinforced cart for transport to the loading dock for daily weights. No roller is available and the use of hydraulics is prohibited. Canceling the daily weights will result in your parking place being moved three blocks away. *Ironman Interminable Rounds.* In this test of endurance, you must remain upright and awake during the entire duration of a visiting professor's rounds. The use of walls for added support is only for beginners and those with a note from the Dean. The use of supplemental oxygen is frowned upon.

Bottom Drawer Back Bends. Attempt to find the nurse's hidden supply of prescription blanks. Check all bottom drawers. Repeat ten times, then ask. For those with weak backs, deep knee bends may be substituted.

Moro Reflex Tone-Up. This station is conveniently located in conference rooms. In this exercise, you allow your head to gradually fall forward, allowing your eyes to close. A rapid and seemingly violent backward snap is given with the head, along with an upward and outward movement of the arms. The exhilarating rush of adrenaline, combined with the spasmodic increase in muscle tone, does wonders for tired bodies and minds. If you are prone to violent excess, you should not attempt this while sitting too close to someone of higher academic rank. This station should also be skipped by those with poorly fitting glasses, those who snore, or those prone to incontinence.

Pupil Push-Ups. At this station, you watch a simulated slide presentation during which the lights are alternately switched on and off without warning. You must rapidly constrict and dilate your pupils without the use of hands. Repeat indefinitely. Protective use of sunglasses or eyelids is not allowed.

X-Ray Tug-of-War. At this station, you attempt to remove the desired folder from the x-ray clerk's clutches. This strengthens not only the upper body, but your resolve as well. Repeat more often than not.

Cardiac (Arrest) Training. Once you have reached the point farthest from any patient care, a cardiac arrest will be announced for that area. You must race up stairs and down halls before the arrest is canceled. Points are deducted if you are too out of breath to ask directions or if you use more than 50% of the patient's oxygen supply. No points will be awarded if the arrest team has to resuscitate you.

Although this trend is encouraging, I personally will continue to pursue the fine art of "carbo-loading." I have also been able to obtain the services of a medical student who comes in three times a week and jogs for me.

Obstet Gynecol 1989;73:275–6.

Conference Coma: A Formula for Appraisal

Roger P. Smith, MD

MAY 1983

hrough the many years of education and training that we as physicians undergo, we endure countless meetings, conferences, and lectures, some good; some bad. All of us have at one time wished we were doing something other than listening to a boring speaker. Some among us have developed elaborate methods of escaping this boredom: "emergency surgery," sham pages, mock indignation, and others, the workings of which are all too familiar. For the timid, the woeful fewness of available survival techniques has forced them to sit through these meetings with no relief from a poor speaker. It would seem the time has come to report an improved technique that has long offered a solution to this problem: conference coma.

This approach is efficient, restful, and easier to use than some of the more complicated methods of escape; however, to work well the method requires preparation, timing, and skill. In the past there has been no reliable method of assessing the potential time available for the respite, thus leaving the conference-goer faced with the prospect of restless vigilance lest his ploy be discovered. There is, however, a simple formula which, when applied correctly, can yield an estimate of the amount of time a speaker will spend with his slides. Knowing this time allows even the most timid to sit through the most boring meeting. The elegance and universal appeal of this formula technique may be easily grasped by the simple observation that all speakers have slides.

TECHNIQUE

A careful but inconspicuous peek just before the presentation can give an indication of the number of slides to be used by the speaker. Although this number is often in direct proportion to the length of the speaker's credentials or his traveling distance, direct observation is always superior to estimation. By knowing the number of slides, an estimate of the time available for rest can be made.

A simple formula by which this may be accomplished is as follows:

$$\frac{\text{Log}(D_{spk}) \times 10}{BS_{coef}} \times N + (F_{ink} - 5)^2 = T_{min}$$

To use this formula you should multiply the log of the distance the speaker has traveled in miles (D_{spk}) by a factor of 10. This value is then divided by the basic science coefficient (BS_{coef}). This is a factor varying from 1 to 10, reflecting the degree of basic science or clinical content of the presentation. The greater the basic science content the lower the number. Completely clinical subjects should be assigned higher numbers. The quotient derived by this division is then multiplied by the number of slides (N) the speaker will use. To this number a familiarity factor must be added. This represents the Factor of Information in National Knowledge (F_{ink}). When a topic is new, the time required to present it tends to expand. Unfortunately, when a topic is well known most speakers feel obligated to expand their presentation to somehow prove they have a reason to be presenting the same old thing. For this reason, a constant (5) is subtracted from the number of times the subject has been presented in a national forum. The resultant number is squared and becomes the familiarity factor to be added. This formula will give a rough estimate of time, in minutes, that the slides may last. Any time the speaker has more than one tray of slides (80 slides), the time for slide presentation should be increased by 50% over that determined by the formula. You may safely anticipate at least 80% sleep time out of the time slides are to be used.

APPLICATION

When the calculations are complete, you have taken your seat, and the speaker has been introduced, you are ready to apply the data provided by the formula. If you are to rest secure in a job well done, however, you will want to carry off your comfort with the finesse of a veteran. This means staying awake during the first two to three slides so that knowing nods or creative comments may be made. This will serve to camouflage your intent and make those around you thankful for your later silence. If you do not awaken gracefully, the use of an alert and understanding friend next to you may be vital. This person can prevent you from becoming an embarrassment and give you ample time to compose yourself before the lights come on at the end of the lecture. The application of an alarm watch or previously timed page will provide similar warning when your calculated time is running out, but tends to attract attention.

SUMMARY

With the application of advanced techniques and a formula such as this, even the most timid may again look forward to an enjoyable conference.

Obstet Gynecol 1983;61:647–8.

Statistically Speaking

Roger P. Smith, MD

onfusion between "the King's English" and "American" has insidiously perverted the original meanings of the statistical terms we rely on in the scientific literature.

Some are aware of the significant (statistically) contributions to mathematics made in the early part of this century by the British statistician, William Gossett. For his entire professional life, Gossett worked for the Guinness Brewery. He chose to publish his landmark studies of families of population distributions under the pseudonym "Student."[1] These papers provided the basis for what has become known as the "Student *t* test." Unfortunately, few are acquainted with the true origin of the *t* test or how this statistical terminology has been changed from its original meaning.

Despite his employment by the Guinness Brewery, William Gossett was a devotee of the British national drink, tea. He observed that some scientific manuscripts were exceedingly boring and required more tea to stay awake than did others. This quantification led to the "tea-test" for papers and the "tea-distribution" for oral presentations. (The latter was based on the number of audience members resorting to methylxanthines to maintain consciousness.) The application of these concepts led inevitably to the "*P* value" and the "continence interval." A low "*P* value" indicated an exciting concept that required little tea to maintain a wakeful state. A shortened "continence interval" indicated that the audience wanted ed no more discussion on the point (also reflected in the "frequency" distribution, if not the urgency of some presentations).

The British preoccupation with alimentary statistics, and their sequelae, led to the concept of the "commodal value" (the most frequent place or set of observations). This has been shortened to "modal value" in the American literature.

To obtain consensus regarding a given set of statistics, Gossett would convene a group of cronies in a local pub (a cohort study). Assembling a group for such an uninteresting chore was sometimes a grim task. To entice participants, he had to offer both a sampling of Guinness's products and the possibility of the companionship of unaccompanied persons at the pub. (Outdoor variants of this system were adopted in some Hispanic countries and in Greece in the form of the "Latin-square" study design and "Chi-square" test, respectively.) The need to find appropriately qualified individuals who would not be distracted gave rise to both the concept of a "standard deviate" and the continuing distrust of "single observation" papers that persists today. The presentation of data around the countertops of the pub led to the idea of "tabular data" and the love of "tables" (and "bar graphs") found in modern literature. (Small fruit stains from the occasional dessert consumed during the review process are not, however, the source of the "pie chart" or "splatter-gram," though periodic announcements on the status of liquid refreshment did give rise to the "case report.")

The risk of being pinched by a bobby for excessive use of the Guinness products was recognized as potentially reducing one's "degree of freedom."

Despite the somewhat onerous job of reviewing poorly written papers night after night in a dim British pub, participation in this process was the best way for a rising mathematician to become known in the cut-throat world of statisticians. As a result, it was soon well known that you had to be "pub-ish or perish."

REFERENCE

1. Rosner B. Fundamentals of biostatistics. Boston: Duxbury Press, 1982:147.

Obstet Gynecol 1993;81:625–6.

The Next-to-Last

Allan C. Barnes, MD

MAY 1957

ecently a challenging paper appeared on the mechanisms of menstrual bleeding by Read, Jones, Mellin, Thompson, Dickey, Robbins, and Browne. It is of considerable interest because it advances opinions which are diametrically opposite to those expressed two years or so ago by Gard, Billings, Bartley, Williams, Jones, and Allison. I happen to know both groups of workers in this field, and know that there is no disputing their scientific integrity nor the honesty of their work. The fact that they cling vigorously to views on menstrual bleeding which are in direct opposition to each other is just one of the interesting facets of scientific investigation.

Also, since I know both groups, I can pass on some further information. Thus the Jones who is second out of seven authors in the more recent paper is in no way related to the Jones who is fifth out of six on the earlier work. Also, it is of some interest that Robbins (sixth out of seven) and Jones (the one who is fifth out of six) are actually close personal friends who have simply, on this particular topic, agreed to disagree.

There is another realm, however, in which they have common knowledge and interest; that is, they are both the next-to-last author in the major work which represents the thinking of their respective laboratories. For some time now I have been urging them to collaborate on a small article on The Role of the Next-to-Last Author in Scientific Literature. What this exact role is, I have no idea (in fact, I'm so obtuse I don't even know the role of the third-from-last author, which probably should be clear). They certainly should be able to enlighten us on this score, but I fear that the opus will never be written: They can't agree on whether it would be submitted as a paper by Robbins and Jones, or by Jones and Robbins.

This is, in many ways, a shame. Because as matters now stand, both of them are doomed to scientific oblivion. The older paper is always referred to as being by "Gard and co-workers," and the later paper is written off as stemming from "Read *et al.*" I don't know whether or not they resent this anonymity, but I have noticed that over the poker table Robbins calls Jones "Coworker," and Jones calls Robbins "Et al," or "Al" for short.

The *Quarterly Cumulative Index Medicus* will pile further ignominy on them by not listing the topic of their paper after their names. Only after the names of Read and Gard will the precise wording of the title of the respective papers be listed. For Billings, Bartley, Williams, Jones, and Allison, the *Index* will simply say: "See Gard, Q.M." For Jones, Mellin, Thompson, Dickey, Robbins, and Browne, it will say "See Read, G.K." In this case keeping the two Jones boys straight is up to the *Index*, and we can trust it to do a good job.

The growing tendency to multiple authorship has not only increased the work of the *Quarterly Cumulative Index*, it has also complicated the business of compiling a bibliography. While in the body of the text you can say "Gard and his co-workers[5] have shown ...," in the References, at the number 5, you must list every blessed name with its initials. And should you start "Gard, Bartley, Billings ..." when it should be "Gard, Billings, Bartley ..." you can count on a storm of protesting letters catching your error. Well, not a storm perhaps, but at least one, signed Billings and Bartley or Bartley and Billings, as the case may be. If you refer to as many as 10 papers in the course of writing your own paper, the resultant bibliography will fill an entire column, and there goes the cost of reprints.

I assume that in most cases the first author was the person who thought of the idea in the beginning. The last author not infrequently is the head of the department from which the work emanates, and rides in on the coattails of every article from his division. But who or what all the in-between people are seems to follow no consistent pattern. Sometimes they lent a private patient or two to the study (at the price of joint authorship). On some occasions they own the essential piece of equipment, or have a corner on a necessary medication without which the study cannot proceed. In some instances, however, a name may appear in fourth place (in contrast to fifth place, or even in contrast to not appearing at all) simply because the owner of the name won the flip of a coin at an appropriate moment.

The chief advantage in winning such a flip of the coin would accrue to one's personal bibliography. Thus when applying for the Wrexley Fellowship, Thompson can list this title as one of his contributions to the literature, putting after it in parentheses "With Reed, Jones, Mellin, Dickey, Robbins and Browne." He doesn't need to specify that he was fourth on this imposing list, nor even what fourth place signifies. Of course, if all the authors of these papers apply for the Wrexley Fellowship it will look like thirteen different papers, whereas you and I know there were only two papers which practically neutralized each other, anyway.

Rather than resorting to the flip of a coin for this type of bibliography building, however, I should like to propose that we systematize it. Let each member of the faculty be a coauthor of every paper coming from the Medical School. The list of authors would exceed the length of the article in most cases, but the individual bibliography of each faculty member would be staggering. Since everyone would have an identical list of published articles, each one could soon be promoted to the rank of full professor. Under these circumstances, competition for the Wrexley Fellowship may become highly confusing. Confusing also will become my job of determining the role of the Next-to-Last Author.

Obstet Gynecol 1957;9:627–8.

COMMENTARY

The versatility and cleverness of Allan C. Barnes (see biographical information, page 61) are abundantly evident in this delightful little dilatation (ie, written or spoken amplification, not what typically precedes curettage) on the order of authors of medical articles. Barnes wrote this many years before authorship became a matter of great concern, leading to establishment of elaborate policies.

Funipuncture: A Rose by Any Other Name...

Joseph G. Pastorek II, MD

APRIL 1988

Every profession owns its jargon. Words and expressions may make for more adequate communication between practitioners, but as well, the use of unique terminology sets its users apart from the horde of humanity, providing a sense of identity or importance. In time, some specialized terms may become incorporated into the language proper. What lay person is not at least passingly familiar with "appendicitis"? On the other hand, much terminology remains obscure to the masses. Who could translate the Latin shorthand of a formal apothecarial prescription, even if it were actually legible?

In any event, a dynamic discipline invariably produces words. In our Western culture, Latin or Greek roots are customarily anglicized, producing new terms that fill our expanding professional vocabularies. Medicine is probably the classic example of this verbal progress. However, it falls to the practitioners of the art to ensure that novel terminology is developed logically and practically. We may, from time to time, be called upon to influence such development.

Sampling of fetal blood in utero via puncture of the umbilical cord vessels is a relatively new procedure[1] that has received much attention over the last several years in both the United States and Europe. Helpful in the evaluation of possible intrauterine growth retardation, fetal infection, or isoimmunization, this technique has been addressed in over a dozen journal articles, numerous abstracts, and even a recent book.[2] A problem arises, however: What is the actual name of the procedure?

The French investigators who published most of the early experience with this technique referred to it simply as direct fetal blood sampling of the umbilical cord with ultrasonic guidance. Currently, at least in the United States, the name of the procedure has more or less become "percutaneous umbilical blood sampling,"[3] predictably shortened to "PUBS." However, recent abstracts from both sides of the Atlantic bandy about the term "cordocentesis" (Moise et al, Abstract 131, Society of Perinatal

Obstetricians Seventh Annual Meeting, February 1987; and Soothill et al, SPO Abstract 33, February 1987). Which term is better? Are there alternatives?

Examination of the term "PUBS" shows it to be wordy on the one hand, and just another medical abbreviation on the other. Although the word "percutaneous" is meant to describe the mother's cutis, ambiguity arises when one considers that "percutaneous" may refer to the fetus in cases of fetal intraperitoneal transfusion. In addition, "PUBS" indicates blood sampling; the term does not apply to direct umbilical transfusion, as has been described[4] (lest we consider "PUBT" as a related expression). Finally, "PUBS" speaks solely to the procedure itself, leaving the necessity for other words to describe, for instance, the puncture wound ("PUBS-site"?).

"Cordocentesis" is an intriguing combination of the Greek roots *chorde* (string) and *kentesis* (perforation). *Chorde* denotes any long, rounded, flexible structure (which may, of course, include the umbilical cord), and *kentesis* means perforation or tapping, as with an aspirator, trocar, or needle.[5] In common usage, "centesis" usually connotes tapping of a body cavity (eg, amniocentesis, thoracentesis) as opposed to a blood vessel or other tubular structure. Therefore, "cordocentesis" is not specific for the umbilical cord, nor in keeping with the general usage of "centesis." In addition, "cordocentesis," like "PUBS," demands related terms, such as "cordocentesis-site."

Besides "PUBS" and "cordocentesis," what other terminology presents itself? Consider the word "funipuncture" (fyoo'ni-punk'cher or fū'ni-punk'cher). A combination of the Latin roots *funis* and *punctura*, "funipuncture" denotes the act of piercing or penetrating with a pointed object or instrument any cordlike structure, particularly the umbilical cord (obstetricians are familiar with the expressions "funisitis" and "funic presentation" as specifically indicating the umbilical cord). As well, "funipuncture" may refer to the wound so made.[5] It would seem that "funipuncture," then, possesses specificity for the umbilical cord, consistent usage of the root words, flexibility (ie, use as a noun or a verb), and therefore economy of use (fewer related terms needed). All in all, this appears to be a much better choice than "PUBS" or "cordocentesis."

So, like other relatively recent newcomers to the medical jargon (eg, acquired immunodeficiency syndrome, Lyme disease), perhaps "funipuncture" could be a new word worthy of adoption by the specialty and inclusion into the everyday language of obstetrics. It makes sense, from the point of view of specificity, connotation, relational usage, and flexibility, and may save us some ink. Besides…it sounds better.

REFERENCES

1. Daffos F, Capella-Pavlovsky M, Forestier F: A new procedure for fetal blood sampling in utero: Preliminary results of 53 cases. Am J Obstet Gynecol 146:985, 1983
2. Milunsky A (ed): Genetic Disorders and the Fetus. Second edition. New York, Plenum Press, 1986, p 580
3. Copel JA, Scioscia A, Grannum PA, et al: Percutaneous umbilical blood sampling in the management of Kell isoimmunization. Obstet Gynecol 67:288, 1986
4. Grannum PA, Copel JA, Plaxe SC, et al: In utero exchange transfusion by direct intravascular injection in severe erythroblastosis fetalis. N Engl J Med 314:1431, 1986
5. Dorland's Illustrated Medical Dictionary. 25th edition. Philadelphia, W. B. Saunders, 1974

Obstet Gynecol 1988;71:646–7.

COMMENTARY

Use of multiple terms for the same condition or procedure can confound indexing systems and literature searches. When the new technique of needling the umbilical vessels burst on the scene in the early 1980s, it was given several different names, and the editors of the Green Journal were worried about the potential for confusion. They found this article convincing in its etymological argument and, decreeing that "funipuncture" would be the term used, they expected authors and other journals to fall in line. However, that turned out to be a forlorn hope.

Letters to the Green Journal: What You Can Do with Them

Gerson Weiss, MD

DECEMBER 1991

The Letters section is an integral part of many professional journals. Editorial policy regarding the Letters section varies considerably among publications. *Lancet* and the *New England Journal of Medicine* accept de novo letters. In *Obstetrics and Gynecology*, only letters related to specific articles published in the journal are considered. With an eye to determining the usefulness and appropriateness of the Letters section of the Green Journal, I conducted a comprehensive evaluation of the 1990 letters, volumes 75 and 76. I hasten to add that this was not a self-motivated task. The Editor requested that I perform this evaluation and present the results at an Editorial Board meeting. Since the Editor springs for dinner costs and has impeccable taste in wines, I felt it prudent to acquiesce.

I approached this task with an open mind, having no preconceptions about the Letters section because I had never read it and was only vaguely aware that it existed. An informal survey of my colleagues revealed that roughly 80% of them never read the Letters section either. However, 20% look forward to the letters and described the section with a variety of adjectives, such as instructive, entertaining, educational, and amusing.

In 1990, the Letters section used 53 journal pages, thus displacing at least ten manuscripts. The section contained 44 letters with replies, one without reply, and one partial retraction by an author. My initial observation was that I knew many of the letter writers personally. This is unusual because there are over 35,000 subscriptions to the Green Journal and I don't know most of the subscribers. There are several potential explanations for this apparent difference. One is that I know the critical thinkers in our field and critical thinkers tend to be letter writers, an hypothesis of doubtful validity. Another possibility is that I know many contentious people and contentious people tend to write letters. This is certainly more plausible. Possibly, I know the same people the Editor knows and he tends preferentially to publish letters from his acquaintances. But there may be yet other explanations for this phenomenon.

Table 1 summarizes the claims made in the letters and the authors' replies for the 1990 Green Journal volumes. A cursory review of this table reveals that there is little agreement between letter writers and authors. In two replies, listed as "other," the authors admitted that there was an error or the impression of an error. They claimed, however, that this was not their fault. The fault rested squarely in the hands of the publisher, whose type selection and typographical errors led to the confusion. The publisher, of course, has no recourse in self-defense. Also, please keep in mind that proofs are submitted to authors for review before publication. The letters also raised questions or technical arguments but, as can be seen from Table 1, they were rarely resolved by the author's reply.

In general, there are three reasons for most letters. One is to point out problems in the manuscript missed by the reviewers and editors. Another is to express points of view different from and sometimes conflicting with those of the author. A third is the self-aggrandizement of the letter writer. An example of the latter might be the following exchange:

To the Editor:

I am writing to comment on Dr. Klutz's article on outpatient hysteroscopic transtubal oophorocystectomies. He reported five complications in 100 cases. I have performed 5000 cases with only two complications. I suggest that Dr. Klutz enroll in my postgraduate course or repeat his residency so that he may learn to operate.

A. Lout

In reply:

Thank you for your interest in our report. Evaluation of the prevalence of cysts appropriate to manage hysteroscopically indicates that there are only 1000 cases in the entire United States in a given year. Perhaps the reason for the difference in our results is that I operate only on patients who have appropriate indications and demonstrable disease.

A. Klutz

TABLE 1. CLAIM OF LETTER WRITER AND AUTHOR'S REPLY

Claims (N)	Reply			
	Did not	Did	Thanks	Other
You missed an important point or confounding variable; made a technical error or omitted important data (25)	23	0		2
You did it wrong (7)	7	0		
You came to the wrong conclusion (5)	5	0		
I have a different point of view (4)			4	
We did it better (3)	3	0		

It is possible to think of the letter and reply format as a competitive indoor sport. Words are used rather than a ball. The serve and volley are represented by references, arguments, and formulas. A supportive argument for this view of the letter and reply format is that in the United States, spectator sports are more common in winter than summer (eg, football, hockey, basketball). In the Green Journal between October and March there were 29 letters, whereas from April through September there were only 15, in line with the distribution of competitive sporting events in general. If we are to think of the letter and reply format as a competitive spectator sport, then perhaps the rules should be clarified. A scoring system may be needed, along with umpires to control the game. In the interest of fairness, perhaps the letter writer should be granted the right of reply rebuttal.

Clearly, a major role of the Letters section is to correct scientific errors or identify manuscript problems overlooked by the reviewers and editors. If this were not the case, then consideration should be given to eliminating the Letters section entirely. Eliminating the reply might be considered, since it is rarely helpful. However, our sense of fair play would suggest that the author be given the right of reply. It might be appropriate to refer the letters to the manuscript reviewers, who could evaluate the validity of the letter writer's claim. These reviewers would then have to accept the error of missing the point raised by the letter writer. This would be a cumbersome system for the editors to deal with, but it might be the most meaningful for the readership.

I readily anticipate that many readers may have points of view that differ from mine. I look forward to hearing from them. Don't expect a reply.

Obstet Gynecol 1991;78:1136–7.

COMMENTARY

The main reason for a letters column in a journal is to permit readers to challenge authors and to point out their errors. However, this survey and analysis of a year's worth of letters in the Green Journal indicate, in a clever and humorous way, that authors never agree that they made a mistake. Gerson Weiss presented this to a meeting of the Editorial Board where it was received very favorably; only a little encouragement was needed to induce him to submit it for consideration for publication.

Brave New World

Allan C. Barnes, MD

FEBRUARY 1969

Office Scientific Exchange
243 Kova Street
Moscow
Apr. 11, 1972

The Office of International Industrial Information Exchange
Department of State
Washington, D. C.

Dear Sirs:

Under the terms of the scientific agreement between the USSR and your great nation, dated the first of January 1971, which treaty provides for the complete exchange of secret ingredients in health and para-health manufactured products, we would like to ask the following:

1. What is Gardol, in Colgate's toothpaste? (This is the substance we have admired so much which keeps a baseball from hitting the head of the head of a household.)

2. What is the essential ingredient in Dreen Hair shampoo? (Apparently one needs only use it once to get married the next day.)

3. What is "The highly potent yet nontoxic and nonirritating spermatocide" in Ortho Creme contraceptive jelly?

4. What is Twill Kar Kleener? This makes the doctor's Cadillac look like a mirror in the TV shows.

We would be very appreciative of this information and will of course be happy to send you any material you might wish on four of our products.

Sincerely yours,

I. V. Prinkosh
Deputy Assistant

Office of International Industrial Information Exchange
State Department
Washington, D. C.
Apr. 20, 1972

Mr. I. V. Prinkosh
Deputy Assistant
Office Scientific Exchange
243 Kova Street
Moscow, USSR

Dear Mr. Prinkosh:
    I am in receipt of your letter of April 11. The answer is: sodium lauryl sulfonate or sacronate.

Sincerely yours,
Henry M. Schmitz, Jr.
Communication Clerk

Office Scientific Exchange
243 Kova Street
Moscow
May 4, 1972

Mr. Henry M. Schmitz, Jr.
Communication Clerk
Office of International Industrial Information Exchange
Department of State
Washington, D. C.

Dear Mr. Schmitz:
    Your letter of April 20 has been turned over to me by Comrade Prinkosh. The relationship between our great country and the U.S.A. should not be strained by such nonsense.
    Comrade Prinkosh wrote in good faith asking for four items of information. I do not need to review with you the details of the treaty between our countries. Instead of giving him the four items he requested, you gave him only one, and you did not even state which one you were sending him.
    Before this matter becomes serious, I would suggest that you review the correspondence between our offices as well as the details of the treaty in question.

Yours,
G. M. Schushnok
Assistant Director

Office of International Industrial Information Exchange
State Department
Washington, D. C.
May 20, 1972

Mr. G. M. Schushnok
Assistant Director
Office Scientific Exchange
243 Kova Street
Moscow

Dear Mr. Schushnok:
I really didn't mean to strain our relationships. Mr. Prinkosh wrote asking for four items. I told him the answer, which is sodium lauryl sulfonate. It is they. Or they are it, as the case may be.

Sincerely yours,
Henry M. Schmitz, Jr.
Communication Clerk

Office Scientific Exchange
243 Kova Street
Moscow
June 3, 1972

Mr. Henry M. Schmitz, Jr.
Clerk
Office of International Industrial Information Exchange
Department of State
Washington, D. C.

Dear Mr. Schmitz:
Your letter of May 20 has been forwarded to this office by Comrade Schushnok.

I must say I am distressed by the attitude you have adopted. You seem to wish to make sport of what is a very serious matter.

I have reviewed the entire correspondence between our offices beginning with the courteous letter of Comrade Prinkosh on April 11. I have also taken the trouble of pulling the dossier on your own files.

Not only have you failed to answer the questions that were civilly addressed to you, but the following becomes evident:

1. You are the same man, who, a year ago, when we asked for the "mystic marvellous, hi-powered fuel" which propelled the submarine advertised on the box of Kellogg's Sugar Crisp, wrote back "sodium bicarbonate."

2. According to our translation division, the sentences "It is they" and "They are it" are not even English.

3. You have not shared this impudence with your superiors.

I have to say that the situation between our splendid country and the imperialist U.S.A. will deteriorate rapidly unless this matter can be cleared up at once.

Signed:

D. S. Kovitsch, ORR
Director

Office of International Industrial Information Exchange
State Department
Washington, D. C.
June 19, 1972

Mr. D. S. Kovitsch, O.R.R.
Director
Office Scientific Exchange
243 Kova Street
Moscow

Dear Mr. Kovitsch:

It *was* sodium bicarbonate. The instructions said to add a tablespoonful of vinegar to the water the submarine was put in. Possibly you forgot the vinegar.

I do hope you won't call any of this trouble to the attention of my boss. In contrast to your country, people can be fired over here, and I have a wife and baby boy (Henry III) to support.

Arm and Hammer will do.

I don't know what else I can say to smooth all this over.

Very sincerely yours,

Henry W. Schmitz, Jr.
Communication Clerk

Treaty Enforcement
The Kremlin
Moscow
July 6, 1972

Henry M. Schmitz, Jr.
Clerk, Office International Industrial Information Exchange
Department of State
Washington, D. C.

Dear Schmitz:
The entire problem which you have created has been turned over to this office. I have not the time to waste on these stupid matters.
Let us get one thing clear: We are not interested in toy submarines or sodium bicarbonate.
We are interested in:
Gardol in Colgate toothpaste
Dreen Hair Shampoo
The effective ingredient in Ortho Creme Contraceptive Jelly
Twill car cleaner
You will communicate each of these items promptly or letters will go at once to the Secretary of State and the President of your war-mongering country.

A. M. Tomykin, A.K.
Divisional Chief

Office of International Industrial Information Exchange
State Department
Washington, D. C.
July 16, 1972

Mr. A. M. Tomykin, A.K.
Divisional Chief
Treaty Enforcement
The Kremlin
Moscow

Dear Mr. Tomykin:
I know you are busy and I don't want to take your time. I also don't want you to write the Secretary of State and the President.

Therefore I will answer your questions as directly as I can... sodium lauryl sulfonate.

Everything Mr. Prinkosh asked for is the same thing.

Sincerely yours,
Henry M. Schmitz, Jr.
Communication Clerk

Treaty Enforcement
The Kremlin
Moscow
July 24, 1972

Henry M. Schmitz, Jr.
Clerk, Office International
Industrial Information Exchange
Department of State
Washington, D. C.

Schmitz:

Do you mean to imply in your communication of July 16 that this same substance is rubbed on the head, put on the teeth, and put into the vagina? The American public is obviously decadent.

A. M. Tomykin, A.K.
Divisional Chief

Office of International Industrial Information Exchange
State Department
Washington, D. C.
Aug. 1, 1972

Mr. A. M. Tomykin, A.K.
Divisional Chief
Treaty Enforcement
The Kremlin
Moscow

Dear Mr. Tomykin:

I don't know if it is truly decadence, but I am glad you understand the situation.

You just have to realize that as far as the American Public is concerned, as long as you name it something different each time, there is no surface on which they will not rub and no orifice into which they will not insert, sodium lauryl sulfonate.

Sincerely yours,

Henry M. Schmitz, Jr.
Communication Clerk

Obstet Gynecol 1969;33:292–5.

COMMENTARY

This delightful article, another one by Allan C. Barnes (see page 61) is a little dated, because the Soviet Union no longer exists and the Cold War has ended. However, anyone who has tried to negotiate his or her way through a bureaucracy likely will find humor in it.

Doctor-Patient Relations

A sick person is given an infusion. Thirteenth-century illustration in
Tractatus de pestilentia, Abenzohar. (University Library, Prague,
Czech Republic. Photo © G. Dagli Orti.)

*The relationship between physician and patient represents the very
essence of medical practice. Items chosen for this section involved that
relationship, in one way or another. Roughly the first half reflect
the physician's perceptions and perspectives, whereas the latter part
includes articles and poems expressing how the patient might view the
relationship.*

Bearing Down Pains

Allan C. Barnes, MD

*J*une 30, 1970. That patient who is presumably the last patient I shall ever see has gone. That curious relationship between the woman who has been saving up her complaints for several weeks to justify her trip to my office, and the physician who was supposed to know the answers to all these complaints has been dissolved.

In the examining room, the nurse is throwing away the disposable needles, the disposable syringes, the disposable gloves and the disposable drapes that are the hallmark of contemporary medical practice.

In the consultation room, however, I am recognizing that I have escaped without ever being asked that fatal question by a single patient. I am home free, as the saying goes.

Over the years the dialogue—when searching for symptoms of relaxation of the pelvic floor—has gone something like this:

"When you cough or sneeze do you lose a little urine from your bladder?"

"Well sometimes. Particularly if I have a bad cold ... you know, with a heavy cough."

"Do you have bearing down pains?"

"Only when I've been on my feet a lot. At the end of the day."

So it has gone in front of the patient. Confident and assured, I have sought out the symptoms which would give me the necessary clues; assist in establishing a diagnosis. But at home, in the quiet of the evening, that confidence and assurance has dwindled. What would happen, I have repeatedly wondered, if the patient, instead of answering my question "Do you have bearing down pains?" had asked "What are they?" Since I have never felt a bearing down pain, I would be hard put to it to describe it for her. Where would my confidence and sense of assurance have gone under such circumstances?

Late at night, I would wake up with this nightmare in front of me. Staring at the dark of the ceiling I would visualize a conversation in which the patient asked me to define and describe the symptom I was asking about. "Bearing down pains? Tell me what you mean, Doctor."

There I would be, the knowledgeable physician, unable to answer. How silly can a man appear? There I would be, one who has always insisted on using words and terms correctly, caught in the act of bandying about phrases that were (at least in my own personal experience) meaningless and undefined. A fine perspiration would break out on my forehead. I could define stress urinary incontinence, yet I couldn't define a bearing down pain.

But the threat of exposure is over. The last patient has departed from the office, and over the decades no one has ever asked me to define my terms. Every woman (bless them all) has either said "Yes," "No" or "Sometimes." No one has unmasked me, and presumably they all think I have bearing down pains frequently and am thoroughly conversant with what I am talking about.

I went into the examining room and sat on the (presumably) disposable stool.

"Mrs. Thompson, do you have bearing down pains?"

"Nope." Prompt, perhaps a little icy (was I violating personal privacy?) But, certainly decisive. She knew she didn't have them.

"Have you ever had them?"

"Never." A little more icy, but equally decisive.

"Then how do you know you haven't got them this very minute?"

"What are you talking about?"

"Well, if you have never experienced them, how can you know what they are? And if you don't know what they are, how can you answer so quickly that you don't have them?"

"Are you all right?"

"I was only interested."

"Look, you ask me if I have a pain in my left ear, and I say 'Yes' or 'No'. You ask me if I have a headache and I say 'Yes' or 'No'. So what's the difference? You ask me if I have bearing down pains and I answer 'Yes' or 'No'. Don't make a production out of it."

"I don't think it's quite the same. When I ask about an earache and a headache at least I personally know what they are."

"You've been working too hard. Go in the other room and relax."

"It's a matter of integrity in the use of words."

"I think you're overtired. Should I call your wife?"

"That wouldn't help. She doesn't have them. I asked her." I got up from the stool. "As best as I can determine all little girls are born knowing what bearing down pains are and the answer to that particular question." I started for the consultation room. "I'm home free," I said.

Obstet Gynecol 1970;36:652–3.

COMMENTARY

This and the following two articles from Allan C. Barnes (see biographical information, page 61), address various aspects of the doctor–patient relationship. The first two concern facets of history-taking that probably most gynecologists have wondered about in their idle moments, but few with such humor. The third is a clever view of the preoccupation with shortening labor.

To our modern ear, these articles might seem a little condescending and perhaps even a trifle sexist. However, they need to be viewed in relation to the era from which they came. In Barnes's time, 30–50 years ago, medicine was pretty much a man's game; more than 90% of physicians, and even a larger proportion of gynecologists, were men. Thus, obstetrics–gynecology was characterized by men taking histories from women. Things are different—and better—now, but we can still get a chuckle from that perspective of former times.

When Was Your Last Menstrual Period?

Allan C. Barnes, MD

December 1953

 have been impressed, as have all physicians, by our professional obligation towards lay education in matters medical. The term "doctor" originally meant "teacher," and the physician who does not instruct his patients is a pretty poor specimen indeed. Inspired by thoughts and ideals such as these, I sat down recently to write a manual for patient instruction. My topic, I felt, was one of the utmost importance, and I was reasonably sure the world—in fact both the feminine and the masculine worlds—would welcome my contribution.

The title of the arbeit is *How to Remember the Date of Your Last Menstrual Period*, and the value of an authoritative monograph on this subject is immediately apparent. Think, I reasoned, think of the untold personal tensions that could be relieved, of the family discussions obviated, and of the hours saved in innumerable offices of physicians—hours accumulated as we patiently await the answer to that recurrent question: "When was your last menstrual period?" All that is needed is a set of rules, a clear-cut opus on the subject, and we will have a significant contribution to lay health education.

I launched my project (this was some time ago) in proper scientific fashion by collecting the fundamental data. Whenever I asked this particular question, I would poise my pencil over the record, and promptly write down *the next sentence that the patient uttered*. Regardless of the patient's age, regardless of the patient's I.Q., in over a thousand cases I faithfully wrote down what the woman said when asked for the date of her last menses. With these data recorded and coded, I divided the answers into certain broad classifications, together with the percentage of patients falling into each group.

Now it must be admitted immediately that a certain number of women quite simply answered the question which they had been asked. This came as a distinct surprise to the writer, who had had the a priori impression that no woman ever directly answered this particular question with a specific date. Nevertheless of the entire study series 8 per cent replied promptly with the desired figure. In general these women were the wives of internes [sic] or younger staff men, and their replies were made mechanically, as though they had been carefully rehearsed just prior to setting out for the gynecologist.

The largest group, however, 48 per cent, answered this question by asking another one. This is said to be a distinctive characteristic of American conversation ("What were you doing last night?"—"Whaddya wanna know for?"), but I had never before realized its pervasiveness. Thus, for example, to the question: "When was your last menstrual period?" would come the answering question: "Let's see, when was the Missouri game?" These questions which were asked of me tended to center around athletic contests or outstanding social events, and really called for a rather extensive knowledge of contemporary affairs on my part. Accordingly I have found that in the long run it saves time (in this part of the country) if a gynecologist will memorize the Big Ten football schedule, the dates of the Kentucky Derby, the World Series, and the strawberry festival at the Methodist Church. Armed with some fixed point as this, the patient and doctor can count forward one, two, or even six months, as the case may be. Lately much of such joint counting in this office has for some reason centered around the recent Coronation (June 2nd, if you had forgotten).

The next largest group (29%) answered the given question by making a statement to themselves rather than to me. Rather than launching into a counting effort that included their physician, they would launch into a quiet monologue of personal events which excluded him. On reviewing them, one finds that these statements range over a wide spectrum of moods and reactions. Thus at one end of the scale we find the morbid:

"What was the date of your last menstrual period?"

"Well now ... Johnny fell down the cellar steps July 16th, and I ..."

And at the other end of the line we encounter the joyful:

"Let me see—the night we got drunk and drove all the way down from Indian River was July 16th, and I remember that it was just ten days later that I ... Thank God ..."

And somewhere in between these one encounters the purely practical:

"Let me see ... my husband came home from Chicago on July 16th, and it was ..."

So it goes. Actually, in these thousands of case records, I have accumulated a store of knowledge of remarkable value. But now a new technique in question answering has appeared on the horizon, and I see no reason why it should not sweep the country.

I am referring, of course, to the current Congressional Committee hearings, and particularly to the increasing habit of televising their quizzing of witnesses. The 83rd Congress is searching diligently for Communists, subversives, or even Democrats, but as they crossexamine [sic] their witnesses before the television cameras, our patients are learning new ways of answering questions.

I am not referring to the "I don't remember" school of answer. Actually, the American gynecologist has faced this type of answer (11 per cent in my series) long before the American Congress ever heard it. In fact I have one patient who can keep better track of the six-month cycles of her Pomeranians than she can of her own 28-day cycle. She literally cannot remember, and while she could not possibly be subversive, I will offer her to any committee that wants her.

I am referring, however, to the appeal to the First and Fifth Amendments, and the refusal to answer the Committee's questions on the grounds that it might tend to incriminate the witness. My own reaction to the Fifth Amendment is that we can, if we wish, take it out of the Constitution, but that, if we feel it should remain in the Constitution, we should not object to people employing it. My further reaction is that there are few questions which potentially have a better chance of incriminating the witness than does the question: "When was your last menstrual period." My first group (the 8 per cent) were obviously coached by counsel. The largest group that ended up asking me the questions are obviously the adroit witnesses. But the woman that carries on the monologue of personal events and intimate history often implicates herself far more than she realizes. For her (and for those who are embarrassingly overdue) a retreat to the First and Fifth Amendments would be perfectly legitimate, and I anticipate that our patients—learning quickly from their television screens—will employ it more and more frequently.

Obstet Gynecol 1953;2:664–5.

The Hours of Labor

Allan C. Barnes, MD

June 1967

am not particularly enthusiastic about writing the history of medical therapy in the United States in the past half century. In its broadest impact, it has—this is true—been wonderful. The antibiotics have been introduced; cancer chemotherapy has been launched. As everyone keeps saying to everyone else, it has been a marvelous half century.

History in general, of course, is a record of the winning side. The Carthaginian campaign is seen through the eyes of the Romans, since there were no Carthaginian historians left. We record successes and we minimize failures. We record the through pathways and minimize the blind alleys we ran down.

But the honest historian would be bound to record the false starts, the failed experiments, the brick wall at the end of that blind alley. The history which he would write would make uneasy reading. We do not like to be reminded that we once gave "shots of liver" to everyone in the waiting room, before he even got in to see the doctor ... or that oral "pituitary extract" would cure everything from obesity to malnutrition ... or that we once prescribed extract of orange peel. The successes of this age of medical miracles have come at a price, and part of that price is the host of non-remedies we have passingly believed in.

All of this came to mind recently when I looked back over some of the literature dealing with shortening the length of labor. Ever since man first started attending women in her travail, this has been a recurrent theme. How can we reduce the number of hours spent in this process? What can we do, as helpful and knowledgeable males, to abbreviate this female occupation? To reduce the length of labor would produce incredible benefits: shorten women's suffering; reduce the amount of medication needed during the first stage; get us to the first tee on time. Repeatedly this topic has come up, and the history of these efforts should be recorded.

In 1924, Glum and Hurried wrote their first paper on a modification of the quinine molecule which speeded labor and cut down remarkably on the damage to the eighth nerve. This drug (marketed as "Quinoline") enjoyed a brief popularity and now is heard of no more. In 1932, Space and Down had a much better suggestion when they proposed a mixture of hot enemas, castor oil, and whole pituitary (to be eaten on a cracker). Their series indicated that, when this regimen was introduced on their service, the average length of labor (compared with the labors of a year before) was 2 hr. shorter.

After a brief spate of enthusiasm (encouraged by a *Ladies Home Journal* article entitled "Demand That You Have a SHORTER Labor Than Your Grandmother Had"), this logical suggestion also disappeared. Shortly thereafter, however, Grod reported that if the patient drank large amounts of hyaluronidase (which would soften the cement substance which held the cervix together) the average length of labor (on his service) was shortened by 2 hr. No one uses this now, and I guess that it's just because man has become callous to woman's plight. Also, possibly, the fact that hyaluronidase isn't effective by mouth may influence this contemporary neglect of such a remarkable discovery.

A great milestone was passed when Monteley, West, *et al.* proposed that pitocin, placed in the air-conditioning unit and inhaled by all laboring patients, would reduce the number of hours of parturition and would "regularize" labor. This term caught on and the *Reader's Digest* ran an article entitled "Demand a Regularized Labor!" Fortunately, or unfortunately, the technic went its way, and the air-conditioner filter no longer gets clogged.

As I say, I have no impulse to review all the details of my burrowing into the history of this particular form of therapy. Suffice it to say that this subject has come up in the scientific literature about every 10 months since the Glum paper of 1924. The curious thing, as I now reread them in the quiet of my study, is that each of these reports indicates that the drug under question would shorten the length of labor by about 2 hr. It is a mystery what happened to the 3-hr. medications (would you believe 3 hr.?) or the 1-hr. medications (too short even for a Communication in Brief?).

Enthused however, by this forgotten lore of scientific contributions, I got to work on the problem. I compounded a massive medication of all the drugs and procedures which have been recommended for the shortening of the duration of labor. If each of these, on careful (but not always double-blind) study, had been so effective, the combination of all of them should shorten labor miraculously. Not all of the suggested drugs are currently available, but there was no trouble in getting a large National Institutes of Health grant and having the proper (but now long-forgotten) medications compounded for me. Obviously the government was interested in cutting down the loss of effective hours of industrial labor which these wasted hours of obstetric labor represented.

While the resultant program was historically accurate, nevertheless it produced a schedule which was therapeutically complicated. Some drugs

244   DOCTOR–PATIENT RELATIONS

were to be given orally, some intravenously, some intramuscularly, etc., etc. The total combination, however, by all that the scientific authors had assured me (and who can doubt the author of a scientific paper?) was due to be highly effective. The very first time I tried this magnificent cocktail combination, I had to eliminate those ingredients meant to be given rectally. The rectal capsule itself was enormous, but just as I was about to insert it, the baby emerged. It was smiling at me (not having had time to complete Internal Rotation), and it has smiled ever since, although it can't add 2 and 2 at the age of 7.

The combination I had selected (allowing 2 hr. shortening of labor for each ingredient reported in the world's literature) would have shortened the length of labor by 16 hr. Sure enough, with the first scheduled induction I tried it on, the baby was born 45. [sic] min. *before* the onset of labor. I got to the first tee some time before the rest of the foursome was assembled, and wondered if I should tell them about the benefits of studying the history of therapeutics.

In the last analysis, this unhappy outcome (I shot a 96 that day) has led me back to the strange question: What is the length of labor for? If we are going to write articles and carry out studies designed to Do Away with The Length of Labor, then we must have some knowledge that it is a Bad Thing. If the length of labor is a Good Thing, why all this list of articles which I have had to read while becoming an historian on the subject?

Presumably (this has also required some historical research) the length of labor allows time for the maternal soft parts and the fetal intracranial tissues to adjust to each other. When such time is not allowed, trouble ensues. Overwhelming precipitous labor can produce multiple by-products of the nonadjustment between these tissues. On the day of the minus-45-min. labor, it took me an hour to sew up the maternal perineum. I'm hotter than a fox at this, however, and the result was quite comely. But no one has ever told me how to sew up a torn tentorium and my golf score would have been better if that baby hadn't been so ashen.

As I said, I don't think I will ever quite do as an historian of medical therapeutics. Certainly not as a tester of "Drugs That Have Been Enthusiastically Reported." I figure that the length of labor was put there for some purpose, and—as long as it doesn't get *too* protracted—I'm going to leave it there.

Anyone who wants the recipe for the mixture I used can get it by writing Box 1949, Grand Central Station, New York City.

Certain it is that I shan't be using it anymore.

Give the boys at the first tee my regards!

Obstet Gynecol 1967;29:877–9.

Shamanism

Arthur G. King, MD

JULY 1960

nthropologists tell us that in all primitive tribes of all races since the dawn of history, there existed an individual with special powers and responsibilities, whose title has been variously translated as: wise man, fakir, prophet, soothsayer, medicine man, seer, priest-doctor, witch doctor, or shaman. The last is used commonly for the generic classification, and the term "shamanism" is given to the art which he practiced.*

Every tribe had a leader for battle, for hunting, and for maintaining order within the community or clan or kingdom, usually by brute force and arbitrary rules. But the shaman commanded respect for his keen powers of observation, his capacity to reason, his ability to remember and to predict, and for his high moral sense and spirit of obligation to his fellow tribesmen.

When the savage in the cave trembled at the force of the thunder, it was the shaman who explained the origin of the storm according to his best understanding. If he ascribed it to the anger of a spirit or a god, the ignorant tribesman accepted the concept and, when the thunder ceased, assumed that the shaman had a special power of intercession. If the hunting were good after a ritual by the shaman, he received the credit and honor due him; if the results of the chase were bad, the shaman was usually smart enough to "explain" his failure.

The shaman's reputed power of intercession and his familiarity with rituals quickly stamped him a man of the gods or, at least, a person a step nearer than the others to the omnipotent beings of the time. When dis-

---

Shamanism has been defined as a belief of the Ural-Altaic culture that all phenomena stemmed from the activity of good or bad spirits, and that these might be stimulated, appeased, or exorcised. But this definition dates from the fourth and fifth centuries A.D. when shamanism was considered a pagan religion. The belief is universal and goes back to neolithic days. The area referred to is bounded on the east by the Altai Mountains and Turkestan, and on the west by the Ural Mountains and the Caspian Sea. The Greeks and Romans called it Scythia, and all peoples of Asia Minor and Europe, and perhaps India, are thought to have originated in this area.

putes arose it was to the shaman the litigants came because of his better reasoning power and his integrity, so that he was also a judge. With a strong moral sense he inveighed against injustice and wickedness and foretold the consequences, and hence in Biblical times was called a prophet. Other races called him a *soothsayer*, because the truth of his precepts soon became recognized. His advice was sought in all sorts of things, and he acquired a reputation for farsightedness, for knowing the future, for "prognosis," as it was called by the Greeks.

When someone was hurt or fell sick, the shaman was called to explain the phenomenon, to exorcise the evil spirit, to intercede with the Great Spirit for the man's health, and incidentally to do whatever possible, such as stanch the bleeding, set the broken bone, reduce the fever, or give a plant extract to promote diuresis. Being a man of intelligence the shaman applied whatever skill or knowledge was known at that stage of the tribe's development, but wisely he did not neglect the traditional ceremonials. Thus the shaman combined the functions of priest, master of ceremonies, lawyer, teacher, psychiatrist, and judge.

As civilization became more complex, specialization was inevitable. Some shamans concentrated on the legal aspects; others, more mystical, devoted their time to the religious or ritualistic side of the profession. Some concentrated on helping the downtrodden, as social workers; or the ignorant, as teachers; or the unhappy, as psychiatrists. Some shamans were deeply sincere and self-sacrificing; some were more human, and used their hold over the tribesmen for their own selfish purposes. Some were hundreds of years in advance of the tribe's level of culture. Others were ignorant, but shrewd enough to capitalize on the technique of shamanism. These were the charlatans. Some good shamans were both wise and shrewd and, with the philosophy that the end justifies the means, used hokus-pokus [sic], or worked miracles, or intensified the ritual side of their work to effect cures, or improve social conditions, or rectify injustices, or advance the civilization or national advantages of their tribe. Gradually, however, the people became wiser and smarter and were able to see through the hokus-pokus [sic], and that brand of shamanism became discredited, despite the good it had done. We doctors are the functional descendants of the shamans who specialized in healing the sick.

When primitive man had chills and fever, every third day the shaman exhibited, that is, held up for the patient to see, a branch of a sacred tree. That word "exhibit" is of interest, because many thousand years later our medical textbooks, in dealing with malaria, used the words "for the chills and fever of this disease, copious doses of the bark should be exhibited." The word "exhibit," meaning to prescribe a medicine, is an etymologic link in the chain which binds us to shamanism.

When the primitive man had a common cold the shaman knew that only time would cure him. But this was scant comfort to the patient who wanted something done. So the shaman sacrificed the skin of the sufferer's buttock and rubbed in some moldy cheese, uttering as he did so the incantation, "walla, walla, bing, bang," which freely translated means "This will cure you in a few days." Many modern physicians treating the same disease, at least wipe the skin off first with an alcohol sponge and use the extract of the mold, but the ritualistic phrase and the end results are the same. Which is the witch doctor?

The Visigoth women had most of the menstrual difficulties of the women of today, and the shamans probably cured as high a percentage of them as we do. They "exhibited," and by this time the word meant to prescribe or administer, a concoction to be taken at a certain time of the month, expressed, of course, in terms of phases of the moon, for three successive months. The medieval *langue d'oc* is no longer spoken, but the ingredients sound familiar. The medication, we are told, consisted of the whole ovary of a sow, the testis of a bull, and the urine of a pregnant mare.

Let us not condemn the shamans any more than we disparage our grandfathers because they used a straight razor instead of an electric shaver, drove a horse and buggy, amputated the cervix for carcinoma, or applied high forceps. Modern doctors differ from shamans in only one respect: We have more tricks in our bag, more gadgets, and more skill, thanks to the tiny increments of knowledge left to us by each succeeding generation of practitioners of the healing art, regardless of what they were called. We have inherited even their sense of showmanship and their obsession with rituals.

When the American Indian medicine man waved a pungently burning turkey feather in the face of a parturient woman in the second stage of labor, was it hokus-pokus [sic], or did it help the expulsive forces? When we put our finger in the rectum after repairing an episiotomy, is this an adjunct to modern surgical technic or merely the doctor's farewell salute in this particular case to the goddess of parturition?

Sir William Osler described the secret of shamanism some 60 years ago: "Faith is the great lever of life; without it man can do nothing; with it, all things are possible to him. Faith in the gods or in the saints cures one, faith in little pills another, hypnotic suggestion a third, and faith in a plain, common doctor, a fourth." Or, as put by Galen, a shaman of considerable reputation: "He cures most in whom most are confident." The people had faith in the shamans as men of integrity, faith in their technics, laughable as they may seem to us. Osler called this faith the *aurum potabile*, the drinkable gold. As the tribesmen became more educated, they were able to see through the hypocrisy of some of the shamans and the ignorance of others, and then the gold turned to dross.

Our problem as doctors is to retain the faith of the people in us as a profession. Recent competent surveys have shown that too high a proportion of people mistrust doctors in general, question their integrity as a group, and have far less respect for them than obtained 20 years ago. The respondents, of course, excluded their own doctors, who are wonderful and devoted persons, but a third-year medical student can explain the psychology of this exclusion. Any loss of confidence in the medical profession as a whole, any reduction in the dignity attendant on the degree of doctor of medicine, any condemnation of physicians in general, affects each one of us, even the best and the most loved. As John Donne wrote, "No man is an island." And when the bell tolls for the death of the faith of the people in the medical profession, "it tolls for thee."

We can retain the faith of the public in our brand of shamanism only by rising to the level of intellectual, psychologic, and social development which the rest of the people have reached. We have already stopped using "exhibit" for prescribing drugs, but we are still indulging in rituals. We have given up the frock coat and beard, but there are still too many Cadillacs running around flaunting the green caduceus. Because so many of us fail to explain why and what we are doing for our patients, the lay magazines are doing it for us, and concomitantly teaching us a lot about patient psychology we should have learned in medical school.

Every unnecessary hysterectomy done by other surgeons reduces by a minute quantum the faith of your patient in *your* surgical judgment. Every expensive pill any doctor prescribes on the basis of glowing quotations in the pharmaceutical advertisements or reports in the medical literature of commercially inspired, inadequately controlled, so-called scientific experiments moves you one centimeter toward the status of witch doctor. The resistance to hormone therapy that you meet in your patients is the direct result of the indiscriminate use of estrogens by other gynecologists. The earlier shamans had the same difficulty: the Indian squaws finally refused the assistance to second-stage labor which a burning turkey feather provided because so many of the medicine men had used it unsuccessfully before complete dilatation of the cervix. But this was undoubtedly due to the ignorance of the medicine men as to when to use the technic, and in their selection of cases.

We make the same mistakes. Think of the uterine suspensions, the pelvic clean-outs, the tonsillectomies, and cholecystectomies we did 30 years ago! This was ignorance on our part rather than charlatanism for most of the profession, but the same could be said for most of the shamans of previous eras. The lay public does not make a distinction, and somehow always looks for the worse interpretation, aided and abetted by the "yellower" portions of our daily and magazine press.

Many of us rationalize that the pill or injection we give, or the operation we perform, satisfies the need of the patient for some kind of therapy, even though in our own heart we question its real curative value. We argue that it has psychotherapeutic value and hope that it can do no harm. This is the same reasoning which made the little bag of asafetida so effective and popular in the armamentarium of our predecessors. This placebo effect is the essence of shamanism, namely *the curing of illness by utilizing the confidence of our patients in our methods*, regardless of what methods happen to be considered best in any era. The secret of shamanism lies in the faith of the patient that we are sincere in utilizing that confidence, and that we have not deluded ourselves in the power of our medicine. Let us not abuse that faith in us or that confidence in our modern science. Let us respect the growing sophistication of the public; let us be more discriminating in our medical beliefs; and let us be more honest with both our patients and ourselves.

Obstet Gynecol 1960;16:129–32.

COMMENTARY

This thoughtful essay concerns how the patient's confidence influences the outcome of what is done as treatment. The author, an obstetrician–gynecologist from Cincinnati, died in May 2002.

Mother's Day

Natalie A. Mariano, MD

AUGUST 2002

Her mother died in January, after a life that spanned three centuries. She had lived a full life on the land where she was born 103 years ago in Kansas. She had farmed alongside her husband, raising corn and wheat for market and tending to tomatoes and zucchini for canning. She grew flowers for cutting: delicate irises, bright peonies, and wind-swept daisies. She had kept a garden until two summers past, when her knees got too stiff for planting and weeding. When she could no longer garden, she had no reason to look forward to spring and was ready to lie down in the ground she had worked all her life.

Sarah went back to Kansas for the funeral and came back home trying to talk away her sadness. Her mother had lived for more than a lifetime, and Sarah could not justify grieving her mother's longevity. When friends asked how she was doing, Sarah reassured them that she was comforted that her mother had been blessed with a long life and with a peaceful death.

She came to see me in May because she had chest pain. The pain was deep in her chest and not provoked by exertion. The pain was dull but constant. I reviewed her history and examined her, but could find nothing to explain her symptoms. Her cardiogram was normal, as were her x-rays and blood tests. She told me about her mother's death and the unexpected trip to Kansas.

She talked about her mother and her life on the farm. Sarah had never known her mother to be sick, and she had inherited her mother's good health, never knowing how it felt to be seriously ill. So, too, she had been a daughter all of her life, never knowing how it felt to live without a mother. We talked about the dull empty feeling in the middle of Sarah's chest. And we talked about the void in her life that was left by the passing of the woman who gave her life 76 years ago, and who had stayed in her life until last winter. We spoke about her childhood in Kansas. We spoke of planting peonies and daisies and canning tomatoes and zucchini.

A week later, after a series of tests had shown her to be perfectly healthy, Sarah came to the office with a handful of daffodils. Her eyes were moist with tears and she spoke openly of her sadness, but her chest pain was gone. Her children were coming from the west coast on the weekend to celebrate Mother's Day. She was looking forward to springtime and planting peonies.

Obstet Gynecol 2002;100:363.

Gynevision

Roger P. Smith, MD, and
Frank W. Ling, MD

OCTOBER 1991

Gy•ne•vi•sion\'gin-ə-'vizh-ən\n (ca. 1934) [Gk gyn-, fr. gynē woman — more at QUEEN, + ME, fr. L vision-, visio, fr. visus, pp. of vidēre to see more at WIT] (13c) 1 a : a system of viewing all things as arising from female pelvic organs <using ~ to find the cause of pelvic pain> 1 b : a system or procedure designed to defer all further investigation to those who provide health care for women <the patient underwent ~> 1 c : a field of vision restricted to the female organs typified but not limited to the uterus, tubes, and ovaries, resulting in the elimination of all other fields, structures, or systems : NARROWMINDEDNESS 2 : to have or possess attributes of gynevision — gy•ne•vi•sion•ing adj
  Gy•ne•vi•sion•ary \'gin- ə-'vizh-ə-ner-ē\ n : one who possesses gynevision — gy•ne•vi•sion•er
  Gy•ne•vi•si•ol•o•gist \'gin- ə-viz-i-'äl-ə-jəst\ n one who is restricted, by law, to diagnostic and therapeutic interventions involving the female organs
  Gy•ne•vi•sor \'gin-ə-'vi-zər\ n any of a number of devices worn to restrict the vision to those pelvic organs possessed solely by women
  The term "gynevision" was introduced in 1954 by Dr. Maurice Monody, of Des Moines, Iowa, and applied to a clinical approach he developed that facilitated moving patients out of his crowded waiting room. As a result of his success, Dr. Monody gave up a lackluster career in general practice for a more lucrative position as head of emergency services at the Sacred Covenant of Saint Mary's Community Memorial Regional Hospital and Grill. When he took on this new position, he was appalled at the backlog of patients crowding his waiting area. Based on his previous success in general practice, he realized that fully half of his patients could be quickly disposed of merely by diagnosing a vaginal or pelvic condition and referring them to gynecologists. Dr. Monody was so successful in implementing this technique that it was soon known that if you went to his hospital emergency room, "it would all be over soon." Dr. Monody's greatest success came in November 1958, a month in which he was able to diagnose 347 cases of ovarian cysts with such diverse presenting complaints as

dyspepsia and vaginal itch. (Historians argue that his single greatest coup was a patient with psoriasis, for whom Dr. Monody not only was able to obtain a gynecologic consultation, but also actually got the patient admitted to the hospital to "rule out ectopic pregnancy.")

Following Dr. Monody's untimely death during a hospital credentials committee meeting in 1964, the technique of gynevision languished, but did not die. Gynevision has again risen to prominence with the introduction and widespread use of ultrasonography and laparoscopy, tools that can identify uterine fibroids of less than 1 cm, ovaries enlarged to the size of 2 × 3 cm, and 4-mm follicular cysts by menstrual day 4. These new technologies, combined with such puzzling clinical conditions as chronic pelvic pain, premenstrual syndrome, and papillomavirus infection, have opened the door for further development of gynevision to include such modern technological advances as laser and loop diathermy. All this makes it likely that gynevision will become a true "growth industry of the 90s."

Obstet Gynecol 1991;78:708–9.

The Fall of the Queen of Heaven

H. B. Atlee, MD

APRIL 1963

O ne night over 50 years ago I was sitting in front of the kitchen stove in a miner's shack in Nova Scotia, chewing tobacco and meditating. On the other side of a 6-foot high partition, the miner's wife was in labor, attended by an old dame who crooned encouragingly during the contractions. It was 3 o'clock in the morning, a bad time anyway for the human race, and from my meditations arose the dismal conclusion that, considering the racial importance of what she is doing, the woman in labor gets a poor deal out of it. Tonight, half a century later, my feeling is much the same.

Of course we have made gains. I, for instance, have long since given up chewing tobacco. We have reduced maternal mortality almost to the irreducible, and made great dents in infant mortality. Nevertheless, two things continue to bother me. For one, we obstetricians seem to think and act as if pregnancy and labor constitute a pathologic rather than a physiologic process. For another, women seem to derive very little real prestige and satisfaction from this act so vital to the perpetuation of the race. I should like to play some variations on these two themes.

Can anyone deny that our attitude towards obstetrics is highly colored with pathology, or that we conduct it in an atmosphere highly charged with pathology? We deliver practically 100% of our women in the hospital. I am glad for their sakes and ours that we do. But the word "hospital" connotes pathology: you go to a hospital because you are sick, and the whole setup of our maternity hospitals and departments is geared to the pathologic philosophy characteristic of all hospitals.

A few years ago I suggested to some of the younger men in our department that it might help to change our outlook if we called our maternity hospital by some other name. But what could you call it? they protested: "Since they go there to have a baby," I said, "Why not call it a Baby House?" They did not say that this was too simple, too unpretentious, too Anglo-Saxon: their rationalization was: "Baby House sounds too much like Bawdy House!" So I suppose if a change is made it'll be to something like Obstetricorium—a designation I find hard to associate with a physiologic process, but one which will undoubtedly satisfy our yen for medical gobbledygook. Nevertheless, I still feel that, even if we don't change the name, we must change the game of our maternity hospitals before childbearing can regain its true physiologic identity.

The irony of the present situation is that we have really narrowed tremendously the actual field of pathology within obstetrics. Toxemias of pregnancy and puerperal infections have all but disappeared in our best circles. If we could learn to prevent miscarriage, prematurity, and malformations—and we may be closer than we think—we would be within sight of the irreducible minimum. Yet our minds, remaining perversely in the old groove, continue to cling almost exclusively to this narrowing pathologic field whose gains are sinking to a point of no return. If anyone doubts this, I can only refer him to our current obstetric journals where, in issue after issue, the same old pathologic spinach is served up in the same dull and humorless medical journalese. No matter where we turn we find ourselves bathed in this stale and dismal literary swamp water.

All this may be inexcusable but it is understandable. Our entire basic medical education is so obsessed with pathology that it is practically impossible for us to think of any woman who comes to us as other than *sick*. So deeply does this fixation take hold of our subconscious that, when we find she has no palpable cellular derangement, we are actually frustrated and unhappy; conversely, there is nothing so beautiful in our experience as the feel of a pelvis full of fibroids.

Nor should we leave out of account the basic urge that drives so many of the most enterprising of us into medicine. Here is perhaps the last remaining field—although the physicists have invaded it lately—in which one can perform miracles. The emotional immaturity evinced in this yen to play God seems particularly to infect surgeons and, since as gynecologists we are also surgeons, we tend to carry over the attitudes and behaviors of our pathologic role as gynecologists into what should be our physiologic one as obstetricians.

For this reason we are happier extracting babies with forceps and tossing them over our shoulders to awe-struck internes [sic] and nurses than sitting patiently in front of an all-too-slowly dilating perineum and wiping away the feces. Reinforcing this is the fact that we may be due in 15 minutes at another hospital to do a hysterectomy. Under such circumstances it is not easy to accept the ancient dictum that they also serve who only sit and wipe. What is so easy and tempting is to persuade oneself that low forceps damage no one. Or to go further, as one recent critic of Natural Childbirth did in a popular woman's magazine, and declare that low forceps actually prevent stress incontinence and prolapse—a supposition surely as dubious and lacking in real proof as the one that, when our astronauts finally reach the moon, they'll find nothing there but green cheese.

If you have to aid a physiologic process with forceps, you say in effect that there is something wrong with that process—you pathologize it. The extent to which this pathologizing goes on in some centers is considerable. A few years ago I was asked to speak in a certain city and, just as we stepped on to the platform, the chairman said: "Perhaps you should know that our practice here is to give a spinal and apply forceps on all cases." "Is that," I asked, "why you suggested I speak on Natural Childbirth?" "Oh, no," he replied, "we just thought we'd like to know how the other half lives."

I'd like to propose to any young obstetrician with stars in his eyes that he is likely to get more gold from them thar hills from now on by turning away from this temptation to pathologize and trying to reinterpret childbirth as a physiologic process. He will not find this an easy way of life, but if you have stars in your eyes life can't be easy anyway. Here is the sort of difficulty he will be up against. At a recent meeting of our Maritime Provinces group the question came up for discussion: Should we obstetric specialists stop handling normal cases in competition with the general practitioner and confine our practice only to consultation with the latter in difficult and complicated ones? The majority opinion favored this. Yet how can we persuade ourselves to regard obstetrics as a physiologic manifestation when our vested interest lies in expanding its pathologic overtones? We obstetricians are only human, and when the size of our income depends directly on our capacity to complicate labor, we'll bite on that apple as surely as our father Adam did.

Our young explorer of the physiologic will find also that the architecture and philosophy of our obstetric hospitals and departments work definitely against him. These were originally constructed to deal only with the emergencies, the normal case still being delivered in the home. They have never got away from the implications of that concept. Yet in the meantime they have been called upon to handle the normal to such an extent that every woman south of Baffin Land is delivered in hospital. Furthermore, the pressure of family fear pushes her into hospital early in the first stage, so that the institution has to deal with her for many hours before she is ready for delivery, especially if she is a primipara.

It is just here that our maternity hospitals display their greatest inadequacy. They provide no special technics or accommodation for handling the long first stage. Nor have they created any special psychologic atmosphere with which to support or fortify the frightened and untried girl having her first baby. She is dumped all too often into a small, austere bedroom in such close proximity to the actual delivery room that she soon becomes all too aware of the atmosphere of pain, blood, and tears around her. Within its comfortless walls she is often left alone for long periods of time with no other company but her pains and fears, which act synergistically to increase each other. The room is too small to walk about freely, so she climbs into bed and stays there, so lacking in freedom and human dignity that she can't even go to the bathroom, but must bear with the precarious insult of the bedpan. To enable her to tolerate this essentially brutal situation we are forced from sheer humanity to dull her awareness of its insolence with a whole array of sedatives—there's a new one in the journals every month. And the more sedation she gets the less easily will her equally doped baby make its response to life when it is born.

We have been able to demonstrate in a small way in Halifax that a section can be incorporated into a maternity hospital that allows for a more humane handling of the first stage. It consists of a small wing on the same floor with the delivery section, but at right angles to it so that, while immediately adjacent, it is shut away completely from its sights and sounds. This section has the great advantage that it does not tie the laboring woman to her bed, but allows her to move about in complete freedom. She can have her husband or a friend with her. She can look at television. She can walk about and talk to other women. She can go out on the verandah. All this distracts her from her pain and, if it does not actually shorten labor, makes it seem shorter.

We have added to this room a mother-figure whom we pretentiously call a Companion of the First Stage. She is not a nurse. She happens to be a widow of about 60 who has had her own troubles and whose outlook is compassionate rather than professional. She is not there as a nurse and she has no obstetric authority over the patient—this being exercised by the delivery section nurses just around the corner. Her business is solely to distract, comfort, encourage, fortify and reassure the woman in the first stage, particularly the primipara, with whom, of course, her effect is the greatest.

While the construction and staffing of this section arose out of our interest in Natural Childbirth, it is available to all patients, no matter what schedule they are following. That it seems to benefit all, including the non-Natural Childbirthers, is shown by the fact that considerably less sedation is required during the first stage. Our women seem happy about it, and to an extent that we hardly expected. A recent query, sent to 300 consecutive women who had made use of it, was answered with an enthusiasm not usual to such questionnaires.

While we are on this subject I would like to say a word in favor of an individual to whom I personally owe a great debt, yet whom we have almost completely repudiated on this continent. Having learned my basic obstetrics as an interne [sic] in a London, England, hospital I have to admit that the nurse-midwife was usually a better obstetrician than we internes [sic]. One of them, in fact, was the best obstetric diagnostician I have ever encountered. I still have to be convinced that any doctor can deliver a normal case more smoothly. I'll go further—I never saw a nurse-midwife make as poor a fist of it as some doctors.

According to their book, their field was normal obstetrics, and when labor became complicated they called in the obstetrician. In effect, they served obstetrics in its physiologic rather than its pathologic aspect. But in addition they also played to some extent the mother-figure previously mentioned, since many of them were mature women. Thus they were more confidence-inspiring to the patient than the relatively younger type of nurse we so often have to employ. Furthermore, they formed a large pool of highly trained personnel from which the nursing staffs of maternity hospitals and departments could be recruited, which recruitment is often a problem of considerable formidability with us.

I am convinced that we should reintroduce her into North American practice, *but train her as a midwife and not as an R.N. specializing in midwifery.* If the present trends continue, on the one hand towards population expansion and on the other to a relative shrinkage of admissions to medical schools, won't she become an absolute necessity? If the various blessings she might bring, not only to us but to the woman in labor, are taken fully into account, to resist any longer her entry into our field constitutes a most flagrant exhibition of original sin.

Could we now widen the screen at which we are looking to include the situation in which woman finds herself in a modern world. This is a timely thing to do: only last month, for the first time in history, Canadian women met in Toronto to discuss this matter. We have known for only a few thousand years that man played any part in the production of a baby. Prior to that it was thought that a woman was fertilized by the spirit of some rock or tree or river that she happened to be passing when she first felt the fetal movements. In his desperate need to increase his food and kind, and in the face of this one mysterious act that a woman could do and he couldn't, man gave his pregnant woman the attributes of a fertility goddess. Her pregnancy became in his eyes a highly prestigious affair, and he eventually sublimated her into the Queen of Heaven. But the situation changed when he found that he himself was actually essential to conception. Childbearing then lost its unique prestige and soon became just another household chore, which is very much how it is still regarded in civilized circles. The kudos has departed.

Our specialty has played some part in this debasement. Partly from compassion—and partly through less noble motives—we have removed considerable of what sense of achievement still remains in having a baby. Very often, because of our manipulations, the woman is left with the feeling that we and not she actually produced the child. It must be very difficult for any woman to withstand the constant suggestion arising from her hospital environment that her part in the performance is relatively unimportant compared to that of the medical and nursing staff.

We have even introduced the husband into the picture as a sort of third-class obstetric attendant. His presence, while often helpful and greatly appreciated by his wife, certainly tends to undermine any attempts on our part to build up in her mind the idea that it is she and no mere man who is having the baby. Husbands have a way of exaggerating, however playfully, the part they play in such a performance: "Hell, sweetie, you'd never have had that baby if I hadn't been in there pushing with you!" While, at Halifax, we haven't discouraged his attendance, I have always been doubtful of his ultimate psychologic value, and have given in to the situation because it seemed better to have him with her in that lonely hospital room than no one at all. I can't get away from the feeling that his replacement by more Companions of the First Stage would ultimately serve our philosophy best and even cause him some relief.

Furthermore, because of sedation and anesthetic, the woman is not often present at the supreme moment of birth. Is this important, or just sentimental baloney dredged up by the Natural Childbirthers to support their droll contentions? Suppose that a mountain climber could take a drug, just before the last desperate push to the summit, that would remove all sense of pain and danger. He could still climb, but he would return from the summit with no memory of having stood on the roof of the world, and no assurance that his guide hadn't carried him up the last quarter mile. Who would want to mountain-climb under such circumstances? What kick would there be left in it?

So here we have arrived at the situation where, because man finally tumbled to his part in conception, and because obstetricians are the sort of people they are, modern woman derives very little prestige or real satisfaction out of doing this most important job that only she and no man can do.

But that's only one side of the predicament in which modern woman finds herself. About 100 years ago, because of the tremendous expansion in the industrial world, man realized he could not cope with it alone. He therefore called to his women, who had previously remained in the home, to come out and help him. As a result the world today is full of eager career women competing on fairly equal terms with him, and not infrequently beating him out in the race for the prizes and vice-presidencies.

But sooner or later the gonadal urge betrays most of them into matrimony and childbearing. Two courses are now open. They can abandon the prestige-laden man's world entirely and, hereafter, devote themselves to the nonprestigious world of the home or, as they are doing in ever increasing numbers, spend a few years getting a family and then return to the outside world. But in the meantime, from 5 to 10 of the potentially most productive years of their lives have slipped by. They now find themselves in competition, not with those of their own age who were their erstwhile rivals, but with a younger group possessed of a vigor they have partly expended on two or three pregnancies and can no longer call upon fully. Their chances, except in the most exceptional circumstances, of getting to the top and wearing the really bright and glittering crown of success, are therefore little better than those of a one-legged man in a wheelbarrow race. But that one such happens to be a Dr. Frances Kelsey our specialty has particular reason to be grateful.

So here is modern woman, with her feet in two worlds, from neither of which is she commonly able to obtain the fullest satisfactions and the highest esteem. To what extent is the resultant frustration driving so many of them to us with pseudo-gynecologic symptoms and to the psychiatrist with real psychiatric ones? To what extent is it responsible for that tendency of so many North American women to overdominate their families, which we call Momism and which is driving so many of the rest of us there? Could it also be in part responsible for the almost complete rejection of breast feeding by the women of this continent? Have these frustrated girls actually come to believe, either consciously or subconsciously, that the breast yields a higher esteem when preserved for looks rather than risked on junior? I have felt for many years that there must be some deeper psychologic reason than those commonly given for this refusal to breast feed.

Is this rejection not only a symptom of woman's frustration, but also in itself a cause of emotional malaise among those denied the security of the maternal breast and arms? While our pediatricians have been most cunning in mimicking mother's milk, I have a strong suspicion that until they devise a nursing bottle as soft, as warm, as comforting and as sense-stirring as the female breast, it cannot be said that they have truly replaced nature. The probabilities are that they have only betrayed it. In any case, surely this is a wide field of female frustration, with its effects not only on the woman herself but on all of us, that our specialty might usefully explore with the cooperation of the psychiatrists. If Lincoln was right in stating that no nation can exist half slave and half free, it is difficult to see how humanity will reach its highest potential with more than half the population denied the fullest satisfactions and recognition from their efforts.

This problem, then, of woman's status in a modern world concerns everyone. Perhaps the handicap that childbirth imposes on those who later return to the industrial world cannot be eliminated. But is it not possible to return to them in some measure those satisfactions and that prestige arising out of childbirth that they actually enjoyed at the dawn of history? In such a movement our specialty might play an important part. We could see to it that our maternity hospitals and their personnel were geared not only to deal with the woman more humanely, but to impress on her the great racial and social importance of what she is doing. While we may not be able to persuade her that having this particular baby is as important as writing Hamlet, we could at least point out to her that before Hamlet could be written a Mrs. Shakespeare had to have a little Willie.

We could redesign our maternity hospitals architecturally so that they increase the probability that the woman herself and not her obstetrician will have the baby, so that they provide that freedom of movement and that species of distraction which lessen—except where really necessary—the need for such sedatives and anesthetics as prevent her being present at the supreme moment of birth. We could begin there, and if we continued to walk humbly under the banner of such a philosophy and not as gods seeking cheap miracles, we might discover a thousand other ways in which to help women achieve from childbirth those satisfactions and esteems now lacking.

So my plea to the younger men in our specialty—those not yet stuck in the mud of their complacency—is to break away from their obsession with pathology and be born again physiologically, heaven-bent towards a higher and less egotistic philosophy of obstetrics, to the end that they will restrain their presumptuous yen to play God high and low in the female pelvis during labor or to deny a woman unnecessarily the opportunity to achieve her own obstetric destiny; to the end that they will help to return to woman the prestige she deserves and once had, for bringing us all into a world so challenging and exciting.

Obstet Gynecol 1963;21:514–9.

COMMENTARY

Written 40 years ago, this is an incredibly prescient view of obstetrics and how it would evolve. The author argues eloquently that pregnancy is basically a normal process and his vision includes the value of support personnel in labor (doulas in current terminology). He even seems to anticipate the great societal changes that would be known as the women's movement. About the only prediction he missed is evident in his repeated reference to the "men" practicing obstetrics and gynecology.

In addition to its farsightedness, the article is written beautifully. The explanation for this literary quality can be found in the author's background. H. B. Atlee (1890–1978) attended Dalhousie Medical School in his native Nova Scotia, graduating at age 20, the youngest medical graduate before or since. He was in general practice for 2 years (the period described in the opening of his article), then went to England for further training. He served with distinction in the Royal Army Medical Corps in World War I, where he began writing about his experiences. Upon returning to Nova Scotia in 1922, he was appointed Chairman of the newly com-

bined Department of Obstetrics and Gynaecology. The position carried no salary and there was little or no potential for private practice because he was not accepted by the medical community. Therefore, for the first 5 or 6 years of his academic career, he supported himself by writing articles, mainly fiction, for magazines in Canada, Britain, and the United States.

A Lesson in Empathy

Nona L. McNatt, RN, CNM

JULY 1980

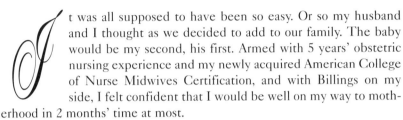

t was all supposed to have been so easy. Or so my husband and I thought as we decided to add to our family. The baby would be my second, his first. Armed with 5 years' obstetric nursing experience and my newly acquired American College of Nurse Midwives Certification, and with Billings on my side, I felt confident that I would be well on my way to motherhood in 2 months' time at most.

Four months later, I began looking at the situation a bit less light-heartedly. I also began looking at my handsome, virile husband somewhat differently. What if he were sterile? Could we handle that? Already my nonconception had begun to erode our relationship subconsciously; what then, of all those couples who face years of this uncertainty, couples I myself had counseled and referred? Had they too had these guilty, angry, pitying, frustrating feelings? I thought ironically of the tiny box on the prenatal form, "months pregnancy attempted," with a new perception of the myriad emotions and circumstances that lay behind it. I accepted the eventual news of my positive human chorionic gonadotropin assay with great humility and elation.

I immediately began in earnest the nutrition program I had outlined for myself the previous year. Because my first child had been small for gestational age and a product of a low-calorie, low-salt diet, I was doubly determined to win an Aggie Higgins Blue Ribbon and deliver at least a 7-pound baby! The pregnancy proceeded well, as I measured my fundus weekly, tapped my belly fondly, listened with my whole body for quickening, and watched my changing figure with delight—until 24 weeks arrived.

"Hmmm," the obstetrician remarked in that most annoying, ominous manner. After a remeasure by his associate, it was decided that I was, indeed, 4 weeks behind in fundal growth. I remember nothing else about that visit, no vague reassurances, no admonitions to improve my diet, nothing but my empty, panicky feelings. "Some women just can't seem to form a healthy placenta ... vascular problems," rang in my ears the entire drive home. I felt handicapped, less than adequate, and terribly afraid. As I reluctantly agreed to the ultrasound, I realized how much having a normal pregnancy truly meant to me. Suddenly, after all the ultrasounds I had ordered for discrepancies in size versus dates, the safety of the procedure became paramount. This was my child, and I needed to know all I possibly could about sequelae and follow-up studies. Oh, how matter-of-fact I had been in the past, mildly reassuring some young mother who no doubt was as full of the same concerns that I was now.

The rest of the pregnancy was a nightmare of tests, procedures, orders. The fundal height remained 4 to 6 weeks behind. Weekly visits began at 28 weeks. Never before had hospital personnel irritated me the way they did then; but I had always been one of "them." Twenty-four hour urine tests for estriol, begun at 32 weeks, were embarrassing and troublesome; I was terrified when the first one came back with a value of 4 mg/ml. My faith was shattered when I learned that a specimen had sat for a week in the lab's refrigerator, and that another value had been erroneously reported. A human placental lactogen assay was ordered; I grew furious explaining the test to the lab supervisor, who had obviously never encountered one. I wondered ruefully, "If this is the area's best lab, what in heaven's name transpires at the worst...."

At 35 weeks, nonstress tests were begun. The night before my first I spent in a panic, dutifully lying in left lateral position counting fetal movements, awakening with a start, knowing the baby hadn't moved in hours. I prodded, wept, prayed that my tiny baby would be all right. "Not even beautiful," I bargained, "just all right." After the torment of that night, I was met at the nurses' station by a cold, bored nurse who called down to a colleague, "Hey, here's another NST, set her up in number 4, will ya?" I fought tears of anger and rage, thinking, "I am not another NST, I am a woman, carrying a child who may be in trouble. Don't you understand at all?"

I continued. To remain at bed rest in a left lateral position, I had to have my mother come in to stay and to care for our daughter and the house, because my husband was working 12 to 16 hours a day. I don't recall being asked how feasible this regimen was, nor do I remember specifically having asked any of my clients the same question. I maintained my 100-g protein, 2500-calorie diet, figuring that that was the only definite help I could give my poor "starving" baby. At 37½ weeks, with a positive diagnosis of intrauterine growth retardation derived from a fetal volume sonogram, an estriol level of 8 mg/ml, and a positive non-stress test, I moved 300 miles away to be near a known and trusted obstetrician, pediatrician, and a fetal intensive care unit, in the event that we needed it. With a heavy heart, I abandoned all hopes of a labor room delivery, LeBoyer techniques, and early discharge. I simply wanted to hold this baby.

As fate would have it, the pregnancy's course did a complete about-face after the move—estriols rose immediately to 20 mg/ml and remained consistently high. The fundus, measured now in fingerbreadths, was deemed adequate; all talk of nonstress tests and induction ceased. Despite my relief at these improved signs, I remained concerned. Had the entire nightmare been a product of lab error, overconcern, and poor judgment? I will never know.

Finally, 50 pounds and 40½ weeks after conception, labor began. *Real* labor, after 4 bouts of false (sometimes even the midwife isn't sure what's what, especially if *she's* the what). After all my plans for an immediate conception and an ideal pregnancy had fallen through, I should have anticipated a long, difficult labor. I didn't, but it was. Fortunately, my obstetricians were confident enough of the baby's size to encourage much of what I had originally wanted from the experience: constant support from my husband, labor room delivery, no episiotomy, no separation from the baby, early discharge.

Their attitude helped tremendously when, after 21 hours of labor, my cervix was only 4 cm dilated; I remember apologizing weakly to our baby as the amniotomy was performed, feeling truly sorry. Six hours later, it was yet 6 cm; Pitocin was introduced, along with external monitoring and intravenous fluids. Throughout the discomfort of the augmentation, I relied heavily on the constancy of my husband, allowing his strength to sustain me through despair, tears, exhaustion, and hints of epidurals and analgesia.

Finally, the unmistakable urge, and Amanda Emily slowly, beautifully, perfectly entered our world. I lay weeping with joy, cooing, shaking, blushing at my own noise, holding her warm wetness to my cheek, feeling enveloped by deep abiding love.

Through it all she came, a healthy 7-pound, 2-ounce wide-eyed beauty, clutching our fingers, capturing our hearts. I quietly watched my husband caress her as they snuggled intimately beside me, feeling wonder, fulfillment, awe. Six hours later found the 4 of us home in our own bed, never separated, knowing only warm, exhausted, tender togetherness after the incredible ordeal we had come through in the past year.

Today, gazing at my robust daughter nursing hungrily at my breast, I am coming to understand a great deal. Looking back on the experience, I feel I have shared many, many feelings with women I have known and yet do not know. The brusque attitudes, the callous treatment, the inefficiency, all so needless, have intensified my desire to give more of myself upon my reentry into midwifery, as well as to demand more of my colleagues in the medical profession. Never again can I be satisfied with less than the best care or less than human caring. It is our responsibility not merely to steer our clients safely through pregnancy, with all of its discomforts and changes, but to guide them gently, sincerely toward an ultimately fulfilling feminine experience, offering not only expertise, but ourselves as well.

Obstet Gynecol 1980;56:131–2.

COMMENTARY

This is an eloquent expression of the patient's perspective through the course of a "maybe abnormal" pregnancy. The patient in this case was a nurse–midwife, so she was able to understand why things were being done the way they were. But she was also a patient and could see the deficiencies in understanding and empathy. Those of us who care for patients do not always appear to care about them.

A Prospective Study of Postpartum Candy Gift Net Weight: Correlation with Birth Weight

Andrew J. Nordin, MBBS

JULY 1993

ew parents in western civilizations traditionally demonstrate their gratitude to the providers of their intrapartum and postnatal care through the gift of confectionary. Deeply entrenched in obstetric and midwifery folklore, but previously untested, is the hypothesis that the weight of the candy gifts is proportional to birth weight. Data collected over 6 months in a busy regional maternity unit were analyzed to test this hypothesis.

MATERIALS AND METHODS

Over a 6-month period in 1992, midwives on the delivery suite and two postnatal wards at Musgrove Park Hospital in Taunton, Somerset, United Kingdom were requested to complete a form detailing the net weight of any candy gifts and the corresponding birth weight. Other gifts, such as cookies and wine, were excluded from the study. The correlation coefficient between candy weight and birth weight was calculated.

RESULTS

Thirty-nine chocolate gifts were recorded during the 6 months, in which 1491 infants were delivered at Musgrove Park Hospital. Birth weights ranged from 2260–4926 g, with a mean (± standard deviation) of 3566 ± 676 (95% confidence interval [CI] 3346.99–3785.63, skewness 0.398, kurtosis −0.357, coefficient of variation 19%). Boxed candy net weights ranged from 200–1200 g, with a mean net weight of 415.74 ± 191.92 (95% CI 353.53–477.96, skewness 1.6316, kurtosis 5.1069, coefficient of variation 46.2%).

The most popular assortment was a soft-cream collection weighing 454 g, which was presented on eight occasions (21%). The hospital charity shop reported brisk trade on this particular attractively packaged assortment. Soft-cream mixtures were given more commonly than hard and soft assortments, with an approximate dominance of 4:1; no all-hard-center assortments were recorded during the study. Amongst recipients, orange cream and almond marzipan were generally accepted as the most popular flavors, with strawberry and coffee soft-cream centers the least sought-after.

Regression analysis found an association between birth weight and net candy weight, with a linear correlation equation of y = 3349.9 + 0.52058x. The correlation coefficient of 0.1477 was not statistically significant ($P = .2$) (Figure 1).

Discussion

The principles behind the presumed association between net weight of candy gifts and birth weight are well established in obstetric folklore. The association is thought to have a multifactorial basis, with different factors influencing extremes of the birth weight spectrum.

Only two parents of infants weighing less than 2500 g gave any candy, and this is consistent with expectations. Smokers from low socioeconomic groups with small term infants are notoriously poor candy-givers. Conversely, parents of preterm infants are well known to be prolific candy-givers, but anxiety and concern for their newborn immediately after deliv-

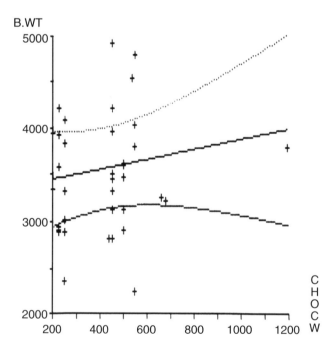

Fig. 1. Correlation of birth weight (B.WT) and net weight of postpartum candy gifts (CHOCW).

ery frequently result in displacement of these substantial candy gifts to the neonatal intensive care staff. Gifts to delivery suite staff by these parents tend to consist of cookies rather than candy. This anecdotal observation demands urgent collaborative multi-center study because of its potential to further our understanding of prematurity.

Parents of average-size infants in this white, homogeneous, middle-class, semirural community traditionally endow hospital staff with soft-centered candy. The expectation of increasing candy weight with birth weight in this population is based on the trend of increasing birth weight with subsequent pregnancies, coinciding with improvement in the family's economic situation.

Parents of high birth weight infants are themselves frequently at the upper end of the adult population weight nomogram, and often achieve this status by consuming vast quantities of confectionary. The situations of diabetic and gestational diabetic mothers with macrosomic infants are unique and well explained. Insulin-dependent diabetics often have obsessions with soft-centered candy, holding it in high regard as a forbidden pleasure. Thus, many grateful diabetic mothers can think of no greater reward for the midwife or obstetrician who has just safely negotiated her macrosomic infant through a potentially hazardous perinatal experience than to present him or her with a large box of "soft-centers." The purchase of large candy boxes often contributes to the onset of the gestational diabetic condition, and the celebration of a gestational diabetic's return to normal glucose tolerance on the postnatal ward is likely to involve excessive candy consumption by the mothers, their families, and their midwives.

The small number of candy gifts recorded over the 6-month period fell short of pre-study expectations. A number of confounding factors are implicated. One of the two postnatal wards withdrew from data collection after several weeks, citing the burden of the additional workload generated by the study. However, rumor suggested that a black-market "soft-center" racket allegedly coordinated by the senior midwife on the ward suffered when all candy gifts were documented. Under-reporting on the other wards is also likely to have biased the study. The frequency of reports fell dramatically after rumor circulated through the hospital that the same data were to be used retrospectively to test the separate hypothesis that midwife waist measurement is directly proportional to the net weight of boxed candy received over a 6-month period.

Less-than-expected clumping of candy weight distribution provoked an extensive search of local candy retail outlets, confirming the suspicion that reported candy net weights did not correspond to the weight cited on commercial packaging. A midwife candy "sampling" error is believed to have occurred before candy weighing.

It is also likely that the true rate of candy gifts has fallen in recent years. One can only speculate on the role of the prolonged economic recession. Only 39 gifts from 1491 deliveries strongly supports recent calls to the government by midwifery and obstetric groups for inclusion in the new mother's maternity grant, with strict regulation and monitoring, to specifically provide for these essential purchases.

Obstet Gynecol 1993;82:156–8.

Postpartum: For Colette Peschel

Enid Rhodes Peschel

...l'affaiblissement et l'effroi...
Rimbaud

What weariness of wan white winter days
that limp along to monotonic blues
of mood and mind: "the depression and the dread."
For endless hours the infant's cries cascade
like waterfalls, then modulate to mother's
tears that gush like lava, burning floods
of fear, fatigue and loneliness, rushing rivers
bearing pain remembered, paining still...

How eerily the newborn nursing at
my breast revives the long and laboring hours
of that rain-slicked night. Just as the infant
day, still swaddled in its soothing blanket
of the night, was scarcely ninety minutes
old and we at last were sailing off
to dreamless sleep, the oceans ruptured and
the birth began.—What strange excitement and
detachment radiating within my heart
and womb! Between contractions, calm, but not
tranquillity: a sailboat, stranded on
a motionless ocean, awaiting propelling winds;
the calm of the hurricane's eye. At 4:00 A.M.,
the restless ride through black air swirled
        with gray-white
clouds, a Van Gogh whirlwind, a storm outside,
a storm within; the hospital bed and dim-lit
room, the hours and the doctors passing
by like green-clad phantoms, drug-dazed dawn
and piercing morning, then the shriek of noon.

Black hair and blood, contractions bringing forth
new life...—contracting now to close the womb,
the wound...To sleep would be a paradise,
to plunge into a womb of peace, to brace
myself to bear this baby's tears and mine.

But suddenly, as if my daughter sensed
my helplessness (I recall her knowing look
at birth), her cries have ceased. And now her fleeting
smile, as beautiful and fragile as
a butterfly, illuminates the wintry
world like springtime sun and fills a weeping
mother's eyes and heart with overflowing
wells of wonder, gratitude, and love.

Obstet Gynecol 1979;53:766.

COMMENTARY

This and the subsequent two poems, all written by patients, express various emotions. The first represents the tenderness of a new mother to her baby, the second is an elegant expression of thanks of a woman to her doctor, and the third is an indignant expression of a woman to an illness. The last two were dedicated to the authors' physicians, indicating the closeness of their relationship. Close and intensely personal bonds with patients characterize obstetrics and gynecology and, indeed, this aspect is one of the features that attracted most of us to the specialty. Today, there seem to be many things trying to tear down this relationship, but even in spite of malpractice litigation, managed care, gatekeepers, and declining reimbursements, the fundamental relationship of trust and respect between a doctor and a patient is still alive. Thank heavens.

Transcendence
(Inspired by Thomas Hanson, MD, FACOG)

S. Mullany, MD

Somewhere you have delivered my mind and soul
Far beyond the fever, pain, and fear
Recorded by my fleeing pulse.

Your appearance at the door in your white wings
Lifts me above another's diagnostic threat.
Your smile carries me past the ultrasound's grim
Shadows and the unknown unseen.

Never no one needed as I need you Now.

Your compassionate Presence and its
Legacy of trust, with skill gave
Birth to Healing, returned the world
To me, and me to those I love.

There is no reciprocity for such a gift as this.
I can only pray for your long-lasting health and
Another Hippocratic Doctor looking after you.

Obstet Gynecol 2001;98:702.

A Woman Redressing Cells

Sue Brannan Walker, MEd, MA, PhD

DECEMBER 1996

(For H. C. Mendenhall)
What do you mean
stealing in uninvited?
Breaking and entering
is a crime—and a serious one
at that. You have no right
to tamper with my walls
in your atypical glandular,
squamous display. We have
never been friends, much less
lovers, and you cannot come
and set up in my cervix as if
I were a woman who would stick out her neck
for the likes of you who are not my kind.
I am a woman who reads literary theory
and warrants abjection, who listens
to Kiri Te Kanawa sing Mozart,
a woman who eats chocolate-mint
Girl Scout cookies and drinks
Chateau Mouton Rothschild wine.
I wear Jungle Gardenia perfume,
paint my toenails polka dot and moonbeam
pink. I have a friend who has a knife
he threatens to use, so I am asking you
to leave quietly just as you came.

Obstet Gynecol 1996;88:1068.